Revenge of the Aesthetic

Revenge of the Aesthetic

The Place of Literature in Theory Today

EDITED BY

Michael P. Clark

UNIVERSITY OF CALIFORNIA PRESS
Berkeley   Los Angeles   London

University of California Press
Berkeley and Los Angeles, California

University of California Press, Ltd.
London, England

Library of Congress Cataloging-in-Publication Data
Revenge of the aesthetic : the place of literature in theory today / edited by Michael P.
  Clark.
    p.   cm.
  Includes bibliographical references and index.
  ISBN 0-520-22002-1 (alk. paper). — ISBN 0-520-22004-8 (pbk. : alk. paper)
    1. Literature—History and criticism—Theory, etc.   2. Aesthetics, Modern—20th
century.   3. Literature—Philosophy.   I. Clark, Michael P., 1950–
PN49.R45   2000
801′.93—dc21   99-29827
                                                                            CIP

Manufactured in the United States of America

08 07 06 05 04 03 02 01 00   10 9 8 7 6 5 4 3 2 1

The paper used in this publication meets the minimum requirements of
ANSI/NISO Z39.48-1992 (R 1997) (*Permanence of Paper*). ⊗

This collection of essays is dedicated to
Murray Krieger
University Research Professor
University of California

CONTENTS

Introduction

Michael P. Clark

The aesthetic can have its revenge upon ideology by revealing a power to complicate that is also a power to undermine.

MURRAY KRIEGER, *Ekphrasis*

The essays in this volume argue for the importance of aesthetic values and formal characteristics specific to literary texts. This theme has taken on a contrarian quality today, as aesthetic issues have often been displaced from a field that only twenty years ago could still be called "literary" theory without drawing the battle lines that these quotation marks imply. In the years following World War II, after a bitter debate between literary historians and the New Critics, the priority of aesthetic value and the privileged status of the literary text had been firmly established among theorists in the United States. From the late 1950s through the early 1970s, that priority was institutionalized in the American academy by the emergence of literary theory as a distinct discourse and field of study that reflected the formalist emphasis on the self-referential autonomy of literary language and its independence from other forms of discourse. Literary theory was distinguished from the biographical and historical positivism of earlier literary criticism on the one hand and, on the other, from most forms of theoretical discourse in philosophy and the social sciences. Through the pioneering historical work of W. K. Wimsatt and Cleanth Brooks, René Wellek, and Murray Krieger, and in influential anthologies by W. J. Bate and Hazard Adams, literary theory traced its genealogical roots back to Plato and constituted the "poem," or literary language in general, as a unique object of knowledge resistant to other analytic perspectives.[1]

The privileged status of literary language among critics and theorists in the United States was first challenged effectively by the rise of poststructuralism in the early 1970s, following the appearance of *The Structuralist Controversy* and the translation of Jacques Derrida's *Of Grammatology*.[2] Initially, the influence of this work on most American critics was limited. Poststructuralism emerged from a Hegelian-Heideggerian tradition that was

I

quite distinct from (and almost incomprehensible within) the Kantian lineage of most Anglo-American criticism at the time. In addition, the term poststructuralism itself denoted less a coherent theoretical program than a convenient historical marker. It grouped together some influential theorists who often had little in common apart from an interest in the constitutive role of linguistic functions in human experience, and a corollary rejection of humanistic touchstones such as "Man" and most philosophical absolutes and metaphysical foundations. Otherwise, their work was quite diverse, and most of it was difficult to classify according to conventional academic categories. In particular, apart from the brilliant exceptions of Roland Barthes and the early Michel Foucault, few of those called poststructuralists directly addressed literary issues in the usual sense, especially as that sense had been narrowed down by the New Critics.

As poststructuralism spread in the United States, however, it was quickly adapted to more specifically literary study by J. Hillis Miller, Geoffrey Hartman, Paul de Man, and others.[3] In their hands, the general antihumanism of the French theorists was focused sharply on literary issues in the form of deconstruction, and it was aimed at one of the most important tenets of American criticism: the semantic independence and autotelic coherence of the poem understood as a closed and internally consistent linguistic system. The poststructural critique of coherence and closure went much farther than a debate over the formal properties of the text, of course. The New Critics' model of literary form had been directly derived from what Coleridge had described as the organic symbol, and the autotelic model of the poem implied—and at times explicitly claimed—a unique status for literary language that was the aesthetic embodiment of the spiritual transcendence and ontic presence associated with the metaphysics of English Romanticism. To challenge the formal coherence of the poem and its discursive autonomy was therefore to challenge the philosophical foundation of Western humanism as it had been derived from the Romantic preoccupation with the symbol and from a Kantian faith in the constitutive power of symbolic categories in general. The threat posed by poststructuralism to Anglo-American criticism was thus real and substantial. It not only targeted the integrity of the literary text but also attacked the entire system of values and intellectual practices associated with that text as "literature."

In less than a decade, deconstruction won this battle and replaced the contextualist formalism of the American New Critics as the dominant theoretical paradigm in the United States. Like poststructuralism in general, deconstruction was as various as the range of its practitioners, and certainly never as programmatic as the simplistic straw men excoriated by many of its opponents. The work characterized as deconstructive was, nevertheless, usually consistent in its critique of structural closure and semantic coherence as formal virtues of poetic language. Those aesthetic attributes were

discounted as mere illusions that obscured the differential (and differentiating) functions at work in all forms of discourse—including the literary
text as an exemplary but not unique instance. Consequently, although most
of the critics associated with deconstruction in the United States continued
to take literary works as their primary examples of such functions, these
works were usually presented as prototypical cases of general linguistic traits
rather than as unique departures from ordinary language. And as literary
language lost much of its specificity, the attention of many critics turned
from the constitutive power of metaphor, meter, prosopopoeia, paradox,
irony, and other attributes most often identified as distinctly "literary" to the
extra-literary and even extra-discursive forces at work in society at large. As
Foucault put it in a reaction against the linguistic focus of his earlier work,
even for the intellectual and cultural historian "one's point of reference
should not be to the great model of language [*langue*] and signs, but to that
of war and battle. The history which bears and determines us has the form
of a war rather than that of a language: relations of power, not relations of
meaning."[4]

This paradigmatic shift in contemporary theory away from language as
the determinative basis of experience toward the extra-discursive ground of
history, social conflict, or "war" was driven in part by a reaction to deconstruction that resembled the historicists' resistance to the New Criticism almost half a century earlier. Deconstruction's focus on language and tropes
obviously recalled the topics, if not the methods and conclusions, that had
preoccupied literary critics in the United States after World War II, and this
similarity resulted in charges that deconstruction was just another form of
depoliticized close reading and so just as reductive and idealist as any formalist theory. These charges were often levied in the name of a historical or
cultural materialism that insisted on subordinating the text to its function
within a broader social context, a function that not only superseded the text
but finally determined its formal properties as well as its thematic content
and social utility. From this perspective, any attempt to consider the text
apart from its context—however that text may be defined—appeared as
aestheticist escapism or as a vestige of Arnoldian idealism intent on isolat-
ing culture from everyday life and then speciously defending that isolation,
both as the realm of universal and timeless ideas and, paradoxically, as the
foundation for whatever social affect those ideas may have in some indefi-
nite, distant future.[5]

This complaint was quickly extended from the specific claims of deconstruction per se to the elevated status of discourse and the signifier that
characterized poststructuralism in general. As a result, the terms of debate
in contemporary literary theory shifted from a dispute about the nature of
literary form to a broader argument about the social function of literature
in the world beyond the text, and about the relevance of literary analysis to

historical analysis and political reform. Against the Arnoldian fear of culture being contaminated by the concerns of the street, many critics of poststructuralism insisted on connecting culture directly to the pragmatic concerns of ordinary life, and then on reading the products of that culture as answers to—or, in the case of much canonical literature, answerable for—the conflicts and injustices of that life. Unlike the earlier reactions against the radical formalism of the New Critics, however, which had usually depended on the relatively simple positivist claims of reconstructive historicism or the expressivist assumptions of straightforward biographical readings, the resistance to poststructuralism was more subtle and conceptually complex. Usually citing Benjamin, Bakhtin, Gramsci, and the later Foucault as its most important predecessors, this newly politicized theory coalesced in the various forms of cultural critique associated with the Frankfurt School and in certain forms of British and French Marxism.[6] Though more varied and conceptually sophisticated than most forms of historical analysis, this work was characterized generally by an effort to treat culture as a primary object of historical analysis rather than as a reflection or expression of some other, determinative cause, and by its tendency to read literary and artistic works primarily in social or political terms, rather than according to the formal categories of more traditional aesthetic analysis.

Whether conducted in Marxian idioms or the broader forms of cultural critique that evolved from Frankfurt and Foucault, this interest in the social import of culture once again opened literary study to historical and ideological questions. By renewing faith in the political efficacy of theoretical work, it also brought a new agenda to the academic study of literature, one that began and ended with the political use of literature to challenge the status quo and effect positive social change. At times, the new cultural criticism identified literary analysis with political action to such an extent that the critic was portrayed as the modern avatar of Sir Philip Sidney's soldier-poet, intent on well-doing and not merely well-knowing.

What Sidney's poet does well, however, is write poetry, and the reluctance of this newly politicized theory to recognize the specificity of the poetic work in the field of social action marks its most significant and most problematic departure from more traditional defenses of the use of poetry. In his *Apology for Poetry,* for example, Sidney celebrates the poet over the historian and philosopher not because the poet knows something about society and virtue that they do not, but because only the poet knows how to embody that knowledge in a form that will lead people to act on the idea of virtue represented in the poem. The poem is fundamentally different both from the philosophical truth or "foreconceit" that it embodies and from the historical action that it would inspire, and it is this difference that imbues poetry with its social significance. Yet, despite a shared enthusiasm for the social and moral utility of poetry—not to mention Sidney's military endorsement of poetry as a "companion of the camps"—few associated with cultural studies would follow Sidney in attributing such independence and power to poetry. Instead, the formal or aesthetic characteristics of poetry and literature in general are often discounted by social and historical critics in favor of less mediated engagement with lived experience, and this suspicion of mediation or representation can be read (and written) too easily as the crude materialism or naive essentialism which opponents of cultural studies so often ascribe to the whole field.[7]

The polemical extremes of this debate have little to do with theoretical subtlety or precision, and attempts to condemn or to promote this range of work under sobriquets such as "race and gender criticism," "subaltern analysis," "postcolonial theory," "cultural studies," and the like inevitably wind up being too facile and reductive to be useful even as dismissive epithets or celebratory shibboleths. Unfortunately, this hyperbolic rhetoric does have a certain currency in institutional politics. In their struggle for professional identity and institutional authority within the university, proponents of cultural studies at times translate the lack of aesthetic autonomy for the literary text into a lack of importance and significance for literary study in general. In the face of that challenge, some belletrists have portrayed this tendency to collapse literature into a generalized form of symbolic determination as indicative of a drive to reduce the rich diversity of literary particularity to a monolithic political theme, regardless of the relevance that theme may have for a specific author or work. The rhetoric of argument at this level is usually that of the jeremiad, and the professed stakes are nothing less than a defense of human rights or the fate of civilization as we know it.[8]

As absurd as the extreme versions of these charges are, the debate has identified an important conceptual limitation that can compromise even the more nuanced versions of cultural analysis, which readily acknowledge the symbolic determination of human experience in the social realm. Although that acknowledgment avoids the simplistic materialism of much historical criticism, it almost inevitably results in literature being treated merely as one discursive form among the many symbolic systems by which subjective identity is constituted at a given historical moment. Without the independent agency or freedom often associated with poetry, however provisionally, in most humanistic traditions, literature is subsumed by a more general symbolic determinism that constitutes, in turn, our sense of the world and our place in it. Contradictions among the various symbolic systems operating at any moment allow for considerable variety in the dominant social forms, but those contradictions inevitably follow the lines of force characteristic of the system as a whole, rather than anything specific to the literary text. Literature as such simply disappears against a general background of material action or symbolic determination, and with the disappearance of literature—in the absence of any unmediated material ground or any other "outside" to that discursive network—the possibility of productive independence, individual autonomy, effective resistance, and difference itself disappears as well.[9]

Since those were some of the values that motivated this challenge to post-structuralism in the first place, the difficulty of finding a ground—either material or symbolic—from which to contest the elevation of the signifier posed a serious limitation to this critique. Yet the challenge was also under-cut by its intended target, which refused to hold still in the position of a more conventional formalism, even in the overtly literary version of decon-structive analysis. For all of its emphasis on close reading and the analysis of tropes, deconstruction not only contested Romantic notions of organic unity and symbolic autonomy usually associated with formalist analysis; it also deliberately challenged the distinction between world and text usually endorsed by both sides of the debate between formalists and their oppo-nents. In his survey of the discursive properties attributed to the literary text by most poststructural critics, for example, Roland Barthes describes the differences between what he calls the "work," as traditionally conceived of by literary criticism, and the "Text," as defined by poststructuralism.[10] Barthes begins by distinguishing between the two on semiotic and formal terms. Whereas the work is treated as a material object associated with and subordinated to some extratextual "meaning" or referent, "the text is held in language: it exists only as discourse" (75). Unlike the meaning-full work, designed to be consumed and converted to usable knowledge, the Text is characterized by the "dilatory" field of the signifier with its "*irreducible* plu-rality," which "practices the infinite deferral of the signified" in favor of "the signifier's *infinitude*" and the "play" that the Text engenders (76, 79). As the essay progresses, however, Barthes insists that textuality is inextricably em-bedded in action and so exists beyond the bounds of formal closure that constitute the "work" as such. The Text "asks the reader for an active col-laboration," Barthes says; one must "produce the text, play it, open it out, *make it go*" (80). This opening out is what links the text to pleasure or *jouis-sance,* and it also establishes its political efficacy as a "social space":

> Order of the signifier, the Text participates in a social utopia of its own:
> prior to history, the Text achieves, if not the transparency of social relations,
> at least the transparency of language relations. It is the space in which no
> one language has a hold over any other, in which all languages circulate
> freely. . . . Discourse on the Text should itself be only "text," search, and tex-
> tual toil, since the Text is that *social* space that leaves no language safe or
> untouched, that allows no enunciative subject to hold the position of judge,
> teacher, analyst, confessor, or decoder. The theory of the Text can coincide
> only with the activity of writing. (81)

As these remarks demonstrate, Barthes is careful to maintain the discur-sive nature of the Text as opposed to simpler materialist claims: the social utopia here is that of the Text, not the world, and he distinguishes between the "transparency of social relations" and the "transparency of language relations" that constitutes that utopian dimension of the textual experience. Still, Barthes deliberately characterizes that discursive space *as* social, and he proposes writing as an activity capable of opposing the repressive codification of the subject in the social roles of judge, teacher, or confessor. Those are the same roles that he earlier associated with the formal properties of the "work"—coherence, reference, even signification in general— and Barthes portrays those properties as the products of extratextual, ideological regulation, operating in the name of precisely those historical or social forces privileged by materialist analysis as distinct from and antithetical to merely discursive operations.

Thus what Barthes's remarks suggest, and what we could find in the work of most poststructural theorists, is an attack on the very notion of "form" as a property of the text apart from its place in the "context" of worldly experience. In Barthes's essay, the form of the traditional work—the work itself—is treated entirely as a product of its situation within the world beyond the text. The specific form of work is, in a literal sense, the material product of those extratextual forces that shape that context, and it is precisely this continuity between the work's form and the social forces that determine it that constitutes the ground, the *material* ground, on which those forces may be contested by "Text." That is why Barthes's reference to the revolutionary and utopian importance of the text as a "social" space is not simply allegorical. Like Lacan's insistence on the materiality of the signifier, and like Derrida's critique of the binary sign as idealist in its inherent subordination of the signifier to the signified, and like the "language games" that constitute social bonds in Lyotard's *Postmodern Condition,* Barthes's Text does not situate the word in the world, as historicists would attempt to do, nor the world in the word, as formalists might argue: it confounds those terms entirely by treating the word as world, by recognizing in the word the weighty materiality of its worldly existence as part of our lived experience. The Text is thus opened to determination by the same "extratextual" forces that govern the rest of our lives, but those lives are in turn influenced by properties of the text that cannot be reduced to ideological formations and social regulation, whether those properties be called *jouissance,* free play, or, more simply, pleasure.

Deconstruction, like poststructuralism in general, therefore cannot be easily categorized and dismissed as "formalism" in the traditional sense. It denies the integrity of form or, more precisely, the coherence of "structure," but, more importantly, it rejects the separation of the work from the world that has historically been the defining characteristic of formalist analysis and its greatest vulnerability in the face of social or historicist charges of linguistic idealism. For some theorists, such as Barthes and Lyotard, that rejection stems from the perception of social relations in semiotic or discursive terms; other theorists writing in the wake of poststructuralism equate the uniqueness and particularity traditionally associated with the literary work with the material specificity usually attributed to historical experience. Commenting on a particular tradition in Islamic interpretation, for example, Edward Said says that its value lies in "dealing with a text as significant form, in which . . . worldliness, circumstantiality, the text's status as an event having sensuous particularity as well as historical contingency, are considered as being incorporated in the text, an infrangible part of its capacity for conveying and producing meaning." That worldly particularity and contingency, Said concludes, "exist at the same level of surface particularity as the textual object itself."[11] With that worldliness incorporated into the text as part of its signifying function, form and content, or work and world, appear not as separate fields to be connected (or not) in the act of analysis, but as reciprocal fields of experience whose significance and visibility are derived from that reciprocity. Treating the worldly situation of the work not as a separable context but as "an infrangible part of its capacity for conveying and producing meaning" means that the formal or symbolic function of the text is effectively continuous with the rest of our experience and so susceptible to the same forms of social and historical analysis as any other event.

At the same time, the peculiarly narrative or textual properties of this "event" demand that those analyses take into account a whole array of issues and questions traditionally relegated to the realm of aesthetics and literary interpretation. As Fredric Jameson famously observed in *The Political Unconscious,* his slogan "Always historicize!" is substantially complicated by the fact that history "is inaccessible to us except in textual form, and . . . our approach to it and to the Real itself necessarily passes through its prior textualization."[12] Similarly, in his influential essay "Dissemination: Time, Narrative and the Margins of the Modern Nation," Homi Bhabha describes the "nationness" characteristic of postcolonial peoples "as a form of social and textual affiliation." Distinguishing his approach from the "historicism that has dominated discussion of the nation as a cultural force," and that "most commonly signifies a people, a nation, or a national culture as an empirical sociological category or a holistic cultural entity," Bhabha claims that "the narrative and psychological force that nationness brings to bear on cultural production and political projection is the effect of the ambivalence of the 'nation' as a narrative strategy."[13]

For Jameson and Bhabha, the reciprocity of work and world as part of our lived experience becomes the proper object of historical analysis because making that connection is integral to the social process. So Jameson insists on the "positive" analysis of narrative closure as a figural projection of utopian longing because that longing can be found at the heart of all class consciousness and therefore constitutes the historical horizon of the text. Similarly, Bhabha focuses on what he calls the "performative" dimension of efforts to teach (or "narrativize") national identity in postcolonial cultures because that performance is the means by which those cultures struggle to define themselves in the wake of colonialist occupation.[14] Unfortunately, in the hands of less careful and subtle critics, that analytic object turned out to be considerably more frangible and fragile than its theoretical origins would support. The reciprocity between work and world that is portrayed here as the object of analysis and the product of specific social actions too often becomes an apodeictic assumption that simply collapses these two poles into one another. Even in Bhabha's account of political marginality, or in other efforts to define the nature of minority discourse such as the introduction to *The Nature and Context of Minority Discourse* by Abdul Jan-Mohamed and David Lloyd, we find many of those attributes often associated with the literary text—hyperspecificity, provisional or local cohesion, ironic self-consciousness and internal contradictions, irreducible marginality, supplementarity, excess, etc.—dissociated from the text and projected directly into the social field as defining attributes of cultural autonomy and political viability among oppressed and marginalized groups.[15]

This tendency to treat social and political marginalization in textual terms and vice versa has produced some important pedagogical and political effects. In particular, it has opened the literary curriculum to a broad and heterogeneous range of works termed "minority literature" as defined by the authors' gender, race, or ethnicity. However, the undeniable benefits of this curricular innovation have been compromised to some extent by the conceptual tautology that informs it and that is inherent in the very phrase "minority literature." Most humanistic formulations of the literary text since the Romantic period insist on the marginality of the text to ordinary discursive practices and social regulation, and, despite its many differences with humanism on most other grounds, poststructuralism too defined the text as an event of absolute singularity. Those attributes continue to be associated with the literary text as such, and as we have seen they have also come to embody (or "incorporate") the experience of specificity and radical particularity that constitute materiality and history as the limit of symbolic determination and ideological generalization. These literary properties of the text thus, by definition, generate opposition and resistance at a plethora of points not mapped by the status quo either as hegemonic or as subaltern. Whether it is defined in the traditional terms of Western humanism or as the disseminative proliferation of difference characteristic of poststructural textuality, literary experience is so utterly unique or "marginal" in itself that it must undermine the very possibility of stable affiliation with any group. The only way such an affiliation may be enforced, other than as a utopian fantasy or as a performative gesture, is by codifying the group in the image of the work through the illusionary, ideological projection of the work's marginality and difference into the world as an attribute of that group's lived experience and social identity. To designate any set of texts as "minority literature" in terms of the authors' historical or social status, therefore, is not only semantically redundant; it also obscures the textual origin of the features that constitute the marginality, as well as obscuring the literary basis of that designation.

This tendency to treat the world in terms of aesthetic attributes is not new: Walter Benjamin, over fifty years ago, described the strategic imposition of conventional formal attributes such as coherence and unity onto the world as a defining characteristic of fascist politics.[16] The overt political values of recent cultural studies are diametrically opposed to the coercive conformity of the fascist agenda, of course. Nevertheless, the contemporary proclivity to read social and political marginality in terms of poststructural textuality exhibits a similar inclination to treat work and world as mirror images of one another: it simply transposes those attributes formerly associated with literary form onto the world and then claims to "read" them in and as material action, thereby codifying in inverted form the very textual properties that distinguished work from world in both Arnoldian humanism and poststructural analysis. The result is an imaginary opposition, in which the functional reciprocity of work and world that makes this transposition possible in the first place is disguised by an ideological scenario that posits the world as distinct from the work and then reads the work in, and on, the world's terms. The resistance to aesthetics in the name of cultural criticism may therefore be read as the product of an imaginary projection of work and world into irreconcilable opposites, when in fact their apparent opposition is produced by symbolic characteristics of the literary text whose status is being contested in the subordination of work to world. The terms of the debate itself, the very notion that "work" and "world" denote ontic realms or modes of experience that can be separated or connected, can be understood in this light as an effect of specific discursive functions that underlie this conceptual opposition and that render its two poles visible; and those functions may well be what constitute literature as such.

The essays in this volume take up this possibility as a point of departure from which a wide range of texts and issues may be read in terms of contemporary debates about the importance of literature to theoretical argument. Though varying greatly in their topics and the historical range of their examples, the authors represented in this collection all insist on some form of dialectical relation between work and world that confounds simplistic distinctions between these two realms, and that contests the facile elevation of either work or world as the determining factor of literary experience. This insistence constitutes a general thesis for the volume that is reflected in its title and summarized by the epigraph from Murray Krieger's *Ekphrasis:* "the aesthetic can have its revenge upon ideology by revealing a power to complicate that is also a power to undermine."[17] Numerous precedents for this position are cited throughout the collection—Vico, Marvell, Friedrich Schlegel, Nietzsche, Celan, and de Man, to name only a few—but most of the essays situate it in reference to the sustained argument Murray Krieger has developed throughout his career. As these essays indicate, Krieger's work has been central to debates about the status of literary and aesthetic form. He has repeatedly and systematically returned both sides of the debate, which he characterizes in his essay for this volume as an "aesthetic" interest in the work vs. an "ascetic" emphasis on the world, to their common ground in a textual encounter that joins world and word even while flaunting their difference.

Although the terms and emphases of his argument have varied considerably, Krieger has consistently focused on what he calls the ironic or "duplicitous" nature of literary illusion as the key element that distinguishes the unique status of the literary work and that constitutes its importance to the world of lived experience. The literary work, Krieger says, presents an illusion of, and to, the world; but unlike the dogmatic proclamations of ideology, literature presents its illusion *as* illusion. In doing so, literature clarifies not only its own relation to the world but also the provisional status of all the other illusions that would pass themselves off as the truth. By foregrounding the provisional nature of aesthetic autonomy in this way, literature offers a unique perspective on the ideological tendency of all discourse to claim for itself the authority of some transcendent foundational truth, whether that truth be offered as history, race, gender, imagination, art, form, or "theory." As Krieger puts it in his essay for this volume, literature is much like what he described in an earlier essay as theater at its best:

> the theater, like trompe l'oeil painting, is not trying actually to take us in. Instead, its devices slyly point to itself: it undercuts its apparent illusionary claims with its textual or subtextual references to its artifice, to the art of theater. In his espousing the anti-illusionary call for alienation, it was Brecht—and not necessarily the rest of us—who was being taken in by traditional theater. Here he is representative of the politicized theorists who would take *us* in by locking us within the ideological limitations of their claims. It is, I believed, the aesthetic that helps rescue us from such traps, because it alerts us to the illusionary, the merely arbitrary, claims to reality that authoritarian discourse would impose upon us; because, unlike authoritarian discourse, the aesthetic takes back the "reality" it offers us in the very act of offering it to us. It thus provides the cues for us to view other discourse critically, to reduce the ideological claims to the *merely* illusionary,

since there is in other discourse no self-awareness of their textual limitations, of their duplicity—their closures, their exclusions, their repressions. I would agree with Brecht that illusion may frustrate, may baffle, may mislead us—but only until the aesthetic teaches us how to put it to use.

Noting the persistence of this theme even in his earlier work, Krieger adds

Because of its fictional character, the literary would be free of any totalizing tendency toward the single-sided. For to me the danger of totalization, and its repressive force, emanates rather from the unrelenting controls that the conceptual—often in the guise of the political—would impose upon discourse. Thus for me it was the aesthetic that held the promise of freeing us from that repressive dominance: the drive to exclusion dictated by the monolithic claims of conceptual discourse can be happily evaded by the drive to inclusion provided by the duplicitous notion of the aesthetic as I had been developing it. The sociopolitical function of literature in its aesthetic dimension, then, is to *de*stabilize the dominant culture's attempt to impose *its* institutions by claiming a "natural" authority for them, and by using (as Brecht in this case properly sees) a false art (a conceptual rhetoric disguised as art) to create the ground for this illusionary naturalization of its claim to power. The aesthetic reveals the fraudulence, and thus the deception, of this attempt.

Not all of the authors in this collection agree about the extent to which Krieger has been successful in this effort to establish a worldly function for the uniquely self-reflective character of literary illusion. The importance of the effort itself is apparent, however, in the extent to which the authors agree that separating the work from the world relies on a false distinction, imposed upon literary experience by theorists who would denigrate art by collapsing it into one side or the other of that binary opposition. On the one hand, this specious logic is evident in efforts to portray literature in terms of an effete aestheticism and then to condemn aesthetic autonomy for its escapist—or all-too-willing—collusion with the status quo. On the other hand, the same opposition also underlies attempts to reduce the literary work to its political themes and then to assimilate the text entirely into a social context, understood either in material or symbolic terms. In the place of that binary logic, the authors in this volume emphasize the paradoxical or, more simply, "poetic" capacity of literature to have an effect on the world beyond its limit by acknowledging the limit as such. That proposition is at times argued as a metatheoretical rejection of any fixed opposition, such as that between text and context, in favor of a non-binary logic peculiar to poetic discourse. At other times, the proposition informs the analysis of specific tropes and rhetorical strategies that constitute the very possibility of literary performance against the pressure of ideology and dogma. At every moment, the essays in this volume direct our attention to the special status of literature in the full range of human experience, and they celebrate the unique vision literature affords for readers able to tell the difference between the work and the world, and able to read what the work tells us about the world in that difference.

The collection begins with Stanley Fish noting the difficulty that critics of Andrew Marvell have had in situating his work persuasively within the historical and social context of its time. Fish argues that Marvell's poetry is best characterized as an "art of disappearance" that would both reform and reject the world of which it is a part. This paradoxical relation of the work to the world is most evident, Fish argues, in Marvell's pervasive imagery of freedom and withdrawal from time and from human relations, but it extends even into the representational mechanisms of artistic media themselves. The very impulse to represent the freedom of poetry from intrusions of the outside world necessarily invokes that world in the images and figures that reject it. Consequently, that impulse inevitably returns both poem and poet to the worldly entanglements that mark the limit of the art. This ambivalence has frustrated some of Marvell's more politically minded critics, Fish observes, though it is far from a simplistic escapism. In fact, it resembles the more complicated aestheticist tendencies implicit in Krieger's work, where the work's paradoxical relation to the world constitutes a privileged perspective on the ideological constraints it would—but finally never can—transcend.

Underlying Fish's reading of Marvell's poetry is an oppositional logic that reads literature as suspended between poetic freedom and worldly constraint. Hazard Adams shows us that same logic at work beneath Krieger's insistence on the "duplicitous" nature of the poem, though what Fish sees as ambivalence in Marvell, Krieger reads as the "self-confessing illusion" of poetry in general. That "illusion," which calls attention to itself and so renders its illusory status visible, shifts poetry from "an epistemological to an ethical arena" by warning us against any cultural delusion "that would legitimize its authority by an appeal to nature" or truth, as Krieger puts it in *Words* about *Words* about *Words*.[18] As Adams claims, however, this paradoxical concept of the poem still defines poetry in terms of the binary opposition of truth and illusion, or presence and absence, and so perpetuates an epistemological bias beneath its ironic embrace of both sides of the opposition. Adams proposes instead what he calls an "antithetical" poetics that resists binary opposition as such. He derives this position from Vico's notion of the "certainty" associated with primitive mythology and poetry. Certainty, according to Vico, had nothing to do with the criterion of "truth" that governed later scientific thought. Adams notes that this certainty possessed a social utility quite apart from questions of truth and credibility, a utility resembling that of the "credible idol" described by Mazzoni. The ethical importance of poetry, Adams concludes, is therefore derived from its capacity to resist the logic of negation that is inherent in all ideological oppositions, including those that would bind the oppositions together aesthetically in a reciprocal or duplicitous relation.

Of all the solutions proposed to transcend the ideological bind of oppositional logic, none was more influential nor propounded more confidently than Romantic organicism and the aesthetic ideology of form with which it is associated. Coleridge's famous definition of beauty in the third essay of the "Principles of Genial Criticism" as "multeity in unity" promises to resolve the dilemma of word vs. world in the poetic image, where "the figure, and the real thing so figured, exactly coincide."[19] Yet deep within the German idealism from which Coleridge borrowed his theoretical formulae was a persistent reluctance to impute that resolution quite so simply to the work of art itself. Friedrich Schlegel occupies an especially controversial position in that tradition, as J. Hillis Miller explains in his essay. That controversy, Miller says, derives from Schlegel's status as "a great theorist and practitioner of irony." Hegel and Kierkegaard denounced Schlegel's irony as "infinite absolute negativity," but Miller follows de Man in stressing Schlegel's definition of irony as "a permanent parabasis," i.e., that moment when an actor suddenly breaks role and addresses the audience in his own voice. Thus, while irony is fundamentally unsettling and vertiginous, undermining the very categories of truth and illusion that constitute secure knowledge, that effect is also enlightening because it reveals the very limits of illusion that hide what remains unknowable.

For this reason, Schlegel insists that any attempt to represent "the highest" must combine enthusiasm, or the embodiment of that highest spirit, with irony, a self-canceling, a-rational attention to the limits of enthusiasm and to the "shimmering through of the aboriginal chaos's madness and stupidity." This combination constitutes what Schlegel calls mythology and serves as an allegory, not of the form of "the highest," but of the form-making or *Bildung* by which we know of it. Myths are therefore "catachreses for chaos," Miller argues, "thrown out to name something that has no proper name," and as such they are primarily performative acts that are "alien to knowledge" because they have no natural correspondence to their referent and must be "worked" into a sign for the chaos to be revealed.

The substitution of ethical effect for the epistemological criterion of truth, which Adams and Miller describe in their essays, echoes one of the oldest and most persistent defenses of poetry against Plato's charge that poets are liars. As Ernst Behler explains in his essay, that defense traditionally proceeds by situating poetry in an aesthetic realm where distinctions between truth and falsehood are inapplicable because there is no pretense of an exact—or any—correlation between language and the world. Behler argues that modern versions of this defense are more complicated because they take what was formerly considered the "aesthetic" freedom of poetry to be characteristic of all forms of human utterance. As developed by the Schlegels, Novalis, Kierkegaard, Nietzsche, Wilde, and others, this position often retains the criterion of truth, but it associates truth with poetry rather than prose because poetry celebrates its derivation from human desire and social interaction and openly admits its dissociation from the empirical world.

If understood simply as the negation of scientific or philosophical discourse, Behler adds, poetry is trivialized, as it is in the radical aestheticism of Wilde's "lying." (Fish suggests that poetry would be similarly trivialized in Marvell's poetry if the poetry's escapist impulse were not constantly frustrated by the text's inevitable return to the world.) Behler prefers Nietzsche's insistence on a reciprocal, dialectical relation between the discourses of poetry and science. That relation does not reverse Plato's elevation of science or truth over poetry so much as it subsumes that opposition in an inclusive dialectic between moral distinctions and artistic conjunctions. Behler also claims that we find vestiges of Nietzsche's position today in the softer forms of Gadamer's dialogic understanding or Habermas's idea of a philosophy that combines "strong propositions with weak status claims." As the essays by Adams and Miller demonstrate, however, the apparent modernity of this dialectical phenomenon may in fact be the product of a contemporary tendency to reduce the arguments of those earlier theorists (including the Schlegels) to a simplistic opposition between the truth of reference and the falsehood of artistic representation, whereas in fact that simplification belies the more complicated understanding of poetic discourse actually found in the work of those writers.

Historically, these complications found their most sustained and sophisticated expression in the long tradition of debate over the nature of ekphrasis. In that tradition, the representational status of art was argued as a contest between the spatial medium of painting and the temporal medium of poetry concerning which medium could best capture the immediacy of life. Contrary to the usual reading of the ekphrastic tradition, Stephen G. Nichols argues in his essay that poets and artists often represented a "complementarity between the iconic epigram and painting" rather than a simple opposition. This complementary relation not only promised to transcend the spatial and temporal limitations of visual and linguistic arts, but also aspired even to master the vagaries of space and time that distinguished the living models from their artistic representation. The French poet Clément Marot explored that complementarity in his work, Nichols says, using poetry's capacity to represent the immaterial, inner life of its subjects in order "to mediate the temporal vulnerability of the body and its likenesses." Similarly, the easy physical mobility of the linguistic medium extended the spatial range of art well beyond the usually fixed status of visual media. Literature thus surpassed the limits of place and position and reached out into the reader's space rhetorically in an effect resembling that of the portraiture that was increasingly fashionable during Marot's lifetime.

What distinguishes the ekphrastic tradition described by Nichols from the ironic or "antithetical" aesthetic described by Miller and Adams is the explicit retention of a referential truth-claim for aesthetics in ekphrasis. Within the ekphrastic tradition, the complementarity of painting and poetry is valuable precisely because it tells us something about the world that even lived experience cannot reveal. Denis Donoghue argues in his essay that the ekphrastic commitment to an epistemological dimension for poetry remains even in Krieger's sophisticated and highly self-conscious adaptation of this theoretical tradition. Donoghue claims that we find traces of this commitment most consistently in Krieger's emphasis on the self-consciousness and ultimate futility of poetic closure within the discourses of organicism and the American New Criticism. Though usually portrayed as an expression of skepticism toward the autonomy of the aesthetic object, this emphasis in fact reflects a vestigial epistemology in Krieger's work, Donoghue says, and he attributes it in part to Krieger's description of formal closure in spatial terms.

Donoghue proposes an alternative to spatial models of form, an alternative that he derives from Paul de Man's elevation of allegory over symbol as the defining trope of poetic language. That shift from symbol to allegory offers the possibility of thinking about form in temporal terms, and as a process that is not dependent on closure for its integrity. Nevertheless, Donoghue notes that de Man's emphasis on the failure of allegory to accomplish symbolic closure still retains a referential standard that measures the language of the poem against the world it fails to reach. Donoghue claims that this standard is less essential to de Man than to Krieger, however, because de Man's treatment of prosopopoeia as the defining trope of poetic language undoes the distinction between external reference and internal signification, portraying objects in the poem as semblances of the world rather than as illusions or hallucinations. We engage those semblances as action and experience, Donoghue says, not as knowledge (or even as knowledge admitted to be ironic, false, or lacking). Understood *as* experience, reading retains its temporal form and is oriented toward feeling and action rather than toward objects in the world. Consequently, as symbol in this temporal sense, the poem "is not a constituent of knowledge but of desire," and so it is free from the taint of epistemology endemic to the ekphrastic tradition.

Donoghue's reading of the debate between Krieger and de Man attempts to shift the terms of the debate from an epistemological connection between the work and the world to an engagement with the work itself as a material act or worldly experience, specifically that of desire. Though

Donoghue does not discuss the genealogy of this move, it clearly recalls Archibald MacLeish's famous dictum, "A poem should not mean, but be." It echoes even more aptly Cleanth Brooks's formalist defense of the poem as "a simulacrum of reality . . . by *being* an experience rather than any mere statement about experience" or even a representation of experience.[20] As Brooks understood, however, any effort to defend the poem as concrete experience or act necessarily subjects poetry (and its defense) to the same ethical and political judgment that may be directed toward any other action in the world. Brooks welcomed that judgment, for although he believed it fell outside the bounds of literary analysis per se, it ultimately justified the unique status of the autonomous poem because that autonomy was what guaranteed the disinterested exploration of all attitudes and emotions associated with whatever action the poem might portray mimetically, or with whatever statement the poem might stage within the context of its closed form.

For all of its formal sophistication, Brooks's aesthetic rather obviously echoes the dominant social ideals of the postwar United States. He envisioned the poem as a symbolic melting pot, in which images, actions, and even words themselves give up their worldly constraints and identities as they are reordered according to a more egalitarian and inclusive—in Brooks's terms, "ironic"—poetic order. It should not be surprising, then, that today, when the metaphor of the melting pot is often read as a rationalization for repressive homogenization and for the suppression of ethnic and racial difference, the aesthetic principle of formal closure would be associated with political totalitarianism and condemned for its collusion with the status quo. That collusion is sometimes read as allegorical (a structural homology between self-contained aesthetic systems and closed social orders) and sometimes as expressive (the work as the manifestation of more pervasive and sinister values of exclusivity and elitism). Either way, the association of formalist aesthetics with repressive politics has been posited both as an inevitable theoretical conjunction and as an undeniable historical phenomenon, and such arguments have been among the most persistent and persuasive challenges to the specificity of aesthetic experience and to the importance of literature as a source of autonomy and resistance to the status quo.

Yet, as David Carroll argues in his essay, this association is reductive, both as a reading of aesthetic form and as a political theory. Formal closure always works against itself in art by disclosing the connection to the world that the work of art would resist. Consequently, critics who argue for the isolation of the work from the world, and those who insist on its worldly status as an expression or reflection of political values, are equally caught within the oppositional logic that the literary work confounds. Carroll compares this aesthetic principle of an open organicism to Jules Michelet's theory of national unity, which borrows directly from aesthetic models of organic form. Contrary to monolithic racial models of the nation, Michelet argued that the spiritual unity of any people is not fixed or closed but in fact emerges in history out of the material differences among races and classes. Unlike totalitarian theories of "unification" imposed upon difference from without, Michelet's "dialectic of division and unification" unifies the nation as an aesthetic ideal and as a historical process that constantly confronts specific differences as the very ground of unity itself. Thus, Carroll concludes, the same obligation to resist ideological closure that Krieger describes as the critic's duty "should also be carried over into the study of history and politics, where the critic should dwell on what in history, as well as literature, resists organic closure and the ideological and aesthetic ideologies that support it."

For Wesley Morris, the historical significance accruing to the failure of aesthetic forms to close off their relation to the world must be understood as the product of a symbiotic relation between modernism and postmodernism. Postmodernism's famous decentering of the subject is but a "second-order" displacement, Morris argues, built upon modernism's earlier decentering of community through the image of an autonomous individual whose imaginative power opposed the oppressively technological form of late industrial society. Postmodernism's celebration of the sign undermined both the autonomy of that individual subject and the organic unity of its symbolic expression, but Morris claims that this "anti-formalism" was "irrevocably bound" to the organic formalism it opposed. Hence, Morris concludes, both movements are profoundly antihistorical in their rejection of the materiality of the world and the pressures of the past that emerge from it.

Unlike postmodernism, however, which exhausted itself in its celebration of difference, modernism's project remains unfinished. Morris claims that modernism's insistent search for a way to resolve differences and conflicts reflects the persistent need to make choices in the world experienced by a subject situated "at the site of contact between ideas of order and sensations, the locus of reality." Such choices require the wisdom born of memory and experience, Morris concludes, not the mere competence to manipulate and negotiate signifying systems, and they depend on a language that recognizes its own materiality in an effort to make a worldly "sense" rather than merely signifying "meaning." We can find that language theorized in Lyotard's *différend*, Morris says, and in Krieger's theory of a poem "that asserts itself as an image of presence." In both cases, we find a metaphor that eludes both the organic ontotheology of modernism and deconstructive difference. Instead, metaphor "operates to differ from difference, not as a guarantee of the good, but as a reminder of our most fundamental human engagement with the corporeal substance of our world."

For Wolfgang Iser, human experience is situated precisely in this gap between the world and the aesthetic forms with which we would make sense of that world; that situation is the focus of what Iser describes as "literary anthropology." Noting the importance of culture and representation in contemporary anthropological theory, Iser argues that literature may be understood as a special form of the fictions by which humans negotiate the "information gap" between their place in the world and the reflective self-consciousness that displaces them from that world. Drawing on the work of Clifford Geertz and Eric Gans, Iser describes anthropological fictions as oriented toward the world but caught up in a "recursive looping" of input and output that measures the fictional model against the world and then revises and retests that model endlessly. He thus describes anthropological fictions as explanatory and integrative, as opposed to literary fictions, which are exploratory and dissipative, "not meant to grasp anything given." Literary fictions represent the world only "as if" it were present to the author and reader.

Because Iser agrees with Krieger that literary fictions "deliberately disclose their fictionality," he claims that they "function as a means of disordering and disrupting their extratextual fields of reference," creating gaps rather than bridging them. In addition, literary texts are always composed of fragments of earlier fictions and must therefore be understood as "an ineluctable duality" in which previous texts are invoked but rewritten, while the pasts they represent are simultaneously invoked in the presence of the text. This intertextuality thus also constitutes cultural memory, and Iser claims that literature gives us a unique perspective on the way that memory functions.

The issue of memory is also crucial to Jacques Derrida's analysis of testimony as a poetic act. In his reading of Paul Celan's poem *"Aschenglorie"* ("Ash-glory"), Derrida argues that testifying or "bearing witness" to an event has much in common with the poetic experience of language as Krieger has described it. That experience, according to Krieger, is characterized by the poem's capacity "to play the unmasking role—the role of revealing the mask *as* mask." In so doing, "in the very act of becoming successfully poetic," the poem "implicitly constitutes its own poetic." Derrida claims that this paradoxical relation of the poem to the act of its own formation, its "poetics," establishes the specificity of a poem and, at the same time, opens the text out onto something beyond its verbal borders: onto the other to whom the poem is addressed, and onto the world.

According to Derrida, testimony bears a similar relation to its own performative basis because it, too, is always about something other than what it is. It is always about an event that took place in some other time and place, and that can only be remembered in its absence. Responsible witnesses, in the same way, are always conscious of an inevitable doubleness in their own roles. They speak about being in another place and time, and their authority depends on their having been there. On the other hand, the act of their speaking, or being able to speak, depends precisely on their no longer being there "as such," so that the position of which they speak is spoken of as absent, past, inaccessible, and irremediably other.

Derrida claims that Celan's poem testifies to this inevitable displacement of the witness's authority in its elliptical allusion to the Holocaust. By refusing to ground its rhetoric in that absent scene of horror, or even to vouch for the authority of the witness—Celan says there is no "witness for the witness"—"*Aschenglorie*" abandons knowledge and instead demands belief through a performative act that situates testimony in relation to the absence that marks the limit of its meaning, even as that absence authorizes those who bear witness to it. In terms of Celan's poem, that limit is death, the deaths of those victims who can never testify to their presence at the event that is remembered in the testimony of the witnesses who speak about them. That limit also marks the limit of interpretation, and the impossibility of ever seizing the poetic reference to which it bears witness by revealing the secret *as* secret. This internal limit characterizes both testimony and the poem, Derrida concludes; it is that to which all poems testify, and that which constitutes the poetic nature of all testimony.

In recognition of his influence on the contemporary defense of literary and aesthetic form, Murray Krieger was invited to reflect on the shape of his career and the extent to which his own "travels with the aesthetic" reflect theoretical debates on this issue from the 1940s to today. Characterizing his intellectual itinerary during these years as a voyage between ascetic and aesthetic values—between an emphasis on the moral and political uses of art and an attention to the properties of the work as an independent object—Krieger argues that these alternatives have "preconditioned" the dispositions of all literary commentators. Posed in this way, the alternatives have also created an unnecessary and misleading opposition between theories of organic closure that celebrate textual autonomy, and theories of direct referential connection between the text and the world that subordinate the text to that world.

Rather than choosing between these alternatives, Krieger proposes a "duplicitous" organicism that "subliminally calls attention to its own illusionary status" and so opens the text out onto the world by calling attention to the fictional status of its aesthetic claims. This "duplicity," in Krieger's terms, preserves the connection between the text and the world in all of its rich specificity, but it performs an even more important social function by exposing the fictional status of *all* discourse, even—especially—those ideological claims that would mask their fictions as natural and true. Thus Krieger confronts the "war on the aesthetic" being waged by "several varieties of sociohistorical theorists . . . replacing theory with historicism and the aesthetic with the sociopolitically ascetic." Such theorists assume with

Brecht that art merely reinforces the gullibility of the public by encouraging them to accept illusion as truth. Krieger insists instead that the aesthetic dimension of art actually sharpens the distinction between truth and illusion and so undermines the totalitarian impulse of all authoritarian discourse, including that of the "politicized theorists who would take *us* in by locking us within the ideological limitations of their claims."

This demystifying power turns the work of art into a potent source of resistance to ideological determination, but the very "self-conscious duplicity" that frees the work from determination by conceptual systems of all sorts also threatens to isolate it from effective dissent and so paralyze us in inaction. Krieger claims, however, that despite the power of this threat, we only ever experience this inaction in passing. The ephemeral character of aesthetic illusion necessarily turns us back to the world even as it satisfies, for a moment, the "elementary desires" for metaphorical unity embodied by the fiction of a natural sign. Thus, Krieger concludes, literature does not protect us from the need to act in the world, and to decide to act, in ways that are inevitably ideological, political, and partial. But it does protect us from becoming captives to the limitations of those actions and the delusions of truth and inevitability that the ideologue would project upon them. "The fictions we entertain within the aesthetic mode of response," Krieger says,

> thanks to the resistance to universals they engender in us, allow us an awareness of existence that enriches, as it softens, our humanity. In the everyday world of action, of decision making, literature, unlike other discourse, does not help us decide so much as it warns us to distrust the decisions we must make. When we are required to choose one path rather than another, it reminds us to tread with a light foot and a heavy heart.

If a "heavy heart" seems like a rather somber burden for a defense of poetry, especially in the midst of fervid calls to action that characterize so much theoretical work today, we might recall the importance that Wordsworth ascribed to "the still, sad music of humanity, / Nor harsh nor grating, though of ample power / To chasten and subdue." Half created and half perceived, a compound of memory and sensation, this is the music that the ear of the poet hears beneath the frantic cacophony of life, and this is the music that constitutes for the poet, "In nature and the language of the sense, / The anchor of my purest thoughts . . . and soul / Of all my moral being."[21] A still music, a gentle power, an anchor of thought in the language of sense—these paradoxes define poetry for Wordsworth as the link between reflection and action, pure thought and moral being, and they situate the poem squarely at the intersection of imagination and experience. That same crossroad is the point at which Krieger claims the aesthetic takes its revenge against ideology by suspending our steps along either path for a moment, and it marks the place of literature in theory today.

The essays in this collection were specially written to honor the work of Murray Krieger and his contributions to the development of literary theory as a field of inquiry and as an academic discipline in universities around the world. The vitality of debate represented here only begins to express the enduring influence of his presence as a theorist, colleague, teacher, and friend.

Michael P. Clark

NOTES

I would like to thank the following people for their help with this book: William Murphy of the University of Minnesota Press, Linda Norton and Jean McAneny of the University of California Press, Damion Searls, and Annelise Zamula. I would also particularly like to thank Professors Helen Regueiro Elam and Emory Elliott for their careful reading of the manuscript and their helpful suggestions.

1. See, for example, René Wellek and Austin Warren, *Theory of Literature* (New York: Harcourt Brace, 1949); Walter Jackson Bate, *Criticism: The Major Texts* (New York: Harcourt Brace Jovanovich, 1952); Wellek's *A History of Modern Criticism,* 8 vols. (New Haven: Yale University Press, 1955–92); Murray Krieger, *The New Apologists for Poetry* (Minneapolis: University of Minnesota Press, 1956); W. K. Wimsatt and Cleanth Brooks, *Literary Criticism: A Short History* (New York: Knopf, 1957); Hazard Adams, *Critical Theory Since Plato* (New York: Harcourt Brace Jovanovich, 1971).

2. Richard Macksey and Eugenio Donato, eds., *The Structuralist Controversy: The Languages of Criticism and the Sciences of Man* (Baltimore: Johns Hopkins University Press, 1972); Jacques Derrida, *Of Grammatology,* trans. Gayatri Chakravorty Spivak (Baltimore: Johns Hopkins University Press, 1977).

3. Among many works by these authors see J. Hillis Miller, *Fiction and Repetition* (Cambridge, Mass.: Harvard University Press, 1982) and *The Linguistic Moment* (Princeton: Princeton University Press, 1985); Geoffrey Hartman, *Criticism in the Wilderness: The Study of Literature Today* (New Haven: Yale University Press, 1980) and *Saving the Text: Literature/Derrida/Philosophy* (Baltimore: Johns Hopkins University Press, 1981); and Paul de Man, *Blindness and Insight: Essays in the Rhetoric of Contemporary Criticism* (New York: Oxford University Press, 1971).

4. Michel Foucault, "Intervista a Michel Foucault," *Microfiseca del Potere* (Turin, 1977); the English text appears in *Power/Knowledge: Selected Interviews and Other Writings, 1972–1977,* ed. Colin Gordon (New York: Pantheon, 1980), quotation from 114.

5. In "The Function of Criticism at the Present Time" (1864), Arnold defined the "rule" for culture as "disinterestedness," i.e., "keeping aloof from what is called 'the practical view of things' . . . by steadily refusing to lend itself to any of those ulterior, political, practical considerations about ideas." Later in the same essay, Arnold adds that "the critic must keep out of the region of immediate practice in the political, social, humanitarian sphere, if he wants to make a beginning for that more free speculative treatment of things, which *may perhaps one day* make its benefits felt even in this sphere, but in a natural and thence irresistible manner." (These citations are from Adams, *Critical Theory Since Plato,* 588, 591, my emphasis.) While

Arnold's critics have been too quick to dismiss such codicils to his general emphasis on disinterestedness as entirely gratuitous and unconvincing, the vague, tentative phrasing in which Arnold couches the possibility of a social effect for culture here certainly begs such a response, especially as those claims have been echoed in theoretical traditions influenced by Arnold. See, for example, the conclusion to Cleanth Brooks's 1949 essay "Irony as a Principle of Structure," where after insisting at length that the language of the poem systematically severs its referential connection to the world and ironically undoes any truth-claims it might contain, Brooks concludes that "(One of the 'uses' of poetry, I should agree, is to make us better citizens.) But poetry is not the eloquent rendition of the citizen's creed. It is not even the accurate rendition of his creed. Poetry must carry us beyond the abstract creed into the very matrix out of which, and from which, our creeds are abstracted" (in Adams, *Critical Theory Since Plato,* 1048). This ambivalence toward the relation between culture and society characterizes a wide range of literary criticism in the United States and remains influential today, though not without challenge. Recently, John Rowe has criticized such attempts to claim an indirect political effect for the autonomy of culture as part of "the Emersonian tradition of 'aesthetic dissent' [that] has defined itself as distinct from those political movements through which historical progress has been achieved in America" (*At Emerson's Tomb: The Politics of Classic American Literature* [New York: Columbia University Press, 1997], ix).

6. For a brief introduction to the major figures associated with the Frankfurt School and an analysis of its sources in critical Marxism, see Andrew Arato and Eike Gebhardt, eds., *The Essential Frankfurt School Reader* (New York: Urizen Books, 1978), especially 185–224 on the issue of culture and materialism. Of the authors associated with this early group, Theodor Adorno was most influential for the development of an aesthetics out of this tradition; see particularly his *Philosophy of Modern Music,* trans. Anne G. Mitchell and Wesley V. Blomster (New York: Seabury Press, 1973), and *Aesthetic Theory,* trans. C. Lenhardt (London: Routledge and Kegan Paul, 1984). Among the British Marxists most influential in the development of a politicized historical analysis, Raymond Williams is certainly foremost, but in the 1970s and 1980s the mode of discourse analysis associated with the Birmingham School was particularly influential; see also the attempt to link certain aspects of poststructural analysis with traditional methods of materialist critique in Rosalind Coward and John Ellis, *Language and Materialism: Developments in Semiology and the Theory of the Subject* (London: Routledge and Kegan Paul, 1977). In the wake of early poststructuralism, French Marxism split radically into at least two major camps, one clinging to affiliations with the Communist party and an already antique empirical materialism, and another that undertook a re-reading of Marx along poststructural lines. Louis Althusser was by far the most significant of this latter group, but see Pierre Macherey, *Pour une théorie de la production littéraire* (Paris: F. Maspero, 1966) for a systematic literary critique developed from this perspective.

7. For an example of such an attack, see John M. Ellis, *Literature Lost: Social Agendas and the Corruption of the Humanities* (New Haven: Yale University Press, 1997).

8. This apocalyptic tone can be found in Ellis, but see also Allan Bloom, *The Closing of the American Mind: How Higher Education Has Failed Democracy and Impoverished the Souls of Today's Students* (New York: Simon and Schuster, 1987), and Dinesh

D'Souza's *Illiberal Education: The Politics of Race and Sex on Campus* (New York: Random House, 1991).

9. Perhaps the best example of this shift toward a monolithic model of symbolic determination can be found in the career of Foucault himself. His early work *Histoire de la folie à l'age classique; folie et déraison* (Paris: Plon, 1961) dealt extensively with the literature of madness (as well as madness itself) as a point of philosophical resistance to the regime of Reason, but the notion of the *episteme* developed in *Les mots et les choses: une archéologie des sciences humaines* (Paris: Gallimard, 1966) and the model of disciplinary society introduced in *Surveiller et punir: naissance de la prison* (Paris: Gallimard, 1975) portrayed historical ages as monolithic systems entirely dominated by a single discourse and a continuous network of institutional practices. Foucault continued to insist on the possible viability of local, temporary points of resistance to these hegemonic systems, but that insistence was not always convincing and has been attacked for its pessimistic concession to the intractable nature of power and oppression in modern society as a whole.

10. Roland Barthes, "De l'oeuvre au texte," *Revue d'Esthetique* 3 (1971); the English text appears as "From Work to Text" in *Textual Strategies: Perspectives in Post-Structuralist Criticism* (Ithaca: Cornell University Press, 1979). Further citations will be made parenthetically in the text.

11. Edward Said, *The World, the Text, and the Critic* (Cambridge, Mass.: Harvard University Press, 1983), 39.

12. Fredric Jameson, *The Political Unconscious: Narrative as a Socially Symbolic Act* (Ithaca: Cornell University Press, 1981), 9, 35.

13. In Homi Bhabha, *The Location of Culture* (New York: Routledge, 1994), 140.

14. See Jameson, *Political Unconscious,* chapter 6, and Bhabha, *Location of Culture,* 147–55.

15. Abdul R. JanMohamed and David Lloyd, eds., *The Nature and Context of Minority Discourse* (New York: Oxford University Press, 1990).

16. Walter Benjamin, "The Work of Art in the Age of Mechanical Reproduction," originally published in *Zeitschrift für Sozialforschung* 1 (1936), translated by Harry Zohn in Benjamin, *Illuminations* (New York: Schocken Books, 1969). For the remarks on fascism, see 231–42.

17. Murray Krieger, *Ekphrasis: The Illusion of the Natural Sign* (Baltimore: Johns Hopkins University Press, 1992), 258.

18. Murray Krieger, *Words* about *Words* about *Words: Theory, Criticism, and the Literary Text* (Baltimore: Johns Hopkins University Press, 1988), 6, 15.

19. Samuel Taylor Coleridge, "On the Principles of Genial Criticism Concerning the Fine Arts" (1814), in Adams, *Critical Theory Since Plato,* 464.

20. MacLeish's line is from "Ars Poetica" (1926); Brooks's remark is from "The Heresy of Paraphrase," in *The Well Wrought Urn* (New York: Harcourt Brace Jovanovich, 1947) and in Adams, *Critical Theory Since Plato,* 1040.

21. William Wordsworth, "Lines Composed a Few Miles Above Tintern Abbey," in *The Poetical Works of William Wordsworth,* ed. E. de Selincourt, 2nd ed. (Oxford: Oxford University Press, 1952), 261, ll. 91–111.

CHAPTER ONE

Marvell and the Art of Disappearance

Stanley Fish

Murray Krieger ends his recent book, *The Institution of Theory*, by pleading guilty to the charge that, even after all these years, he is still an "apologist for poetry."[1] These days being an apologist for poetry means resisting the various historicisms—old, new, cultural, material—whose expansive arguments are made at the expense of the aesthetic, a category (and area) that either disappears in the analysis of "discursive systems" or is identified (and stigmatized) as the location of a status-quo politics anxious to idealize its own agendas. Krieger's strategy is to claim for poetry what our new theorists claim for history and politics: the capacity to complicate, and by complicating disperse, the power of ideological formations. Rather than being in need of demystification, the literary text instructs us in the art—and, far in advance of deconstruction, performs the work—of undoing unities and opening up apparent closures: "totalization is that which the discourse of ideology imposes, and it is that from which, potentially, the counter ideological discourse of the literary text can liberate us" (73). Literature, in short, is "counter theoretical" (87)—where by "theoretical" Krieger means "ideological"—and "in these ideological days, it is the pressure to resist, as well as the role of literature in supplying it, that is sorely needed" (75).

In essence, this is an up-to-date version of Sidney's *Apology* (itself a Renaissance refurbishing of Horace), but with a difference. While both Sidney and Krieger find a special job for literature to do—one beyond the capacities of either history or philosophy—in Sidney's argument that job is hortatory in a positive sense. The reader who, in one of Sidney's memorable examples, comes upon the image of Aeneas carrying old Anchises on his back will be moved to wish himself such a person and therefore be more inclined to act in that same way when the opportunity presents itself. (The moment and the lesson are the essence of humanism.) In Krieger's argument, in contrast, readers are moved by poetry to *refrain* from action, at least of the precipitously ideological kind, and to tarry for a while in the realm of "leisure" or "ideological freedom" that "the poetic fiction" provides (65). Whereas Sidney sees poetry as sharing with history and philosophy a political task, but performing it more effectively, Krieger sees poetry as working against the political projects to which history and philosophy are often attached and instantiating instead a political project of its own, the project of resistance.

It is easy to see why this particular apology for poetry is attractive: given the high value we now place on political commitment, and the suspicion (voiced on all sides) of detachment and disengagement, it is satisfying to find a way of investing disengagement with a political effectivity. Nevertheless, there is another apology for poetry, more radical (although as old as the hills), that one occasionally spies just below the surface of Krieger's argument, especially in those pages where he revisits (nostalgically, I think) the discourse of the New Criticism, rooted in the Kantian ideal of "the transcendence of all our private desires" (60), and in the conception of the work of art as a unique and self-enclosed construct (63), "a self sealing form" so internally complete and totalizing that "it exclude[s] everything else" (71). This stronger version of aestheticism has become suspect because it seeks no compromise with human concerns and indeed pushes them away, and that is why Krieger, as attuned as he is to the critical and cultural currents of the present moment, pushes it away. Nevertheless (although it is presumptuous of me to say so), that stronger aestheticism is really what he wants and I am going to nudge him in its direction by revisiting a poet who wants it too.

That poet is Andrew Marvell, and what makes him a very emblem of the issues Krieger raises is the fact that he is at once the most public and social of men—a tutor to Fairfax's daughter and Cromwell's ward, Latin Secretary of the Council of State, a member of parliament for twenty years—and the least knowable. "I am naturally inclined to keep my thoughts private," Marvell writes in a letter in 1675, and the same sentiment ends a poem ("Mourning") that begins as a meditation on meaning and the possibility of specifying it:

> I yet my silent judgment keep,
> Disputing not what they believe:
> But sure as oft as women weep,
> It is to be supposed they grieve.[2]

The question of record is "what does it mean when women weep?" The closest the poem comes to providing an answer is the word "sure." But what the speaker is sure of is that one may suppose that women's weeping signifies grief; that is, one is sure of a supposition, but the truth (or falsehood) of what is supposed remains hidden. Neither the poem nor the speaker will yield it up, and therefore they don't yield themselves up either. The result is not what Krieger describes as the hallmark of poetry under the New Criticism—every meaning "confronted by its self-contradiction" (63)—but something more stringent and parsimonious, a shrinking away from meaning altogether. "Mourning" does not give us multiple meanings or many judgments, but rather no meanings and a withholding of judgment. Both poem and speaker "keep" to themselves, neither venturing out nor letting anything (or anyone) in.

This is the action (if that is the word) Marvell's poetry attempts (surely the wrong word) to perform, the action of withholding, of keeping to itself, and what is withheld is meaning, the imputation of a significance that originates with the agent who would bestow it. At the most general level this agent is man:

> Luxurious man, to bring his vice in use,
> Did after him the world seduce.
> ("The Mower against Gardens," 1–2)

"After him" means (I am aware of the irony) both "in the wake of" and "in the image of." By seeing, and thus organizing, the world as the categories of his consciousness enable and command him to do, man makes what is primary secondary and what is secondary—the acts of perception and predication—primary. If, as William James famously declares, "the trail of the human serpent is over everything,"[3] it is the smell and slime of that trail from which Marvell recoils in disgust. Man cannot keep his hands, and what is worse, his mind, off of things. His vice is consciousness itself, that appropriative motion which insists on itself as a point of reference in relation to which everything else is then defined. Like Wallace Stevens's jar, human consciousness takes dominion everywhere.[4]

In "The Garden" (23–24), Marvell identifies this prideful taking of dominion with the act of naming, for as John Carey observes, naming, especially of natural objects—which of course are not "objects" in their own eyes—"destroys the unnamed innocence of the thing itself." Things named, Carey continues, "have been interfered with by language."[5] Moreover, man's interference is involuntary; in the very act of seeing, the coordinates of his own perception frame and mark out the relative—not essential—shape and place of all that comes within his view. In "The Mower against Gardens," man encloses: "He first enclosed within the gardens square / A dead and standing pool of air" (5–6). He alters: "With strange perfumes he did the roses taint, / And flowers themselves were taught paint" (11). He adds: "And a more luscious earth for them did knead" (7). "Gardens square" is a double interference; there are no gardens in nature; the squaring of what was not there before is a flaunting and redoubling of an original outrage. The flowers that are taught to paint themselves are no longer themselves; they wear the garment of the landscape artist. The earth that is enriched by human cultivation becomes more than—and therefore different from—what it is; by being kneaded it is given more than it, in and of itself, needs. Giving more is what man inevitably does; that is why he is called "luxurious," that is, excessive, *self*-indulgent, superfluous, above and beyond what is necessary. He simply cannot allow anything to be itself; he cannot leave anything alone.

To be left alone, to not be interfered with, to not be appropriated, is the desire of all Marvellian actors, and it is the frustration of that desire about which they endlessly complain. Two such complainers speak all the lines in "A Dialogue Between the Soul and Body," and despite the apparently agonistic form of the poem, the goal of each is not to triumph, but to decouple. Each desires to be sufficiently distinguished from the other so that a line between them can be cleanly drawn. "Each complains," as Donald Friedman says, "that it has been made what it is by the other and . . . imagines a state of being in which it would be freely and independently itself."[6] The language of tyranny and enslavement that characterizes both speakers does not indicate a desire to be master, but a desire, stronger than Greta Garbo's, to be alone ("Two paradises 'twere in one / To live in Paradise alone" ["The Garden," 63–64]). The soul's complaint is not simply that it feels grief, but that the grief is "another's" (22).

Indeed the point is even deeper than that—since grief itself can only be experienced in relation to loss, deprivation, or disappointment, it is the product of *relationships,* of entanglements; were one to live entirely within oneself, with no motion outward and no intrusions into the space of one's being, grief would not be a possibility. Nor would any of the other emotions be possible, as we see from the equivalent statement by the soul:

> Joy's cheerful madness does perplex
> Or sorrow's other madness vex;
> Which knowledge forces me to know,
> And memory will not forgo. (37–40)

The vexations of sorrow and joy depend on memory, and memory is a function of time, of the disabling ability to recall in the present what has happened to one in the past. Memory is necessary to action (if you don't know where you've been, how will you know where to go next?), and in many if not most accounts of being, memory is honored; but action, engagement with the world of others, is precisely what the body and soul, in their different but related ways, wish to avoid. Indeed, each also wishes to avoid knowledge, for as the verse quite explicitly says, "knowledge forces" (39). That is, knowledge is a commerce on a two-way street: one either knows *about* another or one is known *by* another, and in either case knowledge cannot be

experienced independently; you can only "do" it in the company of someone else, who is either its object or its agent. Knowledge requires extension,
both horizontally to others and vertically in relation to a past that strains toward a future. Knowledge, memory, grief, joy, sorrow are all attributes of the
life lived in time, of an existence that is not accidentally but essentially temporal (available to narration and known only in narration), and therefore
not in and of itself essential at all.

In short, and as I have already said, consciousness itself—the realm of
consecutive and reflective thought—is the chief obstacle to the desired
state of being in these poems. The point is made clearly in "The Coronet,"
a poem in which the speaker's efforts to lay a pure offering at his savior's feet
fail, and fail precisely because they are made, because *as* efforts they originate at a distance from the object of desire and thus apprehend (a word not
innocent) that object from a perspective not its own. In "Eyes and Tears,"
Marvell speaks of the "self deluding sight" that "In a false angle takes each
height" (5–6), and we are meant to realize, first, that any angle is a false
angle in that it cannot be true to the non-angle from which the object knows
itself, and, second, that sight is always self deluding since what it delivers
is the view from some angle. That is why the exertions of the speaker in
"The Coronet" are, quite literally, self-defeating; whatever their direction,
they will come bearing "wreaths of fame and interest" (16); that is, they will
merely reproduce the condition of distance—of non-identity—that makes
them necessary in the first place. The difficulty is summed up in lines that
declare the futility, and indeed sinfulness, of summing up:

> And now when I have summed up all my store
> Thinking (so I myself deceive)
> So rich a chaplet thence to weave . . . . (9–11)

Taken in isolation, line 10 says it all: simply by thinking, by assuming a
stance of reflection (in relation to a past that now configures both the present and the hope of a future), the agent deceives himself as to the possibility of achieving his goal, deceives himself into thinking that, *by* thinking, he
will be able to annihilate the distance thought inevitably declares and extends. Any summing up, any adding up of sums, any putting of things together, any gathering of store, any of the gestures that are the content of
consciousness, only further embeds one in the angled, and, because angled,
false life of temporality, of deferral, of non-coincidence with the essence of
being. The alternative is literally inconceivable and is largely represented
(another gesture signifying defeat) in the poem by words and phrases that
would in other discourses carry a positive value, but here are merely different versions of the same debilitating abilities: to "seek" (4), to "gather" (6),
to "weave" (11), to "find" (13), to "twin[e]" (14), to "fold" (15), to "frame"
(22), to "set with skill" (24), to "ch[oose] out with care" (24), and even to

"care." Opposed to these inevitable shapes of conscious effort are the negative actions attributed to Christ: *un*tying and *dis*entangling ("Either his slippery knots at once untie; / And disentangle all his winding snare" [20–21]). One must, that is, be tied to nothing, entangled only in one's own snare and no one else's, set off in one's own frame, neither measuring nor measured by the frame of some other.

But how would one do that, or, rather, how would one so completely undo entanglements as to achieve this incredible independence? This is the problem that vexes many of Marvell's speakers, among them the Nymph who voices her famous and famously enigmatic complaint. What she is complaining about is, first, change, and then (and ultimately) the corruption that attends relationality: "The wanton troopers riding by / Have shot my fawn and it will die." ("The Nymph Complaining for the Death of Her Fawn," 1–2) The action is abrupt and intrusive; it comes in sideways ("riding by"), as if the characters from another poem have for a moment burst into this one and left behind something to decipher. Why did they do it? "Thou ne'er didst alive / Them any harm" (4–5). What does it mean? "I'm sure I never wished them ill" (7). These questions are barely registered (let alone answered) before there is another abrupt intrusion, this one produced by the Nymph herself who, without preamble, says "Inconstant Sylvio" (25). It is Sylvio who had given her the fawn, but who then, after having "beguiled" her (33), left it behind as a gift marked by his duplicity. Even before the troopers came riding by, he came riding by and in a somewhat longer space of time performed as they would, with motives she can only wonder at. All she is sure of is what he *said*—"I know what he said, I'm sure I do" (30)—but in the light of his betrayal she cannot be sure of what he meant. Indeed the trouble is that he meant anything at all, that she was required to read him, that there was a gap between what he presented (in both his person and his gift) and what he was. (His is the double mind of which the Mower complains ["The Mower against Gardens," 9] even as he displays it.) That is what the world of meaning is, a realm where nothing is coincident with itself but requires for its completion, for its self-realization (which is therefore not a *self*-realization at all), the frame of something other, of some prior history or future goal. In the world of meaning, nothing can be taken at face value because the value of the face always resides elsewhere. (Everything is a sign.)

In the interval between her two encounters with meaning, which are also encounters with deferral, the Nymph turns to the fawn with whom, she reports, "I set myself to play" (37). "Setting oneself" is the language of plan and design, but the design here is to have none, and rather to play, a word that appears prominently in Marvell's poetry where it almost always means non-purposeful activity, activity that is not the product of motives or strategies, activity that is merely consecutive, discontinuous activity in the sense that each of its moments is a hostage neither to the past nor the future. It is therefore, as the Nymph immediately says, "solitary," not bound to anything but itself, and "idle" (40), that is, innocent of teleology.

That innocence, however, is precarious, and the Nymph knows as much, for even before the wanton troopers have appeared she is worrying that the fawn itself might change:

> Had it lived long, I do not know
> Whether it might have done so
> As Sylvio did. (47–49)

That is, in time the fawn too might acquire motives, and present a surface that could not be trusted, a surface that would have to be read in long-range (past and future) terms rather than simply received and experienced. Moreover, insofar as she finds herself imagining a world populated by agents who think strategically, who mean, the Nymph herself is becoming such an agent, someone who cannot take anything for what it is, but must always be looking for hidden reasons and, therefore, harboring such reasons herself. Even when she speculates on the long term effects of the fawn's diet— "its chief delight was still / On roses thus itself to fill" (87–88)—the result she imagines is emblematic of her fears: "Had it lived long, it would have been / Lilies without, roses within" (91–92). That is, not through and through the same, but self-divided, double, duplicitous. Perhaps, then, the fact that the fawn did not live long should be considered a blessing rather than a cause for complaint, for it is only when the fawn grows up, and with it the Nymph, that the idle idyll they now share will be disrupted in ways even more upsetting than the disruption performed by the wanton troopers; perhaps the "short time" (52) when Nymph and fawn enjoyed a love in "play" would give way to the red and white carnal love to which her half-conscious blushes already point. It is significant that the fawn is ungendered, referred to only as "it," an equivocation designed to hold back the time when its "pure virgin limbs" (89) may not be so pure or so virgin.

In her desire (abetted, ironically, by the action of the wanton troopers) to arrest the moment of self-contained and inconsequential play, the Nymph is one with the male speakers of Marvell's two pedophilic poems, "Young Love" and "The Picture of Little T. C. in a Prospect of Flowers." In these poems, an unselfconscious being, that is, a being whose sense of herself is not borrowed from another or from an awareness of what she once was and will someday be, is observed in play by an older man who can observe and reflect on but cannot experience (because he can reflect on) her "simplicity": "See with what simplicity / This Nymph begins her golden days!" ("The Picture," 1–2). Seeing the simplicity, being able to recognize it, is to be unable to live it, for it is recognized as something the observer lacks, and lack—desire to be something other than one is, indeed knowledge that there is something else to be—is the antithesis of the simple state. True (that is, authentic) simplicity is wholly self-sufficient, complete in and of itself, neither signified nor signifying. It is therefore a condition continually threatened, as in these poems, by the future imagined for the young girl by her voyeuristic admirer. Some day, he speculates, she may assume a role in some "high cause" (9), that is, in some epic story; and he can only hope to extend the time "Ere" her "conquering eyes . . . have tried their force to wound / Ere, with their glancing wheels, they drive / In triumph over hearts that strive" (18–21). "Force," "wound," "wheels," "drive," "triumph," "strive"—this is the vocabulary of forward movement, of time that does not provide endless spaces for directionless play but exerts its pressures in ways that inevitably produce alteration; this is the vocabulary of design, and of agents, who, in the course of the unfolding of design, become other than they were, either because they have striven and thus defined themselves by ends not yet in view, or because they have been conquered and become defined by the ends of those who have triumphed.

It is design and an existence defined only in relation to design, in relation to something you are now not, in relation to relation, that the Nymph complaining wants to avoid, and she takes her cue from moments in which the fawn cannot be seen:

> Among the beds of lilies, I
> Have sought it oft, where it should lie;
> Yet could not till it self would rise,
> Find it, although before mine eyes.
> For in the flaxen lilies' shade,
> It like a bank of lilies laid. (77–82)

In order to be seen—captured in another's perspective—the fawn must rise in such a way as to receive definition from a surrounding background; in short, it must appear, where appearance is understood as being set off by something external to it. It follows, then, that in order to escape being defined by another, one must dis-appear, find a mode of being that is not available to the appropriation of sight, and that is what the fawn does when it merges with the bank of lilies so completely that it cannot be picked out. The effect is noted precisely by the Nymph: it is before (in front of, ahead of) her eyes, but not within their sphere of appropriation; the fawn has escaped into a realm where what it is depends on nothing but its own frame of reference.

It is this achievement that the Nymph attempts to match when she resolves "to bespeak thy grave and die" (111). Notice that the claim is not to speak about the fawn's grave, but to speak it, to express it so perfectly that there is no distance between the expression and the thing expressed, so perfectly that expression is no longer expression—a sign of nonidentity—

but tautology. On its face the Nymph's way of making good on her claim is curious: she will have a statue of herself weeping "cut in marble" (112). What could be more an instance of representation and therefore of the distance she wishes to erase than the cutting of a statue? From idea, to medium, to engraver, to tool, to message—with each stage in the process, the condition of mediation, of non-coincidence with the origin, with the thing itself, would seem to be more firmly established. But then the Nymph declares the case to be exactly the reverse:

> . . . but there
> Th' engraver sure his art may spare,
> For I so truly thee bemoan,
> That I shall weep though I be stone,
> Until my tears, still dropping, wear
> My breast, themselves engraving there. (113–18)

The key phrase is "themselves engraving," which means both being at once their own medium and message (a state literally inconceivable) and putting themselves into the grave, i.e., entombing themselves. The relationship between the two is precise: if there could be a mode of representation that scorned the aid of anything external to the thing represented, the result would be the dis-appearance of that thing, since it could only be seen from its own perspective; from any other perspective, from another angle, from angle in general, the thing would be unavailable, would not be present, would be dead, would be *engraved.* The moral is bleak: true life requires representational death; tears that engrave themselves (in both senses) are their own signs and therefore do not signify, they do not point to anything and nothing else points to—is a sign of—them; they are not known by any alien agent; they are not seen, no angle—by definition false—delivers them; they have escaped from the world of meaning.

Or at least that is the desire. As the poem ends the Nymph adds a component to her sculptural tableau: the fawn too will be carved, "of purest alabaster made" (120); but that is just the trouble: it will be "made," fashioned by another and therefore not itself, and it is with this admission, an admission of failure, that the poem comes to its unhappy conclusion:

> For I would have thine image be
> White as I can, though not as thee. (121–22)

That is, although I would like to have thine image be no image at all, have it *be* thee rather than *as* (not quite up to, at a distance from) thee, the best that I, or any other self-conscious agent, can achieve is a whiteness that is still too much on this side of visibility. The project of dis-appearing will always fall short of success if only because the effort itself shows. To be sure, the Nymph is enigmatic—if she never figures out what the actions of either the troopers or Sylvio mean, generations of critics have never managed to figure out what she means—but as an enigma she is still known, if imperfectly.

In Marvell's corpus the desire not to be represented, not to be known, not to be forced by an angle into appearance, is fully realized only by a non-animate agent, "On a Drop of Dew." The poem of this title begins with a simple, but ultimately unfollowable, direction, "See":

> See how the orient dew . . . .

The image seems firm enough until the first word of the second line: "Shed from the bosom of the morn." "Shed" names an action that is already past, and consequently when we look for the object to which the imperative directs us, it has already fled our apprehension, escaped our grasp. I intend this last literally, for seeing is itself a relational activity in which the object is seen—placed, fixed, captured—within the viewer's perspective and not its own. This drop of dew simply does not want to be seen and it repeatedly moves away from the line of vision that would take it in, that would enclose it, and instead it "Round in itself encloses / And in its little globe's extent / Frames as it can its native element" (6–8). This is as precise as it is impossible; a frame is by definition separate from that which it holds in place, but this drop of dew is held in place—is given definition, shape, and identity—by itself, and is its own enclosure; it escapes capture by others by capturing or encasing itself, and the way it does this unthinkable thing—and it is important that it be unthinkable since to be able to think about it is to have framed and enclosed it—is the subject of the next few lines:

> How it the purple flow'r does slight,
> Scare touching where it lies,
> But gazing back upon the skies,
> Shines with a mournful light,
> Like its own tear . . .
> Restless it rolls and insecure,
> Trembling lest it grow impure. (9–13, 15–16)

Each of these lines describes the same motion: a withdrawing, a retreating, a resisting of contact; the drop never quite touches anything, instead it hangs there, suspended in midair, "like its own tear." This description or nondescription is particularly precise and teasing. Tears are framed by faces, but this tear is framed—is seen against—the background of the drop of dew which it also is. "Like" is finally a joke and is at the same time the victim of the joke (like its own tear, like its own joke); even syntax is defeated by this object that refuses to be apprehended by anything but itself.

That refusal takes the physical form of continual oscillation: "Restless it rolls and insecure." In any other context this might be a complaint, but the

state of insecurity—of not being tied down to anything—is what the drop
of dew desires, and restlessness does not name a deprivation but a triumph;
were it at rest, it would be available for sighting, one could get a fix on it,
but as long as it trembles, no sight line can establish a defining relation with
it, and therefore the purity of its self-definition remains uncompromised.
Later, in the second half of the poem, when the drop of dew has been analogized to the human soul, its movement is described in two remarkable, and
remarkably antimimetic, lines:

> In how coy a figure wound,
> Every way it turns away. (27–28)

"Figure" is a mocking word on two levels. First it names that condition of
perceptual clarity—of standing in outline against a background—that the
drop repeatedly refuses; but figure also means figure of speech, a class of
verbal actions characterized by every rhetorician as a deviation or turning
away from direct or literal speech; but of course "coy" means just that, a
turning away, a withdrawing, a delay, and therefore a "coy" figure is a withdrawing or a retreating in retreat or a delayed delaying, an indirection that
turns away. The next line is a gloss on this inconceivable motion: "Every way
it turns away." In what we might call "normal" turning away, one withdraws
in relation to some points of reference—lines of sight—but grows nearer
in relation to others; but this (non-)figure somehow, and we cannot know
how, never turns toward anything; whichever way it turns, it maintains and
increases its distance from anything that is not itself. This is not coyness of
the usual kind, a strategy of delay and deferral designed to make the inevitable coming together even more sweet. This is coyness that is essential,
one might even say defining, except that definition—in both the physical
and conceptual senses—is what it perpetually flees.

What it flees to is its own dissolution, the state in which the effort it must
so strenuously exert, the effort not to be touched, not to be framed, to dis-
appear, is finally unnecessary:

> Such did the manna's sacred dew distill,
> White and entire, though congealed and chill,
> Congealed on earth: but does, dissolving, run
> Into the glories of th' almighty sun. (37–40)

The reference is to Exodus 16:11–22, and it seems straightforward enough
until one notices that while the syntax makes the dew the property of the
manna, it is the dew that distills and what it distills—leaves behind, as a
purified entity—is the manna: "And when the dew that lay was gone up, be-
hold . . . there lay a small round thing . . . on the ground" (Exod. 16:14).
The manna is thus in the impossible but familiar Marvellian position of dis-
tilling itself, emerging not from any prior, governing entity, but from its own

property. Moreover, although it emerges, it does not thereby surrender possession of itself to alien eyes and angles, for as we are told in Exodus, the children of Israel see "a small round thing" and call it manna because "they wist not what it was"; that is, they give it a name indicating their inability to categorize it, a name signifying that it has not been named, captured, framed by something other than its native element (which remains unknown). In the last two lines of "On a Drop of Dew" it returns to that element, disappearing before our eyes, as the Nymph's fawn disappears before hers and as the manna of Exodus disappears even as the Israelites "see" it.

It does this in two steps. First it congeals (39); that is, becomes more concentratedly what it is, adheres to its own particles, turns inward and away from the world; but that is its posture only "on earth," where it is threatened by the danger of alien appropriation. Once in its native element, it quite literally relaxes and gives itself to its proper home; there, one can assume, it is seen by "natives," by those just like it, seen, in effect, by itself. But what we see is its dissolution, its loss of definition; what we see, quite literally and almost in slow motion, is its dis-appearance; not however disappearance into nonbeing, but into a mode of being that escapes apprehension in the two fully relevant senses of that word: being grasped mentally, and being taken into custody, into prison. (As Donald Friedman has finely said, "all of our attempts to capture meaning in form are rendered inappropriate by the 'Glories of th' Almighty sun.'") [7]

One cannot, however, generalize from the drop's escape; after all, it was required to maintain its radically evasive behavior only for a few short hours before rescue arrived with the morn. For all human agents, including poets, the requirement is severer; one must contrive somehow to live many days and years and yet remain aloof from entanglements, from relationships that compromise the purity of self-reference, from relationship itself. One must, in short, contrive to *not* come into focus, to resist the efforts of any agent or discourse to get a fix on you, lest that fix become you by becoming the angle from which you are forced into appearance.

I have already observed that the impossibility of this project—this project of not being implicated in project—is Marvell's great subject, and it is a subject whose uneasy and contradictory imperative informs the greatest of his poems, "Upon Appleton House," a poem consistently at war with its own temporality, with its tendency, inevitable given the structure of language, to mean. "Upon Appleton House" is a poem critics are forever attempting to unify, but unity, rather than being what the poem desires, is the enemy of its non-aspiration, its aspiration not to mean, not to point to anything beside itself, not to go anywhere. Within its frame (far from sober despite the claim of the first line), the enemy is most powerfully present in the person of the subtle nun who is distinguished by her skill at narrative. It is with this skill that she seeks to envelop the "Virgin Thwaites," who oft

> ... spent the summer suns
> Discoursing with the subtle nuns,
> Whence in these words one to her weav'd
> (As 'twere by chance) thoughts long conceived. (94–97)

The parenthesis tells the story (of too much story): what is wrong with the nun's discourse is precisely that chance or randomness is merely pretended; apparently spontaneous speech is in fact the product of a premeditation that takes the form of a verbal net, of something woven in order to entrap. The point is made even more explicitly when the nun's speech is finished. First the narrator at once describes its effect and renders unmistakable its sexual nature by observing that "the nun's smooth tongue has sucked her in" (200); and then Fairfax points the moral (as if it needed pointing) by characterizing the Nun's performance as a cheat (204), as an enchantment, as an imprisoning (206, 208), as something fraudulent (214), and as an art that operates to "alter all" (215). This last is the crucial charge because it specifies the danger inherent in all art. Alteration, in the sense of conferring on something a shape and meaning not properly its own, is the inevitable effect of framing, of positioning an object so that it can only be seen from an angle and not directly.

That is what the nun does when she draws the young Thwaites into a point of view in relation to which her alternatives are already restricted, and indeed it is what is done by any consecutive discourse, that is, by any discourse in which the identity of a moment is a function of what has gone before and what is yet to come. In consecutive discourse, one's person and actions are shaped by a story being told by another (be it the nun or fate or simply time), and it is within the perspective of that other that one lives and moves and has one's being. But if this is what is wrong with the nun's performance, it is difficult to see what the alternative might be, for even if the virgin Thwaites were to escape from the nun's story she would presumably escape into someone else's story, a story no less angled and no less pressuring; and indeed this is exactly what happens when young Fairfax takes the cloister by force and makes his way to where the "bright and holy Thwaites / weeping at the alter waits" (263–64). The passivity of her posture tells us what she waits for: to see who will win the struggle and thereby gain the right to embed her either in a new or in a continuing narrative, the right to make her into a subject. Even as the poem relates Fairfax's triumph it condemns him as no less an agent of design and premeditation than those he defeats.

But one must ask again, is there an alternative mode of action either for the perceiver or the perceived? Is it possible to move about in the world without being a hostage to some purposeful vision in relation to which one's actions and the actions of others are always and already meditated, never being simply what they are? "Upon Appleton House" is, like many of Marvell's other poems, an attempt to answer that question, and one part of his answer resides in the contrast he would draw between his performance and the nun's. Just before he reproduces the nun's extraordinary close-woven discourse, he gives us a self-description of his own: "While with slow eyes we these survey, / And on each pleasant footstep stay" (81–82). Slow eyes are eyes not hurrying in their movement in response to some teleological pressure; slow eyes do not feel at their back time's winged chariot. Similarly, pleasant footsteps are footsteps taken at no behest other than their own; they have no relation either to a previous step or to future steps which may or may not be taken; one can stay on them as long or as little as one likes, and thus they are the very antithesis of the steps—one leading to another—that define a good plot. Pleasant steps are, or wish to be, haphazard. Haphazardness is the poem's goal, and it is that goal (or un-goal) to which the nun's discourse is an affront. That is, her action should not be seen (as it often is) as an interruption of the story of the house of Fairfax, but as an interruption by story, and therefore by meaning, of the mode of slow eyes and pleasant footsteps. The desire of the poem, and of the poet, is not to arrive at the intersection of destiny and choice, but to defer and avoid both.

The career of deferral in "Upon Appleton House" deserves a fuller account than I can give here, although I can say that such an account would begin by rejecting as ironically intended the poem's opening claim to be a sober frame, and go on to observe (as Rosalie Colie and others have before me) the many ways in which sobriety is forestalled and frames are so rapidly and relentlessly multiplied that they never come into focus and therefore fail to provide the focus that would be necessary for sustained perception. Such an account would continue by remarking on the extraordinary self-description of a poet who at least claims to have escaped the demands of his medium, who has been able, or so he says, to hit "chance's better wit" (better, that is, than narration), who languishes "with ease" (593), who securely plays (607), whose side is "lazy" (643), whose foot is sliding (645), whose discourse strives to be like the self-reflecting river a succession of "wanton harmless folds" (633). All these, as I have said, are constitutive of the poet's chief claim, the claim to have fully disengaged, to have withdrawn from all the entanglements that would compromise self-definition and self-sufficiency. In stanza 76 he declares the process of withdrawal successful:

> How safe, methinks and strong behind
> These trees have I encamped my mind
> Where beauty aiming at the heart,
> Bends in some trees its useless dart,
> And where the world no certain shot
> Can make, on me it toucheth not.
> But I on it securely play,
> And gall its horsemen all the day. (801–8)

Only in "The Garden" do we find a more concentrated formulation of the Marvellian desire to not be touched, to be out of the line of any sight, to be so continually out of focus that no dart or beauty's eye will have a chance of hitting what would be its mark; the desire to play securely, that is, without care, without concern that this moment of play be responsive to the moments before it or anxious in relation to the moments that will succeed it. But even before these lines are spoken, Marvell has acknowledged the shadow that hangs over them, the shadow of reflective consciousness. He is after all *reporting* on this supposedly achieved state, viewing it from a reflective distance, "methinking" about it rather than simply living it. He is, as he himself announces, an "easy philosopher" (561), where "easy" is at once a claim to have escaped philosophy's requirement—the requirement to be not loose like the drop but rigorous, consecutive, deductive, hypotactic—and a rueful admission that the escape cannot be made so easily, that it is not so easy to be truly easy, that as a philosopher of ease he is still too much the philosopher, too much aware of his ease to be truly inhabiting it (wearing it as his frame and native element), working too hard at being easy.

He ceases the work the moment the real thing arrives: "The Young Maria walks tonight" (651). The important word is "young": not yet a philosopher trying to think herself back into ease, she is like Little T. C. and the Nymph before the time of either Sylvio or the wanton troopers, unselfconsciously one with herself, complete and entire, like the drop. Without even trying (because she is not trying), Maria is in the impregnable position the poet so bravely (and suspiciously) claims:

> Blest Nymph! That couldst so soon prevent
> Those trains by youth against thee meant:
> Tears (wat'ry shot that pierce the mind)
> And sighs (Love's cannon charged with wind);
> True praise (that breaks through all defence);
> And feigned complying innocence,
> But knowing where this ambush lay,
> She 'scaped the safe, but roughest way. (713–20)

The catalogue of things she escapes is comprehensive: not only the plots and designs ("trains") that men mean (i.e., intend), but meaning itself, the necessity in a world of stratagem of looking behind or above or below phenomena for the significance they do not bear on the surface. Hers is a mind that resists piercing—penetration, violation—by anything, even by true praise, which in the guise of simply mirroring essence makes a claim to have caught it, to have mastered it, to have become its frame. True praise, like feigned innocence, always comes professing its lack of motive, the absence of design, of train; but true innocence responds as Maria does, by *not* responding, by not even registering the "complying" (falsely accommodating) assault.

The poem could end here, but it doesn't. Instead, a detail in the description of Maria's happy state foretells its doom. In her, we are told, self-sufficiency is so perfectly achieved that "goodness doth itself entail / On females if there want a male" (727–28). Her goodness is self-generating and requires mixture with no other in order to produce its offspring, that is, itself. (It is its own tear.) But the deadly word "if"—"if there want a male"—reaches back to the previous line and releases the full and ominous meaning of "entail"—the act of imposing on persons or property an implacable succession of possession and ownership. Something entailed is never itself, for in relation to a sequence it did not originate it always belongs to another, to a story it did not write but cannot evade. That is what happens to Maria:

> Hence she with graces more divine
> Supplies beyond her sex the line,
> And like a sprig of mistletoe,
> On the Fairfacian Oak doth grow;
> Whence for some universal good,
> The priest shall cut the sacred bud;
> While her glad Parents most rejoice
> And make their Destiny their Choice .... (737–44)

The closed society of self-sufficient females lasts barely a stanza before the male who had been almost casually banished returns to supply what Maria cannot: a line, a lineage, a history, a story, whose driving force will take her out of herself—"beyond her sex"—and assign her a role she does not choose. The choice is made in the name of "some universal good" (can we miss the sarcasm here?), some grand epic narrative that first authorizes the ceremonial violation of her unfeigned innocence ("The priest shall cut the sacred bud"), and then calls the violation "Destiny." John Rogers is one of the few to note that these lines "represent an unsettling divergence from a complex of values the poem has established."[8] The values are those of pleasant steps, unhurried time, deferral, ease, all of which are suddenly dislodged by what Rogers correctly terms the "violent action" of the priest who cuts in destiny's name.[9] The destiny in question is most pointedly not hers— she does not even appear in the couplet that announces it—but belongs first to the parents who precede her and then to the male heir she is now obliged to produce. No longer the figure to whom everything in nature resonates, Maria is reduced to being a function—a mere relay—in a narrative to whose inexorable progress she has been sacrificed. It may not be the nun's smooth tongue, but something, surely, has sucked her in.

Like the Nymph, Little T. C., the infant of "Young Love," the unfortunate lover, the solitary wanderer in Eden, the bodiless soul, and the soulless body, Maria is not allowed to remain in the unselfconscious realm of play and leisure where her linguistic virtuosity has full play (all the languages are hers) but is not employed (709) in any purposive direction. She speaks "heaven's dialect" (712), a dialect whose meanings, as Marshall Grossman notes, remain *"in-potentia,"* just hanging there, like the world arrested and hushed (681) for that moment before the "inevitable and necessary splash back into temporality and narrative."[10] The splash back into temporality, meaning, and appropriation is the fate that awaits every human figure in the Marvellian corpus, with the single and unlikely exception of the addressee of his most famous poem, the coy mistress. She is an unlikely exception because the poem is so palpably designed to emplot her, to suck her in. Unique among Marvell's poems, "To His Coy Mistress" is from first to last an argument, and as an argument its goal is to absorb its object—the hearer—into its own structure so that her every action and thought would be conferred and determined by another.

The poem opens by rejecting the unpatterned and slow perambulating of pleasant steps that trace out Marvell's nonprogress in "Upon Appleton House." Here there will be no leisure to "think which way / To walk, and pass our long love's day" (3–4), for each moment is informed by the urgency of a waiting end whose backward pressure turns everything into a beginning or a middle. In its driving insistency, its refusal to let events and persons appear in any terms other than the terms of its own project, the poem is the very embodiment of narrative desire, of the desire to possess, to assimilate, to control. In its mode it is indistinguishable from the speech of the subtle nun, with the difference only that it is more successful, for it so encloses the mistress within its toils that she is never heard from; she is simply the space the narrative appropriates, transforming her before she ever appears into the voiceless occasion of its unfolding.

And yet, from another perspective, a perspective from which the poem excludes us—or is it a perspective that excludes the poem?—the case might be said to be quite different. It is the perspective of the only attribute the poem grants the lady, both in its title and in its second line: she is coy, that is, withdrawing, retreating, turning away. And if coyness is her essence, the only quality predicated of her, then is not her essence fully and autogenously realized in her absence from the poem? Is not the narrative's triumph in silencing really her triumph, for after all, from the beginning to the end, we know nothing about her, we have no line on her, she has escaped our grasp; she has disappeared: she has won.

It might seem an unlikely reading of Marvell that finds the triumphant moments in his poetry shared by (that oddest of couples) the coy mistress and a drop of dew. But in fact, the present essay participates in a strain of criticism at least as old as Jonathan Goldberg's brilliant explication of "The Nymph Complaining," which has borne fruit (sometimes of an oppositional kind) in the work of Marshall Grossman, Barbara Estrin, and Joan Hartwig. Goldberg poses the basic question, the question with which Marvell (in my account) is obsessed: "How can . . . voice preserve itself, its purity, and avoid the contaminating eddies of repetition in which it would cease to own itself?" How, that is, can one "speak of one's own . . . and of nothing else?"[11] And his answer is, string out the story (28), avoid reference, "avoid loss by playing" in a "ritualized and endless sequence" (31) that is "endlessly disjunctive" (33); perform, over and over again "the refusal of going beyond" (which I have described as the refusal of meaning), so that one produces what would seem to be impossible, a text that is "not *really* 'about' something else" (37). In a slightly different vocabulary, Hartwig explores those moments in the poetry where (again impossibly) a cause is its own effect and an effect its own cause "without an intermediate step of transformed substance," "without requiring an intermediary function such as reason to grasp a cause to produce the effect."[12] The immediacy and self-referentiality is such, she notes, that "there is no need to have the mind interfere in the process with thinking" (73), and the result is a surface radically opaque, one that "seems to resist, and often to deny, that there is any level beneath it" (85). In another fine essay, Estrin finds the complaining nymph to be just such an opaque surface, and willfully so. In her utter indifference "to setting anything in the earthly realm aright," she responds to the male world that would appropriate her by creating "enclaves of self-enabling silence" complete with an audience (the fawn) wholly internal to her private meditations: "She has one lover and one reader, the deer's incorporation of her message, eliminating any need to record it."[13] "Firm in her withdrawal" (106), the nymph "plans her silence, substituting deprivation for violation and rendering herself fundamentally inviolable" (118). "Like the dissolving Manna in 'On a Drop of Dew,'" she finds "a resolution in dissolution and evaporating into the heavens from which future readers, reduced to wanton soldiers, are excluded" (119–20).

Of course future readers, especially professional ones, will not take exclusion lying down, and they will labor heroically, as have many under the aegis of historicisms old and new, to reconnect Marvell and his poetry to the world from which they so resolutely turn away. Just what those labors have yielded might be inferred from a discussion that concludes the volume in which Hartwig's and Estrin's essays appear. The discussants are John Klause, Ann Baynes Coiro, and Michael Schoenfeldt, each of whom has an investment in historical/political criticism and each of whom acknowledges a measure of failure. Klause notes the many recent classifications of Marvell as a Puritan libertarian, as a loyalist, as a trimmer, as a classical republican, as a moderate chiliast, but concludes that "a man so baffling as Marvell" may present "something humbling to grand interpretative aspirations" and constitute a rebuke to those who eagerly seek "the historical poet."[14] "Perhaps,"

Ann Coiro begins her contribution, "Marvell's poetry achieves nothing" (238), and is itself a prime instance of what he most values, "graven, permanent words" (240), that is, words which, because they are undecipherable, keep everything to themselves. As "physical inscriptions" rather than efforts at communication, the poems are "inevitably enigmatic because they remain hard and dead when we try to read them" (240). Not only does Marvell "elude us," she concludes, but he "seems to have intended to do so." We may "look upon" his poems, "but we cannot fully understand. . . . The grave is indeed a fine and private place" (243). Schoenfeldt picks up Coiro's note on the half beat: "I have long admired Marvell's poetry but have also found it to elude the very terms in which I try to convey my admiration" (243). He conjectures that the impenetrability to which everyone attests may be "a defensive response to the immense pressures placed upon behavior and speech in an age of political turmoil" (244), but this effort to be politically correct by being political is little more than a gesture (what age has not been an age of political turmoil?), and rings with less conviction than his conclusion: "Marvell's lyrics . . . are difficult to stabilize because they purposefully exclude the interiority they purport to exhibit" (247).

So ends a discussion entitled "The Achievement of Andrew Marvell," itself the end piece of a volume whose first sentence finds the editors (both historically minded critics) declaring: "Andrew Marvell remains the most enigmatic of minor seventeenth-century literary figures" (1). (That is to say, he remains irredeemably literary.) I cannot help thinking that Marvell would be pleased by these reports of the collective failure to "sound" him, and I hope that being reminded of this failure (often spectacularly performed) will give some pleasure, of a decidedly aesthetic kind, to Murray Krieger on this occasion.

NOTES

1. Murray Krieger, *The Institution of Theory* (Baltimore: Johns Hopkins University Press, 1994), 92.

2. Andrew Marvell, "Mourning," lines 33–36. All references are to *Andrew Marvell: The Complete Poems,* ed. Elizabeth Story Donno (London and New York: Penguin, 1972).

3. William James, "What Pragmatism Means," in *Pragmatism: A Contemporary Reader,* ed. Russell B. Goodman (New York: Free Press, 1995), 60.

4. See on this point Donald Friedman's "Andrew Marvell," in *The Cambridge Companion to English Poetry: Donne to Marvell,* ed. Thomas N. Corns (Cambridge: Cambridge University Press, 1993), 283: "The Mower who inveighs against gardens speaks for a purist vision of a nature untainted by human intention; for him man is 'Luxurious,' and gardens a sign of his limitlessly arrogant drive to reform nature in his own image."

5. John Carey, "Reversals Transposed: An Aspect of Marvell's Imagination," in *Approaches to Marvell*, ed. C. A. Patrides (London: Routledge and Kegan Paul, 1978), 136.

6. Friedman, "Andrew Marvell," 291.

7. Donald Friedman, "Sight and Insight in Marvell's Poetry," in Patrides, *Approaches to Marvell*, 320.

8. John Rogers, "Marvell's Pastoral Historiography," in *On the Celebrated and Neglected Poems of Andrew Marvell*, ed. Claude J. Summers and Ted-Larry Pebworth (Columbia: University of Missouri Press, 1992), 220.

9. Ibid., 221.

10. Marshall Grossman, "Allegory, Irony, and the Rebus," in *The Muses Commonweale*, ed. Claude J. Summers and Ted-Larry Pebworth (Columbia: University of Missouri Press, 1988), 202, 203.

11. Jonathan Goldberg, *Voice Terminal Echo: Postmodernism and English Renaissance Texts* (New York: Methuen, 1986), 26.

12. Joan Hartwig, "Tears as a Way of Seeing," in Summers and Pebworth, *Celebrated and Neglected Poems*, 80, 73.

13. Barbara Estrin, "The Nymph and the Revenge of Silence," in Summers and Pebworth, *Celebrated and Neglected Poems*, 102, 104, 103.

14. John Klause, Ann Baynes Coiro, and Michael Schoenfeldt, "The Achievement of Andrew Marvell," in Summers and Pebworth, *Celebrated and Neglected Poems*, 238, 237.

CHAPTER TWO

Ekphrasis Revisited,
or Antitheticality Reconstructed

Hazard Adams

Murray Krieger's *Ekphrasis* is a history, a self-consciously polemical history, of Western culture's shifting and ambivalent commitment to the concept of the natural sign. By the concept of the natural sign Krieger means the idea that a word has a fixed, unambiguous relation to a denoted object and, grounded on a "visual epistemology," is in a sense transparent; or it is a mimesis, a simulacrum; or it is, in the most radical version of *symbolisme*, a miraculous presence. By "visual epistemology," a term Krieger adopts from Forrest G. Robinson's book on Sidney, is meant a knowledge grounded in visual and spatial terms.[1] The history of this notion can be traced back to Simonides's alleged remark that poetry is a speaking picture, but complications set in with Plato's concept of imitation, the competing one in Aristotle, and the spatializing language of early literary theory that lends itself to Simonides's analogy of poetry and painting.

Krieger studies the various moments that arise from these beginnings. He remarks:

> There are those moments in which [criticism] is molded by the pictorial in language and those moments in which it is molded by the purely verbal as non-pictorial; moments in which it is dedicated to words as capturing a stillness and moments in which it is dedicated to words in movement; or even moments dedicated to the more difficult assignment of words as capturing a *still movement*.[2]

The historical argument groups together, in a sort of metaphorical chain, space, the intelligible, logic, mimesis, and painting. Opposed to these are respectively time, the sensible, experience, free-ranging expression, and music. Krieger charts a movement in criticism from the former to the latter and thence to efforts to overcome the opposition. In general, he believes that modern theoretical criticism has sought—"through the two-sidedness of language as a medium of the verbal arts—to comprehend the simultaneity in the verbal figure, of fixity and flow, of an image at once grasped and yet slipping away through the crevices of language" (11). Ekphrasis is one time alluded to as a "temptation" (12), another time as an "ambition" (14). It is both of these because of its implication of the vain possibility that signs can miraculously become or contain the objects they denote. The historical movement is from the naiveté of the sign as pure sensuous mimesis of nature to the sign as intelligible yet still sensuous, making it possible to represent the unrepresentable (26). At this point there begins to develop, gradually, the hegemony of language *over* nature: "As we approach our own time, not only is primacy bestowed upon the arts of the word and of time (instead of upon the arts of picture and of space) but the spreading semiotic interest in texts absorbs all the arts, subjects them all to temporality and makes them all ripe for reading" (26).

The object of Krieger's polemic, we begin to see, is that aspect of poststructuralism which Krieger represents by Paul de Man's deconstructions of romantic symbolism and the notion of presence in the word, de Man favoring, in opposition to these things, absence and what he calls allegory. In a move characteristic of Krieger's tendency throughout his career to swallow and absorb theories opposed to his own, and in a manner not contrary to his own past existentialist tendencies, he accepts absence. But at the same time he argues for the valuable *illusion* of presence—as long as we and the poem know it ultimately *as* illusion. (This makes at least common sense, since no one really wants a painting or a poem actually to be the object it allegedly copies.) But for Krieger none of this obliterates the ekphrastic, which keeps reappearing in new, more sophisticated guises. In his view, postmodernism has not acknowledged its latest version: "the slippery version of the ekphrastic poetic which presses for a verbal play that acknowledges the incompatibility of time and space, while collapsing them into the illusion of an object marked by its own sensible absence" (28). This is really Krieger's own version of postmodernism, explicit in the work I am considering, but also implicit in the essays collected in his *Words* about *Words* about *Words* and subsequent books.[3] Krieger would have other oppositions, too, collapsed: the intelligible and the sensible, logic and experience, mimesis and expression, painting and music as analogues of poetry.

This collapsing of oppositions is always situated in the poem, along with the oppositions' persistence, so that Krieger can refer to an "undoing" that art performs on itself. This undoing makes possible one of art's cultural functions, which is to "stimulate the alienation that warns us away from a culture's delusions [principally the presumption that its governing signs are natural] that would legitimize its authority by an appeal to nature" (260).

De Man characterized language as "duplicitous" and "seductive," as if there were something devilish and evil in it. Krieger adopts the term "duplicitous" for poetic language without, I think, the intention of swaying us to mistrust it, but the suspicion necessarily lingers on, particularly when "duplicity" is coupled with "illusion" and it is implied that existential nothingness or absence is the only reality. The Oxford English Dictionary offers two meanings of "duplicity," the second of which expresses Krieger's intent:

1) The quality of being "double" in action or conduct (see Double); the character or practice of acting in two ways at different times, or openly and secretly; deceitfulness, double-dealing (the earliest and still the most usual sense).
2) The state or quality of being numerically or physically double or twofold; doubleness.

Whereas de Man's usage emphasized the unreliability of all language, Krieger's points to the potential unreliability of any language presuming a one-to-one relation of sign to object, and he reserves "duplicity" for that peculiar doubleness in poetic art that knows itself as such and so declares itself. The ethical side here is the lesson that the poetic, by its implicit confession, warns us not to trust in the naturalness of any language— or the illusion. But there is a risk of denigrating human culture generally as illusion and therefore self-deceiving.

Krieger has come a long way to return, with a difference, to a word made popular and familiar by the New Criticism: irony. (I shall come back to this.) In Krieger's return—with, of course, the important difference that he explicitly gives a cultural or social role to poetic irony—he clarifies his long-standing allegiance to the New Critics, while also addressing contemporary cultural critics and maintaining a vestige of his existentialism. Thus de Man is swallowed whole and poetry apparently saved.

Yet Krieger is also Kantian. For him, things in themselves cannot be known (or uttered), but the terms of not knowing carry a negative suggestion not present in Kant—duplicity, illusion, and even paradox (*Ekphrasis* 22). These terms render him closer to de Man than I think he would really like to be.[4] They are terms that cannot help privileging, and are spoken from the point of view of, the very same spatialized logic of the natural sign of which he is suspicious. It is difficult to see how language can be duplicitous (at least in the first sense) if things in themselves cannot be known, since there is no criterion to determine duplicity except within a strictly empirical system such as Kant constructs for the understanding. But an existential stance does not allow us this luxury as a way to truth.

Of course, if things cannot be known in themselves, language would be duplicitous if it claimed to know, though duplicity usually refers to a conscious lie, a pretense rather than an error. There is always the possibility, of course, that if things can't be known, language might be right by chance; but we could never know that it is. The existential negative and the Kantian constitutive cohabit uneasily, and the problem may be that the defense of poetry cannot finally be made in fundamentally epistemological terms. But let me follow the Kantian line a little farther before I suggest that the whole issue must be shifted from the epistemological to the ethical arena. (This, I think, is what Krieger has actually done, without explicit acknowledgment, in offering poetic art as a self-confessing illusion.) I shall eventually approach this sort of stance by way of Vico and Cassirer, discarding (to the extent that it can be discarded) the epistemological approach and the language of duplicity and illusion for a theory of ethical and empirical fictions.

The neo-Kantian line that proceeds through von Humboldt and Cassirer and does not leave untouched twentieth-century critics as diverse as Ransom, Wheelwright, and Frye shifts the epistemological question from perception to language. In Cassirer, the problem of language as illusion is given a positive twist in an argument drawn out of von Humboldt, but with a deeper source in Vico (about whom more later).[5] The negative, so to speak, is accepted:

> Instead of dealing with the things themselves man is in a sense constantly conversing with himself. He has so enveloped himself in linguistic forms, in artistic images, in mythical symbols or religious rites that he cannot see or know anything except by the interposition of this artificial medium.[6]

But this very envelopment produces both culture, with its positive as well as negative potentialities, and the set of interrelated human creations that Cassirer calls symbolic forms—myth, religion, language, art, history, and science (though Cassirer seems not to see that language is not separable from the others but rather fundamental to them). The positive turn is that Cassirer views human culture, which is structured by these forms, as a process of liberation. At the end of *An Essay on Man,* recognizing the "tensions and frictions," the "strong contrasts and deep conflicts between the various powers [these symbolic forms] of man," he hints at a possible Heraclitan "harmony in contrariety, as in the case of the bow and the lyre" (228). The issue is not whether any of these forms are simply wrong epistemological paths, leading inevitably to delusion, but rather that in each there can be a constitution of the real. Nevertheless, Cassirer still puts the issue in strictly epistemological terms, whereas it might better be put in terms of ends (as I believe Krieger very nearly or perhaps actually does). This would mean that we need not merely a theory of symbolic forms but one of fictions that have different (not exclusively epistemological) cultural purposes.

For this, it is helpful to return to Giambattista Vico.[7] Krieger points out that one of modernism's tenets (and one he would defend) is that poetry is a special and thus privileged form of discourse (though it is never quite clear why to be special is to be privileged). Terms like "defamiliarization"

and "deviation" are employed in some versions of modernism to characterize what Krieger describes as a "structured resistance that obstructs and
complicates, thus leading [language] to serve an other-than-normal form
of discourse" (*Ekphrasis* 186). If we take a Vichean historical view, we are
obliged to reverse the idea of deviation and declare that modernism's
normality is really the special, deviating form and, in the early stages of human culture at any rate, the poetic is the normal. This view was to influence
Cassirer's conjunction of language and myth, which he regarded as "near
of kin" (*Essay on Man* 109). Recourse to a story of origins is unfashion-
able and from one point of view futile, but it may be worth some thought
nevertheless.

Vico's story tells us that language began in fear of nature, that the first
men were poets (by which he meant that they thought in a certain way), and
that they were so because of their incapacity to create abstract universals.
The first human fable for each people was that of a Jove, generated out of
terror of the sky. Mythologies were the proper language of fable, and metaphors were fables in brief. This does not seem to be an auspicious beginning
for any privileging of the poetic. Vico is ambivalent about these primitive
men, whom he calls giants and thinks of as severely limited in intellect. But
he also attributes a vast sublimity to their imaginative acts. Incapable of abstraction, the first men created what Vico calls "imaginative universals."
Their wisdom was a "vulgar wisdom," a "crude metaphysics," the result of a
wholly corporeal imagination, in which the particular had to serve as a universal. Unable to form "intelligible class concepts of things," these first men
created particular poetic characters. They endowed physical substances
with life by extending their own bodies into them: "In all languages the
greater part of the expressions relating to inanimate things are formed by
metaphor from the human body and its parts and from the human senses
and passions."[8] (Cassirer makes the same point.)

The ancient gods and goddesses were human fables. In an important
passage, which I shall quote at length, Vico gives Cybele, Berecynthia, and
Neptune as evidence:

> By means of these three divinities . . . they explained everything appertain-
> ing to the sky, the earth, and the sea. And similarly by means of the other di-
> vinities they signified the other kinds of things appertaining to each, denot-
> ing all flowers, for instance, by Flora, and all fruits by Pomona. We nowadays
> reverse this practice in respect of spiritual things, such as the faculties of the
> human mind, the passions, virtues, vices, sciences, and arts; for the most part
> the ideas we form of them are so many feminine personifications, to which
> we refer all the causes, properties, and effects that severally appertain to
> them. For when we wish to give utterance to our understanding of spiritual
> things, we must seek aid from our imagination to explain them and, like
> painters, form human images of them. But these theological poets [Vico

posits a primitive poetic theology], unable to make use of the understanding, did the opposite and more sublime thing: they attributed senses and
passions . . . to bodies, and to bodies as vast as sky, sea, and earth. Later, as
these vast imaginations shrank and the power of abstraction grew, the per-
sonifications were reduced to diminutive signs. (128)

The poetry of these giants, which is really a mode or form of symbolization
in Cassirer's terms, was wholly lacking in the important quality that Krieger
attributes to poetic art, the self-consciousness that it is fictional. But Vico's
theory is a theory of fictions, and he makes a hard and fast distinction between the "certainty" that such fictions provide and "truth": "Philosophy
contemplates reason, whence comes knowledge of the true; philology observes that of which human choice is author, whence comes consciousness
of the certain" (63). The world of civil society comes from human minds, is
made by men, and is grounded on the making of fables according to poetic
logic. Because the giants could not *understand* nature, they made their fiction of it, creating culture.

Poetic logic thinks *in* tropes, the four principal ones being metaphor,
metonymy, synecdoche, and irony. But irony came later and introduced the
possibility of poetry in the sense in which Krieger uses the term. Vico remarks: "Irony certainly could not have begun until the period of reflection,
because it is fashioned of falsehood by dint of a reflection which wears the
mask of truth" (131). This marked a great change, since the earliest men
were not able to feign anything false; their narrations were true to the extent that one can think of anything as true in a logic that does not include
the false. But Vico does not pursue the study of irony and work out the developing interrelation of trope and reflection that his description of irony
implies. Instead, he goes on to consider the four tropes together:

> From all this it follows that all the tropes (and they are all reducible to the
> four types above discussed), which have hitherto been considered ingenious
> inventions of writers, were necessary modes of expression of all the first po-
> etic nations, and had originally their full native propriety. But these expres-
> sions of the first nations later became figurative when, with the further de-
> velopment of the human mind, words were invented which signified abstract
> forms or genera comprising their species or relating parts with their wholes.
> And here begins the overthrow of two common errors of the grammarians:
> that prose speech is proper speech, and poetic speech improper, and that
> prose speech came first and afterward speech in verse. (131)

Important in all of this is the notion that, from a poetic point of view, poetry (in Vico's sense of tropological thinking) is the ground of all language
and thus its normal form. The supreme deviation would not be poetry as we
know it today but the special language devoid of tropes, mathematics. The
fourth Vichian trope of irony marks the development of a reflective capac-

ity that assumed the power to discover truth and falsity according to reason and science, relegating poetry not even to the province of a suspect certainty, but to the level of sheer opinion. However, irony is not what Vico refers to as a mere "figure," that is, an artificiality to be read *through* to whatever rational truth lies behind its veil. In romantic parlance such figures came to be called allegory, and denigrated, but Vico uses the term "allegory" to mean an imaginative universal rather than a figure for an abstract universal:

> The mythologies . . . must have been the proper languages of the fables; the fables [like Jove] being imaginative class concepts, as we have shown, the mythologies must have been the allegories corresponding to them. Allegory is defined as *Diversiloquium* insofar as, by identity not of proportion [which would be like a simile] but (to speak scholastically) of predicability, allegories signify the diverse species or the diverse individuals comprised under these genera. So that they must have been a univocal signification connoting a quality common to all their species and individuals. (128)

Vico's distinction between truth and certainty was one between rationality (including the rational theology of his own time) and the poetic thought that constructs what Northrop Frye calls "myths of concern," fundamental to the structure of culture.[9] For Vico these would have been fictions, in the sense of human makings neither empirically true nor false, not the lies Plato accused the sophists and poets of perpetrating. A little extension of Vico through Kant leads to a general theory of fictions which unsettles the notion that the discourse of reason or science is normal. A theory of fictions or, in Cassirer's version, symbolic forms requires each fiction or form to function by its own laws, what Kant called categories.[10] All of these fictive forms are "languages" or employ language (in different ways and to different ends), although these can never quite be dissociated one from another, even if a culture may have attempted such a dissociation by suppressing one form or another.[11]

The Vichian moment of irony marks the very consciousness of fictionality that Krieger makes the cornerstone of his defense of poetics and of poetry. Without that consciousness, irony would be impossible. Consciousness of the fictive spread into all but the most naive forms of modern life, though it was not much theoretically developed until Bentham, and then it was applied principally to science and the law.[12] The theory of fiction as it applies to science as a form has its own special kind of irony. Science knows its projections are fictions but nevertheless posits a nonfictive external nature as an objective otherness beyond itself, declaring it to be the thing itself and knowable by empirical means. Yet this thing is a fictive constitution framed in the special language of number, a language that for other purposes was the dream of Plato, entirely free of the troublesome tropes that Vico makes the basis of poetic logic. Forms other than the poetic tend to mistrust the trope, and John Locke's view is tacitly behind this mistrust:

> If we would speak of things as they are, we must allow that all the art of rhetoric, besides order and clearness, all the artificial and figurative application of words eloquence hath invented, are for nothing else but to insinuate wrong ideas, move the passions, and thereby mislead the judgment, and so indeed are perfect cheats.[13]

Locke admits that what he calls wit and fancy are nice for entertainment, but trivial and unrelated to serious pursuit of truth. In them men find "pleasure to be deceived."[14] For Locke, tropes may at best be illustratively heuristic. In fundamentalist forms of religion, tropes are taken as literal truth (or, in more sophisticated forms, as having a literal *level*), and read as what Krieger calls in one place "straight-line discourse."

Vichean irony and Krieger's poetics offer fictions in which there is no deceit because deceit requires an objectivity by means of which a criterion of truth can be determined. We are dealing in Vico with what he calls "certainty," and until there was irony there could be nothing opposed to the certainty of fable. But with the object as the emerging criterion, certainty and the parvenu truth came into an opposition in which one sought to negate the other and control the intellectual realm.[15] The certain became subject to the criteria of empiricism and rationalism. Irony can be seen as poetic logic's answer to this effort to subdue certainty, but poetic logic cannot be sustained on epistemological grounds alone and, indeed, could never in Vico's terms have been fully epistemologically motivated. Arising, according to Vico, out of fear, poetic logic expressed communal concern amid eventually constituted tribal orders. To consider irony only from an epistemological point of view would be to play by the rules of the alleged enemy and would have to end in some form of fundamentalist faith or in existential negation, as it does in de Man and in many other cases. A vestige of this fate remains in Krieger's accommodation of de Man. The existential Krieger must give up all truth except absence, but the Kantian Krieger would recover a constituted form, though only as a maker of illusion. Then, at the critical moment, Krieger reinvigorates the aesthetic illusion as that which insists that all constitutive forms, particularly the forms we want to call natural—natural law, natural science, naturalistic writing—are equally the makers of illusion. The aesthetic illusion, in its elegance, in its irony, is the only honest illusion, a beacon illuminating the naturalistic and hegemonic pretensions of all others. So what was thoroughly negative in de Man is turned half way toward the positive in Krieger.

I should like to place alongside this view—a sameness with a difference—a concept of the poetic as "antithetical," a term I appropriate from Yeats. (Krieger employs the term once in *Ekphrasis* [188], but in an entirely different sense: to characterize postmodern critics opposed to the aesthetic.) Modern poets, by whom I mean here those who have come since the invention of irony, cannot inevitably fail to lie, as Vico claimed the earliest poets could. But critics at least since Sidney have taken pains to argue that the question of truth and falsity is irrelevant to what the poet is about. Yet the tendency of criticism and theory to revert to epistemological terms has remained compelling. Antitheticality is a rising up neither of a countertruth nor of a falsehood: it is the poetic tendency to propose ethical oppositions to the fixities of what I, following Blake, call negations, that is, binary oppositions in which one side would suppress the other.[16]

One could say, of course, that Aristotle already shifted the ground of literary apologetics away from epistemology, in his remark about it being better to paint the hind with horns than to paint it inartistically. But the shift did not hold, since Aristotelians generally reverted in later dramatic criticism to rigorous insistence on the unities of time and space, returning to canons of imitative accuracy. Most turns toward ethics since Aristotle defend poetry with the notion that it presents an allegory of moral teaching, as is the case (with a certain amount of backing and filling) in Sidney's *Apology*.

In Renaissance criticism, the closest thing to an ethical defense based neither on canons of accuracy nor on recourse to moral allegory is Giacomo Mazzoni's argument in behalf of the credible idol and that aspect of poetry he identified with the "civil faculty." Mazzoni opposes "credible things," which may include the marvelous, to the true and the false, the possible and the impossible. In other words, he establishes an antithetical contrary to these binary oppositions (negations). For Mazzoni, the civil faculty "not only professes to understand the justness of human actions but also the justness of the cessation of human actions," that is, play, amusement, game, pleasure.[17] Mazzoni identifies imitation with the delight that Aristotle attributed to it, more than with accuracy as such. The idol should be "correct," but its correctness is grounded on accurate representation of the credible marvelous, not of natural objects. Pleasure is directed toward the socially useful: "Perfect poetry is game and is modified by the civil faculty; insofar as it is recreation it has delight as its end [cessation], but insofar as it is modified or, so to speak, characterized by moral philosophy, it puts delight first in order to provide a later benefit" (101). The benefit is to the "civil community," so Mazzoni is doing more than reuttering the old Horatian maxim of delightful teaching: heroic poetry spurs soldiers to glory; tragedy instructs the great about the downfall of great persons; comedy consoles those with but modest fortunes (103). These values are perhaps not ours, but we can read them as part of an attempt to avoid the subjugation of poetry to the expression of abstract moral code expressed in allegorical particulars.

The concept of imitation—except when hedged around by someone like Mazzoni, who opposes the denigration of the false by the true in liter-ary criticism—is part of a Platonic negation, since imitation is always false. Mazzoni offers the credible marvelous as a contrary antithetical to the Pla-tonic negation of phenomena on the one hand and imitations twice re-moved from truth on the other: "Since the poet has the credible as his sub-ject, he ought therefore to oppose credible things to the true and the false, the possible and the impossible, by which I mean that he ought to give more importance to the credible than to any of the others I have enumerated" (78). In Vichian modern times, after the development of irony, one discov-ers the growth of negating dyads—the true and the false, the good and the evil, the soul and the body, the object and the subject—in which the first in each dyad is favored and would negate the second. In short, ideology is negation. In Krieger's *Ekphrasis,* space and time are a negation; after the domination of space, time takes over the negating role. What rises up in the apologetics for modernist art is, I think, a contrary antithetical to this nega-tion, as, using another terminology, Krieger indicates. Literary criticism be-gan by favoring space, lurched all the way to favoring time, but Krieger him-self favors a third situation: "The special and two-sided role assigned the language medium in poetry allows it to supervise the paradoxical coexis-tence of time and space, of the sensible and the intelligible, of mimesis and free-ranging expression" (*Ekphrasis* 206).[18]

The ethical role of poetry does not lie in its presentation of moral codes, whether these codes are cunningly held behind a "natural" veil or allegori-cally abstracted from a poetic surface. To so assume would be to accept the negation we characterize as the split of content and form, with form negated. Nor is poetry's ethical role to raise up the suppressed half of every dyad and overthrow the previous hegemony. An example of this is the over-coming of spatial form (painting) by temporal form (music) as the princi-pal analogy for poetry only to reestablish negation and threaten a cyclical changing of places from space to time and back. Nor is poetry's role to com-promise between the two terms of the dyad in an effort to obliterate their difference or to transcend them. Such obliterations would be the oblitera-tion of history, the devaluation of all that, for example, we can learn from past negations and past discourse about poetry. Negations are necessary to our thought and, in fact, a category of certain symbolic forms—if they were not present we would invent them. They are expressions of difference which tend to suppress sameness. Hence they are pernicious only if they are not vigorously opposed. To suppress the negation is to repeat the crime. Poetry can provide a sustaining active contrary to the negations, however useful, that began to be developed, in Vico's story, when human beings in-vented irony along with self-consciousness.

Prior to that critical moment, poetic logic ruled life. The model here is metaphorical thought, in which it was possible to think and live the identity of metaphor. But identity was not sameness. In Bronislaw Malinowski's story, the savage mind could declare its identity with animals, yet it did not mistake this as sameness by attempting to cohabit with lions and crocodiles.[19] Identity, if we must define it by recourse to our negating vocabulary, is sameness and difference at the same time and in the same place. It is expressed in the logic of metaphor. Poetry became antithetical in opposition to the dominating differences of our culture and the suppression of sameness, much as modern science had to struggle against the stifling sameness of established myths of concern.

Poetry, then, and criticism are not properly grounded on epistemology, but can offer the ethical stance of positive antitheticality characterized by the trope, and contrary to the negation of difference and sameness. The poem knows both sameness and difference in the trope. Criticism, which would be of the progeny of irony in Vico's story, may proceed from a commitment to absence (difference), as in Krieger's existentialist tendency, but it ought to take poetry's point of view to the extent that it can. Therefore, I would hold that the poetic illusion as offered by Krieger is still a little too much like delusion, because he drags an epistemological bias out of his argument with de Man, whereas poetry's arena is the ethical realm, in which existential truth-illusion is the negation to be antithetically opposed. Sidney, and particularly Mazzoni, were struggling in this direction; Krieger has succeeded in getting farther. What he poses for poetry is ultimately an ethical function.

Even with the accommodation of the postmodern that Krieger is prepared to make in his swallowing of de Man, his argument will not be satisfactory to those who represent postmodernism's postdeconstructive phase. The reason is that postdeconstruction, in which must be included the new historicism, varieties of feminism, and the new pragmatism, has generally attacked, from one fixed political ideology or another, all that Krieger represents by the natural sign, even the fictively natural sign. Having begun as antagonists of some ideological fixity, postdeconstructive critics end up asserting a new one in the pay of their own desires, which would be declared natural if the word were in fashion.

So I salute Murray Krieger. He has traveled his own route through the history of aesthetics. He has maintained, but not blindly, his loyalties. My own route and my language have been somewhat different—his focus has been principally on theory, mine on poetry—but we end with similar ethical roles for both. I maintain my language, he his: as Blake said, opposition is true friendship.

NOTES

1. Forrest G. Robinson, *The Shape of Things Known: Sidney's Apology and Its Philosophical Tradition* (Cambridge, Mass.: Harvard University Press, 1972).

2. Murray Krieger, *Ekphrasis: The Illusion of the Natural Sign* (Baltimore: Johns Hopkins University Press, 1992), 3.

3. *Words* about *Words* about *Words* (Baltimore: Johns Hopkins University Press, 1988); *A Reopening of Closure: Organicism Against Itself* (New York: Columbia University Press, 1989).

4. An earlier Krieger's use of the term "miracle," following Ransom, put him closer than he wanted to be to the *symboliste* tendencies in New Critical theory. His essay "'A Waking Dream': The Symbolic Alternative to Allegory" (*Words* about *Words* about *Words*, 271–88), directed toward de Man, expressed his liberation from, and historicization of, a purely miraculous symbol. On the notion of the romantic version of the miraculous symbol, see my *Philosophy of the Literary Symbolic* (Tallahassee: Florida State University Press, 1983), especially chapter 1.

5. It is puzzling that Cassirer does not make much mention of Vico, even though there are echoes of him in Cassirer's work.

6. Ernst Cassirer, *An Essay on Man: An Introduction to a Philosophy of Human Culture* (New Haven: Yale University Press, 1944), 25.

7. I shall dwell on Vico because I believe that Krieger's theory, like Vico's, is best seen as a theory of fictions. In *Philosophy of the Literary Symbolic* and later work I have followed a Vichian direction, while Krieger's has been through the history of aesthetics generally and the New Critics. The line of fiction theory I have followed is not mentioned by Krieger. Vico and Blake are mentioned once and in the same sentence in *Ekphrasis*, but (if I understand the sentence) they are misread, being assigned to "a Neo-Platonic mythic anthropology . . . in which all differences are dissolved, or rather have not yet come to exist" (166). Cassirer appears nowhere, nor do Frye (with the exception of a footnote in the appendix) or Wheelwright.

8. Giambattista Vico, *The New Science of Giambattista Vico,* trans. Thomas Goddard Bergin and Max Harold Fisch from the third edition (1744) (Ithaca: Cornell University Press, 1968), 129.

9. Northrop Frye, *The Critical Path: An Essay on the Social Context of Literary Criticism* (Bloomington: Indiana University Press, 1971).

10. One might think of Vico's tropes as "categories" of a poetic logic. A somewhat different effort to offer the characteristics of a poetic logic is present in Philip Wheelwright's *The Burning Fountain: A Study in the Language of Symbolism* (Bloomington: Indiana University Press, 1954).

11. I use the word "dissociation" deliberately to recall T. S. Eliot's famous phrase "dissociation of sensibility," which can be read as a suppression of poetic logic (including the trope of irony).

12. See C. K. Ogden, *Bentham's Theory of Fictions* (New York: Harcourt, Brace & Co., 1932). The next major effort after Bentham's, neo-Kantian in character, was Hans Vaihinger's *The Philosophy of "As If,"* trans. C. K. Ogden (New York: Harcourt, Brace & Co., 1925). Neither Bentham nor Vaihinger had the slightest notion of what to do with poetic fictions. In the one place where he mentions them, a footnote, Vaihinger relegates them to "figments."

13. John Locke, *An Essay Concerning Human Understanding* (1690), chapter 10, section 34, excerpted in *Critical Theory Since Plato*, rev. ed., ed. Hazard Adams (Fort Worth: Harcourt Brace Jovanovich, 1992), 268. Here we have duplicity again, which

further suggests that Krieger's usage is ironically offered from the point of view of the enemy. There is less irony, perhaps none, in de Man's usage.

14. Ibid.

15. This situation is what prompted Frye to speak of the "myth of freedom" (Vico's "truth") growing up to oppose the "myth of concern" (Vico's "certainty"). Later these myths changed places, and concern expressed the worry that the myth of freedom, which came with the development of modern science, is no longer free but itself oppressive. Frye takes the Blakean view that the oppressor is not free but a prisoner of his own epistemological certainty.

16. On antitheticality in Yeats, see my *The Book of Yeats's Vision* (Ann Arbor: University of Michigan Press, 1995). On antitheticality, contraries, and negations, see my afterword essay in *Critical Essays on William Blake*, ed. Hazard Adams (Boston: G. K. Hall & Co., 1991), 193–204.

17. Giacopo Mazzoni, *On the Defense of the Comedy of Dante: Introduction and Summary*, trans. Robert L. Montgomery (Tallahassee: Florida State University Press, 1983), 89.

18. There is an amusing parody of the spatialist-temporalist disagreement in Joyce's *Finnegans Wake*, a modernist work that is deliberately antithetical to this negation: Professor Jones attacks the temporal emphasis of Bitchson (Henri Bergson), which, he argues, should be dealt with "*ill tempor*" (James Joyce, *Finnegans Wake* [New York: Penguin, 1976], 164).

19. Bronislaw Malinowski, *Magic, Science, and Religion and Other Essays* (Boston: Beacon Press, 1948), 8 ff.

CHAPTER THREE

Friedrich Schlegel and the Anti-Ekphrastic Tradition

J. Hillis Miller

Murray Krieger's magisterial account, in *Ekphrasis,*[1] of what his subtitle calls "the illusion of the natural sign," does not mention Friedrich Schlegel. Friedrich's brother August Wilhelm is, however, referred to briefly in the chapter on "The Verbal Emblem II: From Romanticism to Modernism" (198). August Wilhelm Schlegel's "appreciations" of Shakespeare are said to be a source for Coleridge's influential argument that Shakespeare's works are organized as "organic forms." The assimilation of artworks to natural living forms is as old as Aristotle, as Krieger observes. The notion that a good work of art or literature will manifest organic form takes on a new life, however, in romanticism and in its derivatives down to the New Critics, as Krieger better than anyone else has shown.

Friedrich Schlegel is, however, mentioned twice in passing in Krieger's *A Reopening of Closure: Organicism Against Itself.*[2] He is both times given low marks. In the first reference, his "literary organicism" is associated with that of Hegel, Carlyle, Croce, and the New Critics. In all these, literary organicism is said to have given rise to unfortunate reactionary political analogies (34–5). I should have thought Schiller or Fichte would have been a better example of that than Friedrich Schlegel, who is anti-Schillerian and even anti-Fichtean, in spite of the deep influence of the latter on his thought.[3] In the other reference, Krieger associates Friedrich Schlegel with "restlessness" and a "continual need for movement" "that keeps the post-Kantian version of organic form from settling into the confinement that the more simple notion of closure propounded by those who would reject organicism would impose upon it" (41). That sounds positive enough, but the next sentence gives this restless movement a more sinister tone. The sentence associates Friedrich Schlegel with Novalis, Solger, and Tieck, and with a "romantic irony" that introduces a radically destabilizing element into the dynamic movement of romantic organicism:

> When, in the wake of Schillerian play, we turn to the several accounts of romantic irony proposed by German writers like Novalis, Friedrich Schlegel, Solger, and Tieck, we again observe the intrusion of a destabilizing element, provoking a trembling apprehension of uncertainty and doubling, a vain search for balance between an awareness of inside and outside that cannot with security know which is which. (41)

Irony is set by Krieger against organicism, even a dynamic, forward-moving organicism. Irony introduces an unsettling uncertainty and doubling for which organic metaphors are no longer appropriate, or at any rate no longer appear in Krieger's language. I propose to look a little more closely at what Friedrich Schlegel says in order to identify just how he forms part of an anti-ekphrastic tradition that has a peculiar notion of the "natural sign," to say the least.

Friedrich Schlegel's place in intellectual history is equivocal. On the one hand he is recognized as a key figure in romanticism. An immense secondary work on his writings exists. The many-volumed *Kritische Friedrich Schlegel Ausgabe* is a monument of twentieth-century scholarship.[4] On the other hand, if Paul de Man is right, and he usually is in such matters, this enormous effort has been to some degree an unintentional work of covering up what is most threatening and disquieting about Friedrich Schlegel's work.[5] Schlegel's conversion to Catholicism in 1808 and his rewriting of crucial passages in his own earlier work provided the model for this coverup.

What is so dangerous about Friedrich Schlegel's writings that it would lead sober scholars to turn away from what he says or to make him say something radically other than what he does say? One answer is to recognize that Schlegel was a great theorist and practitioner of irony. The threatening aspects of irony always call forth their repression. Schlegel's fragments are ironic through and through, as are his other major works.[6] Many of the fragments, moreover, in one way or another attempt to define irony. Hegel, who understood Schlegel (to a considerable extent at least, for example his derivation from Fichte), and detested him, as did Kierkegaard, though for somewhat different reasons, gives a clue. As Kierkegaard says in *The Concept of Irony*, "As soon as Hegel mentions the word 'irony,' he promptly thinks of Schlegel and Tieck, and his style is immediately marked by a certain resentment."[7] Passages denouncing Schlegel appear in Hegel's *Aesthetics,* in *The Philosophy of Right,* in the *Lectures on the History of Philosophy,* and in "On 'Solger's Posthumous Writings,'" all repeating more or less the same indignant reproaches. In *The Philosophy of Right,* for example, Schlegel is anathematized as "evil, in fact, evil of an inherently, wholly universal kind."[8] In the essay on his deceased colleague Solger, Hegel speaks of "the wanton disregard of things that are sacred and of the highest excellence such as marks the period of Friedrich von Schlegel's 'Lucinde,'" and of "the most brazen and flourishing period of irony."[9] As for Kierkegaard, his *The Concept of Irony* contains a long section sharply attacking Schlegel's *Lucinde* and Schlegel's concept of irony generally.

Why is Schlegel's irony so dangerous? Why does it arouse such intellectual violence and resentment? Hegel's remarks about Schlegel in the section of the Introduction to the *Aesthetics* entitled "Irony" suggests one answer. Irony is here defined by Hegel as "infinite absolute negativity."[10] This definition is later echoed and used again with a slightly different valence by Kierkegaard in *The Concept of Irony*. Irony is a power of the ego that just says no to everything. In a famous formulation Schlegel defined irony as "*eine permanente Parekbase* (a permanent parabasis)."[11] This is itself an ironically self-contradictory definition, since parabasis, the momentary breaking of dramatic illusion when one of the actors in a play comes forward to speak in his own person, must have some fictive illusion to suspend, whereas permanent parabasis would be perpetual suspension with nothing left to suspend. Paul de Man, in "The Concept of Irony," after having said that it is impossible to give a definition of irony or to state its concept, nevertheless ultimately defines irony as follows: "if Schlegel said irony is permanent parabasis, we would say that irony is the permanent parabasis of the allegory of tropes" (179). As Hegel recognizes and as Paul de Man demonstrates in detail in "The Concept of Irony," Schlegel's conception of irony derives from Fichte. "[T]he *ego*," says Hegel, in discussing Schlegel's derivation from Fichte,

> can remain lord and master (*Herr und Meister*) of everything, and in no
> sphere of morals, law, things human and divine, profane and sacred, is there
> anything that would not first have to be laid down by the *ego* (*nicht durch Ich
> erst zu setzen wäre*), and that therefore could not equally well be destroyed by
> it. Consequently everything genuinely and independently real becomes only
> a show (*ein Schein*), not true and genuine on its own account or through it-
> self, but a mere appearance (*ein bloßes Scheinen*) due to the *ego* in whose power
> and caprice (*Gewalt und Willkür*) and at whose free disposal it remains. . . .
> [T]he divine irony of genius [is] this concentration of the *ego* into itself,
> for which all bonds are snapped and which can live only in the bliss of self-
> enjoyment (*nur in der Seligkeit des Selbstgenusses leben mag*). This irony was
> invented by Friedrich von Schlegel, and many others have babbled about
> it (*haben sie nachgeschwatzt*) or are now babbling about it again. (Ger., 13:94,
> 95; Eng., 1:64–65, 66)

Hegel's scandalized distaste is overtly directed at what he sees as the immorality and obscenity of *Lucinde,* the way it makes light of the marriage bond. *Lucinde* was deplored also by Kierkegaard as an extreme example of the sort of immorality to which unrestrained irony leads.

Somewhat more covert, however, though it surfaces openly enough in his remarks on irony in Solger, Hegel's perhaps deeper objection to Schlegel's irony is that it puts a stop to dialectical progress. If irony is infinite absolute negativity, saying no to everything, it is therefore a permanent suspension or parabasis. Once you have got into this state of suspension you cannot get out of it or go on progressing through some *Aufhebung* or sublation toward the eventual fulfillment of the absolute Idea. Irony is antithesis without any possibility of synthesis at a higher stage. It is an aporia in the etymological sense: a dead end or blind alley in thought, beyond which it is impossible to progress. "To this negativity," says Hegel, "Solger firmly clung, and of course it is *one element* (ein *Moment*) in the speculative Idea, yet interpreted as this purely dialectical unrest and dissolution of both infinite and finite (*als diese bloße dialektische Unruhe und Auflösung des Unendlichen wie des Endlichen gefaßt*), only *one element,* and not, as Solger will have it, the *whole* Idea" (Ger., 13:99; Eng., 1:68–69).

Kierkegaard's way of putting this was to say that, on the one hand, Socrates's irony came at an appropriate moment. It was the infinite absolute negativity that destroyed Greek culture and made way for the coming of Christ and Christianity. Christ's advent will lead ultimately to the second coming, the last judgment, and the end of history. Schlegel's irony, on the other hand, has come at the wrong time. It is anachronistic. It puts time out of joint. It is a radical danger to Christianity and to its historical progression, since it threatens to stop or suspend that progression. It must therefore be eliminated at all costs. Unfortunately for Kierkegaard, he had a great gift for irony in the Schlegelian sense, Danish parson though he was. He spent his whole life trying unsuccessfully to expunge it from himself by ascribing it to this or that pseudonymous alter ego, for example the "Either" of *Either/Or.* Kierkegaard was a master of double diegesis and therefore subject to what Plato saw as its intrinsic immorality. This immorality is inseparable from the irony intrinsic to double diegesis or, as we should call it, indirect discourse.

Another reason, however, makes irony dangerous. Paul de Man demonstrates that it is difficult, if not impossible, to state in so many words a "concept of irony," though he ends up doing so nevertheless. Why this difficulty? It is because irony is, in the end, or perhaps even from the beginning, when there is no more than a "touch of irony" in a discourse, unreasonable, incomprehensible. Irony is *"Unverständlichkeit"* or "incomprehensibility" as such, as Schlegel's essay "On Incomprehensibility" abundantly shows in its comic failure to be entirely reasonable and perspicuous about irony. Everyone knows that irony is a trap for the unwary or for the naively trusting, such as those government officials who took Defoe's "A Short Way with the Dissenters" seriously and were angry enough to put Defoe in the stocks when they found out he was being ironic, saying one thing and meaning another. Nothing is more embarrassing, or more enraging, than to be caught out taking an ironic remark seriously or "straight." But irony is also, and more dangerously, a trap for the wary. It is particularly dangerous for those who think they understand it, who think they possess a valid "concept of irony" and can therefore protect themselves from it. This includes all the learned scholars, myself also here, who have been so courageous, or so foolish and foolhardy, as to write about irony, that is, to try to make it clear and understandable. Irony cannot be understood. It is the un-understandable as such.

Fragment 108 of Friedrich Schlegel's "Critical Fragments" says this with deceptively clear irony. The reader will note that the strategy of the fragment is to assert in various ways that irony is dangerously unreasonable because it consistently defies the principle of contradiction. "Socratic irony," says Schlegel,

> is the only involuntary (*unwillkürliche*) and yet completely deliberate (*besonnene*) dissimulation (*Verstellung*). It is equally impossible to feign (*erkünsteln*) it or divulge (*verraten*) it. To a person who hasn't got it, it will remain a riddle even after it is openly confessed (*nach dem offensten Geständnis*). It is meant to deceive (*täuschen*) no one except those who consider it a deception and who either take pleasure in the delightful roguery of making fools of the whole world or else become angry when they get an inkling they themselves might be included. In this sort of irony, everything should be playful and serious, guilelessly open and deeply hidden (*verstellt*). . . . It is the freest of all licenses, for by its means one transcends oneself; and yet it is also the most lawful, for it is absolutely necessary. It is a very good sign when the harmonious bores (*die harmonisch Platten*) are at a loss about how they should react to this continuous self-parody (*diese stete Selbstparodie*), when they fluctuate endlessly between belief and disbelief until they get dizzy (*bis sie schwindlicht werden*) and take what is meant as a joke (*Scherz*) seriously (*Ernst*) and what is meant seriously as a joke.[12]

As Georgia Albert, who has written brilliantly on this fragment, observes, "*schwindlicht*" means "dizzy" all right, but it also has overtones of "swindle" and "lie or deceive."[13] The attempt to master irony leads inevitably to vertigo, as though one had lost one's footing in reason, no longer had "understanding" in the literal sense of something solid to stand on under one's feet, had been swindled or become a self-swindler, deceived or a deceiver self-deceived, in an endless unstoppable oscillation or rotation, like being caught in a revolving door.

That the reader of the passage is himself or herself caught up in the dizzying alternations it names, led by it not to a masterful understanding of irony but to an experience of *Unverständlichkeit*, is the most unsettling aspect of this fragment. If you do not understand the passage you are led to fluctuate endlessly between belief and disbelief. If you understand it you are plunged into dizzy incomprehension by your very act of understanding. Either way you have had it, which is a way of saying that the aporias central to

Schlegel's thought are not tame impasses in logic or mere matters of word-play. As Schlegel observes in "On Incomprehensibility," "Irony is something one simply cannot play games with. (*Mit der Ironie ist durchaus nicht zu scherzen.*) It can have incredibly long-lasting after effects. (*Sie kann unglaublich lange nachwirken.*)" (G538) [14] It might be safer to leave it alone. But how can one be sure, in a given case, that one is not speaking ironically without meaning to do so, or that one's interlocutor is not an intentional or unintentional ironist?

Another of Schlegel's formulations, this one about the creation of a "new mythology," ascribed to Ludovico,[15] the speaker of the "Rede über die Mythologie (Talk on Mythology)" in *Gespräch über die Poesie (Dialogue on Poetry)*, turns on the multiple meanings of a particularly rich family of words in German: *Bild, bilden, Bildung, anbilden, umbilden*. *Bild* means form and is translated as such in the English version. It also means figure and metaphor, as well as portrait or picture. *Bilden* means to form, but also to educate. *Bildung* is formation but also education—formation in the sense of informing submission to a discipline or curriculum. A university education, for example in Humboldt's idea of it in his plan for the University of Berlin, is devoted not only to teaching knowledge (*Wissenschaft*), but also to *Bildung*, to the formation of citizens of the state. *Anbilden* means conform, while *umbilden* means transform.

Schlegel uses play on these various words to express a double paradox. On the one hand the original "chaos," as he calls it, from which everything else has derived, already has form or has been given various cultural forms. We should make use of those pre-existing forms in our new mythology. On the other hand chaos is without form. It is rather a place of constant transformation. The proper way to give poetic expression to this is to produce a new mythology that is itself in constant transformation. Moreover, this new mythology must be radically inaugural, innovative, not dependent on any pre-existing forms. On the one hand the new mythology will be constative. It will seek the best indirect expression of what is always already there but usually escapes our consciousness and can never be directly expressed. On the other hand the new mythology will be performative in a radical sense. It will be a speech act that is a new start. It will invent "the highest," not in the sense of discovering it but in the sense of casting out new forms that reshape the original chaos and are deliberately manipulated transformations of it.

"In regard to the sublime (*wegen des Höchsten*)," says Ludovico, "we do not entirely depend on our emotions (*unser Gemüt*)" (G501).[16] To translate "*das Höchste*" as "the sublime" is daring, perhaps even a sublime daring, since the usual German word for the sublime is "*das Erhabene.*" Schlegel probably just means "the highest" in the sense of the most elevated, the most out of reach, and the most valuable in itself, that unspeakable of which mythologies are allegorical expressions. It is somewhat misleading to bring in all the Kantian, Burkean, and Hegelian associations of the sublime. To say we do not entirely depend on our emotions in regard to the highest is to say that irrational feelings—love and imagination as manifested in *Lucinde,* for example—are not the only way to get in relation to the highest. The other way is to "take part everywhere in what is already formed (*an das Gebildete*)" (G501; DP85). Schlegel has Ludovico go on to say that this means we should "develop, kindle and nourish the sublime (*das Höchste*)," in two ways: "through contact with the same in kind, the similar (*des Gleichartigen, Ähnlichen*), or if of equal stature (*bei gleicher Würde*) the hostile; in a word, give it form (*bilden*)" (G501; DP85–86). This is an odd and not entirely perspicuous formulation. Its somewhat covert logic seems to be the following: Since the highest is itself a place of contradictions, we should develop, kindle, and nourish it not only by things that seem to be similar to it, but also through appropriately grand things that are hostile to it, such as Schlegel's details about bodily love in *Lucinde.* Just as Schlegel's fragments generate their explosive wit by bringing together in the tight space of a sentence or two logically contradictory expressions, so the highest, since it cannot in any case be spoken of directly or literally, must be spoken of simultaneously in what is like and unlike it. Or rather, nothing is really either like or unlike it in the usual sense. To express it simultaneously in the like and the unlike is to give it form, to shape it, in an act that Schlegel calls "*bilden.*" Since it does not have fixed form in itself, any form we give it will be both adequate and inadequate.

The notion of "giving form" to the highest, Behler and Struc's translation of "*bilden,*" is crucial here. The highest does not in itself have a form comprehensible to human consciousness. The function of any mythology, whether that of the Greeks or that of the new romantic mythology in the process of being created, is to give form not so much to the formless as to something that is a place of constant transformation. That something has forms, if forms they can be called, that are alien to human consciousness. Schlegel's expression of this necessity is somewhat hyperbolic or even shrill: "If the sublime, however, is incapable of being intentionally created (*Ist das Höchste aber wirklich keiner absichtlichen Bildung fähig*), then let us give up any claims to a free art of ideas (*freie Ideenkunst*), for it would be an empty name" (G501; DP86). A free art of ideas would be intentional (*absichtlich*) creation, the *Bildung* of the new mythology as an allegory of the inexpressible.

What it means to say mythology is a *Bildung* whose essential trait is constant transformation is indicated in the next paragraph of Ludovico's discourse, as well as in a consonant passage in *Lucinde* that I shall not discuss here.[17] Giving form to the highest is not a single static gesture, but a perpetual process of metamorphosis. This is so because that for which the allegorical myth stands is itself not a fixed unity, such as the Platonic One, or the Christian Godhead, three in one. Schlegel's "highest" is the locus of constant transformation.

"Mythology," says Ludovico, "is such a work of art created by nature (*ist ein solches Kunstwerk der Natur*)" (G501; DP86). The translation here makes a not wholly justified choice by saying "created by nature." Which is it, subjective or objective genitive, in the phrase "*Kunstwerk der Natur*"? The phrase must contain the possibility of both. The German might mean "work of art created by Nature," or it might mean "natural work of art," or it might mean "artwork representing nature," as when we say "That is a picture of so and so." The German literally says "artwork of nature," just that. This point is worth dwelling on because of a fundamental, and highly traditional, ambiguity in Schlegel's use of the word "*Natur.*" The word, in his usage, means nonhuman nature as intermediary between human beings and the aboriginal chaos. It also means human nature. It also means, especially given the avowed influence of Spinoza's pantheism on Schlegel's thinking in the "Talk on Mythology," a single continuous realm that includes "the highest" as well as nature in the limited senses of physical nature and human nature. An "artwork of nature" arises from, represents, and is continuous with nature in this complex sense.

Ludovico goes on to say that in the "texture (*Gewebe*)" of a mythology that is intertwined with nature in this way, "the sublime is really formed (*ist das Höchste wirklich gebildet*)" (G501; DP86). The sentence contains undecidable alternative possibilities of meaning. "*Gebildet*" may mean either the creation of something that was not there at all before the mythology brought it into being, or it may mean that the mythology gives form to the formless chaos that was always already there. The rest of the sentence does not decide one way or the other, but it helps the reader understand why it is impossible to decide. In such a mythology, says Ludovico, "everything is relation (*Beziehung*) and metamorphosis (*Verwandlung*), conformed and transformed (*angebildet und umgebildet*), and this conformation and transformation (*Anbilden und Umbilden*) is its peculiar process (*Verfahren*), its inner life and method, if I may say so" (G501; DP86). Far from being a fixed set of mythological stories, the new mythology will be, like romantic poetry in general in Schlegel's idea of it (the two are more or less synonymous), dynamic, never finished, constantly changing. A celebrated fragment, fragment 116 of the *Athenaeum Fragments,* is the best expression of this. "Romantic poetry," says Schlegel,

is progressive, universal poetry. . . . Other kinds of poetry are finished (*fertig*) and are now capable of being fully analyzed (*zergliedert*). The romantic kind of poetry is still in the state of becoming (*im Werden*); that, in fact, is its real essence: that it should forever be becoming and never be perfected (*daß sie ewig nur werden, nie vollendet sein kann*). . . . It alone is infinite, just as it alone is free; and it recognizes as its first commandment that the will [in the sense of arbitrary wilfulness; the German word is *Willkür*] of the poet can tolerate no law above itself. (*Sie allein ist unendlich, wie sie allein frei ist und das als ihr erstes Gesetz anerkennt, daß die Willkür des Dichters kein Gesetz über sich leide.*) (G38–39; E31–32)

This refusal to accept any law above itself is one feature of Schlegel's thought that outraged Hegel, but one can see its necessity. If the new mythology is going to be forever becoming and never perfected, it can move toward its infinitely distant goal only by rejecting whatever has come before and working in a radically inaugural way. If it is to progress, it must, in an absolutely free and wilful creative gesture, be a new law unto itself. That means rejecting any pre-existing law.

This freedom and wilfulness must enter into the intimate texture of the new mythology. This means that if, on the one hand, it is characterized by establishing new and hitherto unheard of relations (*Beziehungen*) among the elements that enter into it, on the other hand these relations must not be fixed. They must rather be in a constant state of change. This change takes two forms, as is indicated by the two forms of "*bilden*" that are employed: "*anbilden*" and "*umbilden,*" conformed and transformed. Each new element must be conformed to the one to which it is related, but this process is also a transformation of the new element that is assimilated into the dynamic system.

The alert reader will notice that what Schlegel is describing here is nothing more or less than a tropological system. Metaphor and the other master tropes—synecdoche, metonymy, and prosopopoeia—as they work by substitution, condensation, displacement, naming, and renaming, are the primary linguistic tools whereby the process of giving form by conformation and transformation, in a perpetual metamorphosis, is accomplished. The consonance of Schlegel's formulations here with an admirably exuberant affirmation of the poet's power in Wordsworth's "Preface" of 1815 will confirm this. Wordsworth is talking about a series of figurative metamorphoses in a passage from his "Resolution and Independence." The passage and its commentary might have been written as an exemplification of what Schlegel says about the way the poet gives the law to himself and continually transforms things in a sovereign exercise of his tropological power. What Wordsworth says is a comment on the following passage in "Resolution and Independence," as he cites it in the Preface:

As a huge stone is sometimes seen to lie
Couched on the bald top of an eminence,
Wonder to all who do the same espy

By what means it could thither come, and whence,
So that it seems a thing endued with sense,
Like a sea-beast crawled forth, which on a shelf
Of rock or sand reposeth, there to sun himself.

Such seemed this Man; not all alive or dead
Nor all asleep, in his extreme old age.

.   .   .

Motionless as a cloud the old Man stood,
That heareth not the loud winds when they call,
And moveth altogether if it move at all. (ll. 57–65; 75–77)

Here is Wordsworth's commentary on these lines:

> In these images, the conferring, the abstracting, and the modifying powers
> of the Imagination, immediately and mediately acting, are all brought into
> conjunction. The stone is endowed with something of the power of life to
> approximate it to the sea-beast; and the sea-beast stripped of some of its vi-
> tal qualities to assimilate it to the stone; which intermediate image is thus
> treated for the purpose of bringing the original image, that of the stone, to
> a nearer resemblance to the figure and condition of the aged Man; who is
> divested of so much of the indications of life and motion as to bring him to
> the point where the two objects unite and coalesce in just comparison. After
> what has been said, the image of the cloud need not be commented on.[18]

All this aspect of Schlegel's theory of myth seems admirably positive and op-
timistic. This is the side that has been most often stressed by those critics
and scholars who approve of Schlegel and who want to affirm his importance as one of the founders of romanticism or of what we should call today
aesthetic ideology in its modern form. Things are not quite so simple with
Friedrich Schlegel, however, nor quite so cheerful.

A darker side of the motif of transformation emerges a little later in the
"Talk on Mythology" and in the echoing passage in *Lucinde* to which I referred earlier. The reader will remember that the function of the new mythology is to form allegories, indirect expressions, of "the highest," or of
what Schlegel calls "chaos." Works contributing to the formation of the new
mythology must be in constant transformation because what they indirectly
represent is not fixed but is in constant, senseless metamorphosis, subject
to deformations beyond the human power to comprehend. "Senseless" is
the key word here, and I must now show why it is justified and why this senselessness gives a dark tone to Schlegel's notion of mythology.

The paragraph about the way the highest is really formed by a mythology
that is a constant process of metamorphosis is followed by a passage that
amalgamates, in an act of transformation and conformation of its own, the

"marvelous wit of romantic poetry which does not manifest itself in individual conceptions but in the structure of the whole," meaning the works of Shakespeare and Cervantes, with mythology. "Indeed," says Schlegel, "this artfully ordered confusion (*diese künstlich geordnete Verwirrung*), this charming symmetry of contradictions (*Widersprüchen*), this wonderfully perennial alternation of enthusiasm (*Enthusiasmus*) and irony which lives even in the smallest parts of the whole, seem to me to be an indirect mythology themselves" (G501; DP86). Having said that the wit of romantic poetry lies in the structure of the whole, not in individual parts, Schlegel now says that the alternation of enthusiasm and irony is vitally present even in the smallest parts of the whole. It must be both at once, in another example of the symmetry of contradictions of which Schlegel speaks. The wit of romantic poetry is present in the asymmetrical symmetry of the whole, something slightly askew or amiss in the whole structure that makes it explosively witty, as a fragment is witty. Unlike an example of harmonious organic unity, with each part contributing to a whole that hangs together—with nothing in excess, as Aristotle says should be the case with a good tragedy—a work of the new mythology will be made up of parts that mirror the paradoxical witty structure of the whole. It is not simply that one part is not consonant with some other part, though perfectly coherent and self-consistent in itself. Each smallest part is itself riven by the same kind of contradictions that dominate the larger structure. It repeats those contradictions in miniature, as each part of a fractal repeats the pattern of the whole. It is not that one part is enthusiastic and another part ironic, but that even the smallest part is enthusiastic and ironic at once.

The next sentence gives that asymmetrical symmetry a name that has a complex resonance in Schlegel's thought and in that of German romanticism generally.[19] He says both romantic witty poetry and the new mythology are organized as an arabesque: "The organization [of both romantic poetry and mythology] is the same, and certainly the arabesque (*die Arabeske*) is the oldest and most original form of human imagination (*der menschlichen Phantasie*)" (G501; DP86). As other passages in Schlegel show, he thinks, when he says "arabesque," as much of Raphael's arabesques—complex designs of beasts, flowers, and foliage—as of the Muslim designs to which Raphael was alluding. In either case an arabesque is, like the airy flourishes of Corporal Trim's stick in *Tristram Shandy,* a tangle of lines whose interleaved wanderings are governed by a center that is outside the design itself and that is located at infinity. An arabesque is a complex of asymptotic curves.

The words enthusiasm and irony are not chosen at random. Enthusiasm: the word means, etymologically, "possessed by a god." Insofar as witty romantic poems, poems that are an indirect mythology themselves, are enthusiastic, they contain or are possessed by that "highest" to which they give indirect, allegorical expression. Irony: we know what that means. It means incomprehensibility, vertigo, a dead end in thought, the permanent suspension or parabasis of dialectical progression. A mythology must be both enthusiastic and ironical at once, in defiance of reason. It must be enthusiastic in order to be inhabited by the highest. Since that highest is also chaotic, however, it can only be adequately allegorized in a mythology that is self-canceling, against reason, or alogical. Schlegel's name for this kind of discourse is "irony." This combination is itself contradictory and ironic. How could a person or a discourse be at once enthusiastic and ironic? Each feature would suspend or cancel the other.

The necessity for this impossible combination is made clear in the two sentences that follow. These are the climactic formulations of the whole braided or enchained sequence of assertions I have been following. Both romantic wit and any mythology must be enthusiastic in the precise sense that they allow the highest to shimmer through, according to that figure of "*sinnliche Scheinen*" used already earlier in the "Talk on Mythology," in the paragraph just before my citations begin. At the same time what shines through must be expressed ironically because it is, like irony, senseless, absurd, mad. It must fulfill Paul de Man's definition of irony in "The Rhetoric of Temporality": "Irony is unrelieved *vertige*, dizziness to the point of madness."[20] In de Man's witty sentence, "unrelieved" must be taken not only in the sense of unremitting, without relief, but also as an unostentatious translation of the Hegelian term "*Aufhebung*" as "relief." "*Aufhebung*" is more or less untranslatable, since it means simultaneously cancel, preserve, and lift up. It might, however, be translated as "relief." Unrelieved vertigo would be a dizziness that could be defined as an infinite absolute negativity incapable of dialectical sublation, lifting up, or relief. "Neither this wit nor a mythology can exist," says Schlegel,

> without something original and inimitable which is absolutely irreducible (*ohne ein erstes Ursprüngliches und Unnachahmliches, was schlecthin unauflöslich ist*), and in which after all the transformations (*Umbildungen*) its original character and creative energy (*Kraft*) are still dimly visible (*durchschimmern läßt*), where the naive profundity (*der naive Tiefsinn*) permits the semblance of the absurd and of madness, of simplicity and foolishness (*den Schein des Verkehrten und Verrückten oder des Einfältigen und Dummen*), to shimmer through (*durchschimmern läßt*). (G501–2; DP86)

These are strong words—the absurd, madness, simplicity (in the sense of simplemindedness), and foolishness. As de Man observes in "The Concept of Irony," these words sharply undercut any strongly positive, humanistic reading of the passage as a whole, such as might seem to be authorized by what is said earlier about the ability of a mythology to represent the highest allegorically, as well as by many other passages in Schlegel that seem to give a cheerful allegiance, in accordance with aesthetic ideology generally, to a progressive view of history as moving closer and closer to a union with the highest under the guidance of romantic poetry and the new mythology. The endpoint of the new mythology's insight is, on the contrary, the shimmering through of the aboriginal chaos's madness and stupidity. As de Man also observes in the same place, Schlegel rewrote these phrases to make them even stronger. Originally he wrote "the strange (*das Sonderbare*), even the absurd (*das Widersinnige*), as well as a childlike and yet sophisticated (*geistreiche*) naïveté," rather than "the semblance of the absurd and of madness, of simplicity and foolishness (*Schein des Verkehrten und Verrückten oder des Einfältigen und Dummen*)."[21] This revision in the direction of a starker confrontation with the senselessness of chaos also gives little support to the assertion by the "many critics," alluded to in Behler and Struc's introduction to their English translation of the *Dialogue on Poetry,* who "have seen in this demand for a new mythology the first symptom of Schlegel's later conversion to Catholicism" (DP27). Catholicism is a broad and catholic religion, but there is no way it can be made to jibe, even distantly, with the conception of a chaotic, impersonal, mad "highest" presented in the *Dialogue on Poetry.*

The "something original and inimitable which is absolutely irreducible" is that aboriginal chaos. The words "original," "inimitable," and "irreducible" must be taken in strong or literal senses. This "something" is radically original in the sense of being the transcendent source of everything, not just in the weaker sense in which we speak of "poetic originality." It is inimitable not in the sense that Charles Dickens was known as "the inimitable Boz," but in the literal sense that it is impossible to represent it directly in a mimesis. It is "unspeakable," and can only be spoken of indirectly. It is absolutely irreducible in the sense that it cannot be reduced by analysis to its component elements. Though it is the locus of a constant self-differentiation, it cannot be adequately differentiated, analyzed, or reduced by human language. Nevertheless, its original character and creative energy still shine dimly through all the formations, conformations, and transformations that characterize a mythology. It shines through because this mythology combines, in an oxymoron, naiveté with profundity. The new mythology is naively profound, or profoundly naive, like a fairy story. It is profound without knowing that it is profound. The combination of naiveté and profundity makes it both enthusiastic and ironical at the same time. What shines through, however, as should be stressed, is not the original absurdity, madness, simplicity, and stupidity of chaos, but only its *Schein*, that is, both a distant, indirect gleam of it and its "semblance," as the translation puts it. Probably that is a good thing, since the closer one gets to that original chaos the closer one gets to absurdity, dizziness to the point of madness. Mythology, it may be, is a protection as well as a means of insight.

Nevertheless, what Schlegel stresses in the final sentence of the enchained sequence I have been following is the irrationality of poetry and the way it puts us within chaos. The sentence, in its use of the word "*aufzuheben,*" is a parodic anticipation of Hegelian dialectical sublation. In Schlegel's case the *Aufhebung* does not raise us to a higher level in an endless progression toward the far-off fulfillment of union with absolute spirit, the Idea, nor does it move toward the achievement of Absolute Knowledge. It transplants us into a mad chaos. It leads to total non-knowledge. Hegel was right to be appalled.

As opposed to Paul de Man, who stresses the madness of ironic language in Schlegel, I want to argue that Schlegel's difference from Hegel arises from a different intuition about what is beyond language: Schlegel's chaos as against Hegel's Idea. Everything follows, I claim, from that difference. Every feature of Schlegel's nonsystematic system makes sense (a strange kind of nonsensical sense) when everything he says is seen as swirling around those "wholly others" he called chaos.

Here is that final sentence, the last link in this non-concatenated chain:

> For this is the beginning (*Anfang*) of all poetry, to cancel (*aufzuheben*) the progression (*Gang*) and laws of rationally thinking reason (*der vernünftig denkenden Vernunft*), and to transplant (*zu versetzen*) us once again into the beautiful confusion of imagination (*die schöne Verwirrung der Phantasie*), into the original (*ursprüngliche*) chaos of human nature, for which I know as yet no more beautiful symbol (*Symbol*) than the motley throng (*das bunte Gewimmel*) of the ancient gods. (G502; DP86)

About the stuttering repetition of the prefix "*ver-*" here—in "*vernünftig . . . Vernunft* (reasonable reason)," in "*versetzen,*" and in "*Verwirrung,*" already used a few sentences earlier—there would be much to say, but I defer that here. If "*aufheben*" means not just cancel, but preserve, and raise up, thereby suggesting that poetry is a kind of higher reason, the passage makes clear that this higher reason is not rational, clear, but an irrational confusion. The translation affirms that poetry "transplants" us into that original confusion, but "*versetzen*" means literally, according to the dictionary, "set over, move, transfer; move from one grade to another in school; pawn, hock; reply." The word, in one of its valences, as meaning "transpose," is almost a synonym for "*übersetzen,*" translate. The prefix "*ver-,*" as in this verb, is antithetical, both an intensive and a privative. "*Versetzen*" can mean to put forth or deposit as collateral for a loan, in short, to put in hock, as well as transpose, set across. In Schlegel's usage here, "*versetzen*" affirms that poetic words have a magic power to transpose the reader into original chaos, just as if he were being translated into another language home where another mother tongue is spoken. That new language, however, is the language of madness and foolishness.

This encompassing irony, a kind of ultimate irony of irony, will allow, finally, understanding, if I dare to use that word, of another recurrent motif in Schlegel's work, namely the definition of poetry as magic. In the dialogue leading up to Ludovico's presentation of the "Talk on Mythology," Ludovico asserts that "poetry is the finest branch of magic (*der edelste Zweig der Magie*)" (G496; DP80). After Ludovico's talk, Lothario (who is sometimes said to represent Novalis) asserts, apropos of Dante, that "Actually, every work should be a new revelation (*Offenbarung*) of nature. Only by being individual and universal (*Eins und Alles*) does a work become *the work* (*wird ein Werk zum Werk*)." A moment later he stresses the word again, speaking of the "independence and inner perfection for which I simply cannot find another word but the work (*als das von Werken*)" (G507; DP92). The word "work" here means primarily a work of art, of course, Dante's *Divine Comedy* in one example Schlegel gives. The insistence on the word, however, gives it alchemical or magical overtones. The great "work," for medieval alchemy, was the transmutation of base metals into gold. That transmutation was a figure for the transfiguration of the human spirit by a kind of magic into something worthy of salvation or even into a kind of deity. If poetry is the noblest magic, this means that poetry does not promise or give knowledge. It works performatively to bring something about, as though it were a magic formula. It is a feature of magic formulas, however, that they are, at least superficially or to profane ears and eyes, senseless, stupid: "Abracadabra! Hocus-pocus!" says the magician, and something happens, a pack of cards is turned into a pigeon. Schlegel's conception of mythology is ultimately performative, not constative. A work of mythology is a speech act that works through its senselessness to reveal, in a magic opening up, a gleam of the semblance of chaos. It thereby works to transform its readers through this revelation. We do not come to know anything through a myth. We are made different, magically. The mythological work works.

The final irony, however, is that since this transformation is brought about not by knowledge but by a magic speech act, there is no way to know, for sure, whether the revelation is a true one, or only a semblance, a *Schein*. "Hocus-pocus" is a slang term for the beguiling procedures of a fraud. The pack of cards is not really turned into a pigeon. It is a sleight of hand. The paradox of all speech acts appears here in a hyperbolic form. It is hyperbolic because the speech act in question deals with the highest destiny of humankind. It is the speech act enabling all other speech acts. The performative side of a speech act is alien to knowledge. It makes something happen, but just how, by just whose authority, and just what happens can never be known for certain. Another way to put this is to say that mythologies are for Schlegel forced and abusive transfers of language, thrown out to name something that has no proper name, something that is unknown and unknowable. The rhetorical name for this procedure is catachresis. I therefore call Schlegel's myths catachreses for chaos. For Schlegel, what cannot be known for certain is whether new mythological works create a spurious semblance of the highest out of hocus-pocus, language's magic power to project new virtual realities, or whether such works open doors allowing us to glimpse a semblance, a *Schein,* of that pre-existing, perennial, wholly other realm Friedrich Schlegel calls "chaos." Nothing could be more important to know, but we cannot know. We can, however, believe, and bear witness, one way or the other. This is the way Schlegel's assertions about myth embody the threat to rationality and dialectical thought that made Hegel so indignant.

I have also shown, so I claim, the paradoxical place Friedrich Schlegel has in the history of ekphrasis or in the history of what Murray Krieger calls the illusion of the natural sign. On the one hand, catachreses for chaos are by no means signs that have a natural correspondence to their referent. They must be "worked" to come to stand for chaos. On the other hand, any sign under the sun has a natural capacity to be worked in this way, for example the details about sexual intercourse in *Lucinde* that so scandalized Hegel and Kierkegaard. The lowest can stand for the highest, or, as Ludovico puts it, the highest can be given form by what appears opposed to it as well as by what appears most like it.

NOTES

1. Murray Krieger, *Ekphrasis: The Illusion of the Natural Sign* (Baltimore: Johns Hopkins University Press, 1992). Numbers after citations refer to page numbers in this edition.

2. Murray Krieger, *A Reopening of Closure: Organicism Against Itself* (New York: Columbia University Press, 1989). Numbers after citations refer to page numbers in this edition.

3. For a brilliant essay on this topic see Werner Hamacher, "Position Exposed: Friedrich Schlegel's Poetological Transposition of Fichte's Absolute Proposition," in *Premises: Essays on Philosophy and Literature from Kant to Celan,* trans. Peter Fenves (Cambridge, Mass.: Harvard University Press, 1996), 222–60. Hamacher's essay, which I saw only after finishing my own, overlaps to some degree with my reading of Friedrich Schlegel.

4. *Kritische Friedrich Schlegel Ausgabe,* ed. Ernst Behler with Jean-Jacques Anstett and Hans Eichner (Munich: F. Schöningh, 1958–).

5. See Paul de Man, "The Concept of Irony," in *Aesthetic Ideology,* ed. Andrzej Warminski (Minneapolis: University of Minnesota Press, 1996), 182: "The best crit-

ics who have written on Schlegel, who have recognized his importance, have wanted to shelter him from the accusation of frivolity, which was generally made, but in the process they always have to recover the categories of the self, of history, and of dialectic, which are precisely the categories which in Schlegel are disrupted in a radical way." The two examples of this de Man gives are Peter Szondi and Walter Benjamin, two names to conjure with. To these names may be added the even more august names of Hegel and Kierkegaard. If all these dignitaries got Schlegel wrong, how could we expect to do better?

6. These include, along with the three sets of fragments, the *Gespräch über die Poesie* (*Dialogue on Poetry*) (1799–1800); the essay entitled "Über die Unverständlichkeit (On Incomprehensibility)" (1800); and the strange autobiographical novel *Lucinde* (1799).

7. Søren Kierkegaard, *The Concept of Irony*, trans. Howard V. Hong and Edna H. Hong (Princeton: Princeton University Press, 1989), 265–66. Lee Capel's translation has "indignation" rather than "resentment": "As soon as Hegel pronounces the word 'irony' he immediately thinks of Schlegel and Tieck, and his style instantly takes on the features of a certain indignation" (Søren Kierkegaard, *The Concept of Irony*, trans. Lee M. Capel [Bloomington: Indiana University Press, 1965], 283). Friedrich Schlegel makes Hegel indignant.

8. G. W. F. Hegel, *Elements of the Philosophy of Right*, trans. H. B. Nisbet (Cambridge: Cambridge University Press, 1991), 182.

9. Cited in Kierkegaard, *The Concept of Irony*, trans. Hong and Hong, 547.

10. "Unendliche absolute Negativität," G. W. F. Hegel, *Vorlesungen über die Ästhetik*, *Werke* (Frankfurt am Main: Suhrkamp, 1981), 13:98; *Aesthetics: Lectures on Fine Art*, trans. T. M. Knox (Oxford: Clarendon Press, 1975), 1:68. Henceforth Ger. and Eng., respectively.

11. "Die Ironie ist eine permanente Parekbase,—": Friedrich Schlegel, "Zur Philosophie" (1797), Fragment 668, in *Philosophische Lehrjahre I* (1796–1806), ed. Ernst Behler, *Kritische Friedrich Schlegel Ausgabe* 18:85.

12. Friedrich Schlegel, *Kritische Schriften* (Munich: Carl Hanser, 1964), 20–21, henceforth G, followed by the page number; Friedrich Schlegel, *Philosophical Fragments*, trans. Peter Firchow (Minneapolis: University of Minnesota Press, 1991), 13, henceforth E, followed by the page number.

13. See Georgia Albert, "Understanding Irony: Three *essais* on Friedrich Schlegel," *MLN* (1993), 825–48. The comment on "*schwindlicht*" is on 845.

14. "On Incomprehensibility," in *German Aesthetic and Literary Criticism: The Romantic Ironists and Goethe*, ed. Kathleen Wheeler (Cambridge: Cambridge University Press, 1984), 37.

15. Ludovico is thought by some scholars to be modeled on the philosopher F. W. von Schelling, but there is no way to be certain about that.

16. Friedrich Schlegel, "Dialogue on Poetry," in *Dialogue on Poetry and Literary Aphorisms*, trans. Ernst Behler and Roman Struc (University Park: Pennsylvania State University Press, 1968), 85, henceforth DP, followed by the page number.

17. See Friedrich Schlegel, *Lucinde* (Stuttgart: Reclam, 1973), 78; *Lucinde*, trans. Peter Firchow, in *Friedrich Schlegel's Lucinde and the Fragments* (Minneapolis: University of Minnesota Press, 1971), 104.

18. William Wordsworth, *Poetical Works,* ed. Thomas Hutchinson, rev. Ernest de Selincourt (London: Oxford University Press, 1966), 754.

19. See Karl Konrad Polheim, *Die Arabeske: Ansichten und Ideen aus Friedrich Schlegels Poetik* (Munich: F. Schöningh, 1966).

20. Paul de Man, "The Rhetoric of Temporality," in *Blindness and Insight,* 2d ed. (Minneapolis: University of Minnesota Press, 1983), 215.

21. De Man, "The Concept of Irony," 180–81.

CHAPTER FOUR

On Truth and Lie in an Aesthetic Sense

Ernst Behler

The question of truth and lie in an aesthetic sense raises problems of the most fundamental character about poetry and literature. We are immediately reminded of Plato, who claimed that poets are liars, and take refuge in Aristotle, who was more favorably disposed toward fabulation. However, whereas Aristotle's justification of philosophy succeeded quite well when he proclaimed, in the first sentence of his *Metaphysics,* that by nature all human beings strive for knowledge, his attempt to rehabilitate poetry in his *Poetics* by claiming that all human beings like to imitate was less convincing.[1] Attacks on poetry and defenses of poetry have succeeded one another in the Western world ever since. Furthermore, imitation, mimesis, and the implied representation of nature all relate to a conception of poetry and literature that has long been discarded, at least since the beginnings of romanticism. Nevertheless, Aristotle's notion of poetry is certainly not restricted to this narrow concept of imitation and the truth of nature, especially when he distinguishes poetry from historical depiction (AR 1451b, 3–4) because of the role the imagination plays in poetic creation, or when he establishes the principle of structuring with a beginning, middle, and end (AR 1450b, 3–4) and in terms of space and time, according to human dimensions (AR 1459a, 1–20). The debate about truth and lie in poetry therefore finds its origin on classical grounds and could very well be enacted there.

Borrowing my title from Nietzsche's essay "On Truth and Lie in an Extra-Moral Sense," I am approaching the topic from a modern perspective instead. More specifically, my departure is taken from a theory of language emerging towards the end of the eighteenth century in writings by Rousseau, Herder, and especially the early romantics. Nietzsche's "On Truth and Lie" is surely the most intensified expression of the romantic theory of language and inevitably raises the question of truth and falsehood not only in poetry, but also in philosophy and virtually all realms of human communication. Friedrich Schlegel, Novalis, Kierkegaard, Baudelaire, and Oscar Wilde all touch upon truth and falsity in their literary reflections, and I will touch on them all in turn.

I

Before leaving antiquity, however, I should like to make several observations about the ancient world, because both Friedrich Schlegel and Nietzsche, the two poles of my discussion, drew inspiration for their own conceptions of truth and lie in literature from classical authors. Schlegel considered the world of ancient drama as "completely torn away from the real world" and having a system of reference entirely of its own.[2] Reality is to be understood here in the ancient sense, as being equivalent to truth as revealed in the three forms of myth, history, and the surrounding world of nature. Drama, by being torn from these relationships, however, does not establish itself in a world of lies for Schlegel, but in a realm where the notions of truth and reality are nonexistent or irrelevant. Whereas "even the most artful epic and lyric poems of the Greeks still have a foothold and ground" in myth, history, and reality, drama establishes its position beyond such relationships.

This special status of drama is obvious not only in its deliberate alteration of pregiven mythologies, but especially in the most fundamental task of dramatic representation, namely, to "let the most distant appear as immediately present" (FS 1:502). Referring to a statement by Quintilian (Inst. II, 8), Schlegel says:

> By virtue of an inner unity connecting independent parts created out of
> pure appearance, the dramatic genre is preeminently and in the full sense
> poetic art, which, in the view of the ancients, consists in the accomplishment
> of lasting works. (FS 1:502)

For Schlegel, this purely aesthetic character of a true work of art has to find a correspondence in a "purely artistic point of view," an entirely aesthetic attitude of the critic free from any truth-related or morally inclined interpretation (FS 1:xcix). Two terms used by Schlegel in this context (FS 1:298) are revealing. The first is the metaphor taken from the ancients, of weaving or knitting, a carpet for example, and describes the creation of poetry as the knitting together of various threads to a pleasant unity without any extra-aesthetic consideration. The second is that of a gracious mobility of alternation, noticed especially in Sophocles, one of motion and tranquillity, action and peace, agitation and reflection, but also of truth and lie. This alternation of opposites results in a pleasant and ever-shifting unity. Schlegel is following Kant's proclamation of the autonomy of the beautiful in its complete lack of any moral, rational, or practical consideration, and he is attempting to give this conception more substance by referring to ancient examples. His discussion of the lies in Homer, however, relates more directly to the Greek world and refers to statements by the ancients themselves, such as Pindar, who had said:

> I believe that Homer, while agreeably narrating, said more about Ulysses
> than the latter really suffered. For Homer's lies, by virtue of their deft art,
> have a certain dignity about them. Wisdom deceives, in a tempting manner,
> through its poems. (quoted in FS 1:454)

Even those who defend Homer's veracity, Schlegel continues, had to admit that deliberate deception was not out of the question for this poet, of whom one could say what he had said about Ulysses: "Thus, deceits he many composed, similar to truth" (FS 1:455).

Nietzsche, in contrast to Schlegel, concentrated more on the origin of the concept of truth among the Greeks and found it lacking among the earlier philosophers, the Pre-Socratics. "The proclamation of truth at any price is Socratic," he said, and he found it extraordinarily difficult to reconstitute the "mythical feeling of free lying" in oneself. "The great Greek philosophers still live entirely in a conviction of being justified in lying," Nietzsche continued, attempting to make this attitude plausible with the remark: "Where one has no true knowledge of anything, lying is permitted."[3] These philosophers embarrass us when we deal with the problem of "whether philosophy is an art or a science" (FN 7:439). In Nietzsche's opinion, these "older philosophers," unlike the Socratics, "are partly guided by a drive similar to the one that created tragedy" (FN 7:442). "Thales is long gone," he observes, "yet an artist standing at a waterfall will admit that he was right" (FN 7:441). The same applies to Heraclitus, of whom Nietzsche says: "Heraclitus will never become antiquated. He represents poetry beyond the limits of experience, a continuation of the mythical instinct; he also speaks essentially in images" (FN 7:439). Nietzsche concludes by remarking: "Striving for truth is an infinitely slow acquisition of humanity" (FN 7:450).

Nietzsche finds an ambivalence in the concept of truth to still exist in Plato, and says in his lectures on rhetoric at Basel University:

> Most remarkable is *Republic* 376e: here Plato distinguishes two types of
> speech, those that contain truth and those that lie: the myths belong to
> the latter. He considers them justified and reproaches Homer and Hesiod
> not for having lied, but for not having lied in the right manner.[4]

Nietzsche is referring here to the section in the *Republic* dealing with the education of the guardians of the city when they are still children. An agreement is made indeed to begin their education with those tales that are false (ψεῦδος) and contain lies, as in fables and in myths (μῦθος) (377b). Homer and Hesiod are of no use here (377d) because they did not falsify in a pleasant manner, but rather told the greatest lies about things of the greatest concern. Nietzsche goes on to consider *Republic* 414b, where the discussion turns to "those opportune falsehoods" and "noble lies" by which the ruler, or at least the rest of the city, can be persuaded. Nietzsche finds this type of argumentation in Plato himself, when he introduces "entire myths" in order to establish the right opinion in the mind of his disciples (N 418–19). Nietzsche comments:

> Plato's polemic against rhetoric is directed first against the bad purposes of popular rhetoric and then against the gross, insufficient, and unphilosophical training of the orators. Based on philosophical education and used for good purposes, that is, for philosophical purposes, he approves of rhetoric. (N 419)

These are some of the observations which later motivated Nietzsche to write "On Truth and Lie in an Extra-Moral Sense."

With Aristotle we come to a stricter distinction between lying and veracity. In his *Nicomachian Ethics,* Aristotle distinguishes three positions in relation to truth and reality: one of exaggeration and bragging, named ἀλαζονεία in Greek; the opposite one, of understatement and modesty, called εἰρώνεια in Greek; and a third midway between the two, for which Aristotle finds no designation but which he labels truthful, veracious, sincere, ἀληθεντικός (AR 1127a, 13–1127b, 32). Through Aristotle truthfulness or veracity became one of the homiletic virtues, which together with friendliness and rhetorical skill relate to conversation, communication and, in a broader sense, to social intercourse in general. Veracity is an attitude of the magnanimous person, the paradigm of Aristotle's ethics, who exercises truthfulness in the first place but also irony when he is in contact with people (AR 1124b, 30–31). Veracity as a homiletic virtue clearly has the flavor of an art of living and not yet the Christian character of a virtue established on the grounds of personal intention. It was St. Augustine who introduced this understanding of *mendacium* and *veritas,* mendaciousness and truthfulness. This is the consideration of truth and lie in a moral sense which took shape during the coming centuries.[5]

II

The result of this long process up to the period of romanticism can best be seen in Kant's *Foundations of the Metaphysics of Morals* published in 1797, and proscribing lying as the "greatest offense of the duty the human being has toward himself."[6] This can be considered the apex of the ethics of intentionality, but also an expression of the system of rationalism and the Enlightenment, which constituted the last reliable and accomplished system of knowledge in our history. At the same time, however, forces were making themselves felt that eventually led to a breakdown of this system.

One example from the French Revolution is particularly illuminating in this regard. Kant had illustrated the absolute obligation never to lie with a casuistic example according to which a servant had to confirm the presence of his master to a police patrol even if the master had ordered his servant not to reveal his presence (KA 4:425). While reading this text, Madame de Staël was reminded of a similar situation during the Reign of Terror when she offered shelter to many of her friends in the exterritorial building of the Swedish Embassy in Paris, her *palais* in the Rue du Bac.[7] One day a patrol approached this building to arrest Mathieu de Montmorency, a close friend of Madame de Staël's, whereupon Madame de Staël, in order to save him from the guillotine, denied his presence. Today we could imagine far more serious examples from the time of the Holocaust. In the same year that Kant's *Metaphysics of Morals* appeared, Benjamin Constant, Madame de Staël's companion at that time, published his text *Des Réactions politiques* and pointed out the "devastating character" moral principles would assume if they were absolutized and cut off from their social basis. "We have proof of this in the most direct result a German philosopher has drawn from this principle," Constant wrote, intensifying Kant's casuistic example: "He goes so far as to pretend that if you deny to murderers the presence of your friend who has taken refuge at your house, such a lie would be a crime."[8] Constant first published his *Des Réactions politiques* in a Hamburg journal, and Kant answered in the same year with his essay "On an Alleged Right to Lie out of Philanthropy." He complimented Constant for his attempt to deal with moral principles from the point of view of a practical politician, but found a relativizing of moral principles by the "French philosopher" of which the "German philosopher" could not approve (KA 8:425–30).

Two years before this debate, August Wilhelm Schlegel, who was living in Amsterdam at the time, published a series of essays entitled "Letters on Poetry, Meter, and Language" in Schiller's new periodical *Die Horen*. These letters of 1795 are the first expression of the early romantic theory of language, and approach the phenomenon of human language in the context of poetry and poetic meter. Schlegel's theory has a distinct position within the broad European spectrum of language theories at the end of the eighteenth century: he refers to authors such as Moritz, Herder, and Rousseau, who represent a more sensualist orientation; to Charles de Brosses and his theory of a mechanical formation of language from animal sounds, the most prominent language theory of the Enlightenment; but especially to the Dutch author Frans Hemsterhuis and his *Letter on Man and his Relationships.*[9] In good scholarly manner, Schlegel distinguishes three possible theories of language: (1) language has arisen from the imitation of signs of nature and their constant perfection, the rationalist theory of the Enlightenment; (2) language has originated from inner "sounds" of feeling and emotion, the theory of eighteenth-century sensualism; and (3) language developed from both the imitation of nature and inner sounds, of reason and sensuality, the theory of Hemsterhuis which Schlegel adapts (AWS 7:118–19).

So far there is nothing particularly exciting in Schlegel's language theory. The more dynamic aspect of his theory emerges, however, if one asks what distinguishes his theory from that of Hemsterhuis, who also had attempted this synthesis. Then it becomes obvious that Schlegel does not limit the realm of sensuality and feeling to an early stage in the formation of language, one of "crude sensuality" and "untamed passion," one that was lost and overcome during the process of language development and civilization. He maintains instead the presence of this sensual, poetic element of language up to the most advanced stages of language formation and scientificity (AWS 7:120–21). In addition, Schlegel considers language to be "the most wonderful creation of human poetic power," the "great, not yet accomplished poem in which human nature represents itself" (AWS 7:104). Language is a proto-poetry of humanity, an original manifestation of the creativity of the human being, his first spontaneous contact with the world. In this relationship with the world, the human being is not passive, but actively involved, exercising a primordial ποίηδις. This ποίηδις operates on a deeper level, however, than Kant's forms of intuition and categories. In this sense, language, as a poetically mediating principle, is the true condition of possibility for our orientation toward the world. Language is furthermore a general medium of communication among people. Language is not a product of reason alone, but of a more comprehensive power also embracing feeling, sensuality, and above all the imagination. This original language or protolanguage is the source of the languages of developed cultures, more perfect in terms of precision and usefulness but without that original power. A bond of communality links all human beings, and that bond is more important for communication than anything else. This is the "true, eternal, general language of the human race," the protolanguage operative in all developed languages. What matters to Schlegel is that this metaphorical character of language always remains present, and that even on the most developed level of speech we still speak in metaphors (AWS 7:116).

August Wilhelm Schlegel's thoughts on the interrelationship of language and mythology emphasize these poetic and metaphorical qualities of language. The first sentence of his 1796 Jena lectures on *The Philosophical Doctrine of Art* establishes such an interconnection: "Myth is, like language, a universal and necessary product of human poetic power and, as it were, a proto-poesy of the human race."[10] Mythology is a "metaphorical language of reason and its kindred power of imagination," a poetry deriving from the proto-poetry of language and forming the basis for poetry in the specific sense. However, independent of this relationship to poetry in the specific sense, mythology is an essential equipment of the poetic and metaphorical organization of the human mind. Mythology not only belongs to an early and bygone phase of humanity, but forms, just like language, an essential component of the human being, a structural principle of his mind. Even at the most elevated status of reason, even in the disciplines of science, the human mind mythologizes.

III

One can say that August Wilhelm Schlegel reflects more upon what is possible with language, whereas his fellow romantics, Novalis and Friedrich Schlegel, reflect more on the limits of language and communication. An especially interesting piece of this type of reflection is a brief text, a fragment, by Novalis, entitled "Monologue." With just a few strokes he emphasizes the roguish character of language that constantly prevents us from achieving what we want to accomplish with its help, namely a complete and ordered communication of our ideas. People assume, Novalis argues, "that their talk is about things" and ignore "what is most distinctive about language, namely, that it is concerned solely with itself" and that "the capricious nature of language" will cause them to say "the most ridiculous and mistaken things." Yet as soon as someone speaks without a specific purpose, "just in order to speak, he pronounces the most magnificent and original truths." That is why "a number of serious people hate language," but they should know "that it is with language as with mathematical formulas": "they constitute a world by themselves, they play only among themselves, express nothing but their own marvelous nature, and for that very reason, they are so expressive and mirror the singular interplay of things."[11] Up to here, the fragment reads like an exercise in language critique, in language skepticism. At this point, however, Novalis reverses the direction of argumentation and focuses on the great capabilities of our language. For it is precisely this nonintentional, involuntary use of language which is the essence of poetry. A true writer is simply "one who is inspired by language" (NO 2:673).

Friedrich Schlegel entertained thoughts about language very similar to those of Novalis. One essential means for attaining a full comprehension of the world and perfecting our understanding, Friedrich Schlegel argues sarcastically, would be a "real language" that would permit us to "stop rummaging about for words and pay attention to the power and source of all activity" (FS 2:365).[12] Such a language would appear as the appropriate endowment of an age that proudly congratulates itself on being the "critical age," and that raises the expectation that everything will soon be criticized "except the age itself." Christoph Girtanner, a prolific writer from Göttingen, had already put forward this idea of a "real language," holding out the glorious prospect that "in the nineteenth century man will be able to make gold." With Girtanner's prediction and Schlegel's comments, we are at the close of the eighteenth century, when all sorts of expectations were held for the future. He had always admired "the objectivity of gold," Schlegel assures us, and "even worshiped it." In every part of the world "where there is even a little enlightenment and education, silver and gold are comprehensible, and through them, everything else." Once artists possess these materials in sufficient quantity, we can expect them to write their works "in bas-relief, with gold letters on silver tablets." "Who would want to reject such a beautifully printed book with the vulgar remark that it is incomprehensible?" Schlegel asks (FS 2:365). The problem, however, is that Girtanner is dead and the nineteenth century has begun without a fulfillment of the promises of gold and real language. At this point, Friedrich Schlegel begins to wonder whether incomprehensibility and the lack of a real language is really "something so unmitigatedly contemptible and evil" (FS 2:370). One could argue that "the salvation of families and nations rests upon it," and also that of "states and systems" as well as the "most artificial productions of man." "Even man's most precious possession, his own inner happiness, ultimately depends on some point of strength that must be left in the dark but nonetheless supports the whole burden, although it would crumble the moment one subjected it to rational analysis." In an inverse type of reflection, all of a sudden becoming serious, Schlegel declares: "Verily, it would fare badly with you if, as you demand, the whole world were ever to become wholly comprehensible" (FS 2:370).

This argument is drawn from Schlegel's essay "On Incomprehensibility," and its relationship to the theme of truth and lie seems obvious. As a matter of fact, in an earlier letter of November 1792 to his brother, Friedrich Schlegel had developed the entire argument under the heading of lying. This letter begins with the statement "I believe to be able to justify lies, if you only don't mind the harshness of the word." He then proceeds to show, just as in "On Incomprehensibility," that lies give energy to the young and wisdom to the old; that lies make society possible and that the power of empires, the cogency of philosophical systems, and the happiness of marriages rest on them; that without lies no friendship is possible, and that even a correspondence like the two brothers were conducting at that time would not be feasible without the occasional ornaments of lies (FS 23:71–73).

Following Friedrich Schlegel, Kierkegaard expressed this skeptical attitude toward objective truth not in terms of incomprehensibility, but more in terms of uncertainty, using the indirect communication of pseudonyms and masks as his style. We encounter one of these masks in the figure of a "private thinker, a speculative crotcheteer," who, as in a tale by E. T. A. Hoffmann, lives in "a garret at the top of a vast building, in his little refuge," and is seized by "a dim suspicion that there was something wrong with the foundations": "Whenever he looked out of the little garret window, he shudderingly saw only busy and redoubled activities to beautify or enlarge the structure," and "whenever he communicated his doubts to someone, he perceived that his speech, because of its departure from prevailing fashion, was regarded as the bizarre and threadbare costume of some unfortunate derelict." If such a "privately practicing thinker and speculative crotcheteer," Kierkegaard continues,

> were suddenly to make the acquaintance of a man whose fame did not directly ensure the validity of his thoughts for him (for the poor lodger knew that he could not draw the conclusion from fame to truth), but whose fame was nevertheless like fortune's smile in the midst of loneliness, when he found one or two of his difficult thoughts touched upon the famous man: ah, what joy, what festivity in the little garret chamber.

The "hope of understanding," first the "hope of understanding nature" and then the "hope of understanding oneself," and perhaps the "hope of understanding the nature of the difficulty, and then perhaps of being able to overcome it," would grow upon the encounter with the renowned thinker.[13] This renowned thinker is of course none other than Lessing, but not Lessing the "scholar," the "librarian," the "poet," the "master of dramatic dialogue," not Lessing the "aesthetician" who drew the line of demarcation between poetry and the formative arts, not Lessing the "sage," the "teacher of tolerance"—but that Lessing who understood the mystery of the religious in all its subjectivity and had left us no result of this understanding (K 60). From the "objective point of view" of truth, Lessing has long since been left behind: he is merely a vanishing little "waystation on the systematic railway of world history," but not from the subjective point of view. To be sure, "Lessing was no serious man": his entire mode of communication is without earnestness, lacking "true dependability" and presenting things in a "mingling of jest and earnestness, which makes it impossible for a third party to know which is which." "Does all this sound like a serious mind?" Kierkegaard asks, and answers that it is precisely because of these qualities of dissimulation that he expresses his infinite gratitude toward Lessing (K 65–66).

For Baudelaire, in his "On the Essence of Laughter,"[14] the sign system of truth is perfectly intact when we are dealing with classical comedy, Molière's for instance. This comedy assures us that the disturbance of order which incites our laughter will be reestablished and has really never been disturbed, because this is the comedy of representation, of imitation, the "signifying comic." Here we laugh at the misfortune of others, never at ourselves, and we laugh after the occurrence of the comic event has taken place, after we have understood its meaning and truth. The "absolute comic," in contrast, does not grant us any such reference point. The absolute comic draws us into the suspension of all systems of reference, beyond truth and lie, and incites absolute laughter. In "The Painter of Modern Life," Baudelaire deals with the theme of a "representation of the present," and indirectly points to the deep paradox, even impossibility, of the attempt to represent the passing moment of presence and all the suggestions of beauty and eternity it contains (BAU 1:683–84). The eighteenth century's prime error was to have taken nature as the ground, source, and type of all possible Truth, Goodness, and Beauty. On the contrary, nature is for Baudelaire the source of all that is disgusting and abominable, whereas "everything beautiful [is] the result of calculation." "Evil happens without effort, naturally, fatally," he says, whereas "Good is always the product of some art of deception." "Fashion" should therefore be considered "a symptom of the taste for the ideal," as should cosmetics, or even the "dandy." A more thorough philosophy of "maquillage" would tell us that the need for it is not in order to correspond to nature and truth, but an "absolutely opposite need," namely, "the need to surpass nature" (BAU 1:714).

Oscar Wilde, in his 1899 "The Decay of Lying," carries these thoughts even further. People tell us, he argues, that "art makes us love nature more than we loved her before," but our real experience is that "the more we study art, the less we care for nature": "What art really reveals to us is Nature's lack of design, her curious crudities, her extraordinary monotony, her absolutely unfinished condition."[15] Wilde defines the relationship between art and lying on the basis of a deep artfulness in lying: a "fine lie" is simply that "which is its own evidence," and the same goes for art. Wilde says: "If a man is sufficiently unimaginative to produce evidence in support of a lie, he might just as well speak the truth at once" (W 35). Furthermore, the relationship between art and lie has been established by the foremost philosophical authorities, by philosophers such as Plato and Kant. Plato immediately saw that lying and poetry are both arts. Kant is the one who once said that the "only beautiful things" are those that "do not concern us": "As long as a thing is useful or necessary to us, or affects us in any way, either for pain or for pleasure, or appeals strongly to our sympathies, or is a vital part of the environment in which we live, it is outside the proper sphere of art" (W 45).

The next step in this attempt to remove all veracity from works of art is to negate any dependency of art on nature as a firm reference point for truth. Wordsworth is the best proof of this, namely that nature "has no suggestions of her own": "Wordsworth went to the lakes, but he was never a lake poet. He found in stones the sermons he had already hidden there" (W 47). But the ultimate point of Wilde's text is to show that the classical relationship between art and nature has been totally reversed, i.e., that art does not imitate nature, but nature imitates art. Wilde's text is totally in keeping with his subject matter: brief, unsubstantiated lies. According to this motto that nature imitates art,

Schopenhauer has analyzed the pessimism that characterizes modern thought, but Hamlet invented it. (W 56)

Nature follows the landscape painter, . . . and takes her effects from him. (W 61)

The extraordinary change that has taken place in the climate of London during the last ten years [i.e., London fog] is entirely due to a particular school of Art [i.e., impressionism]. (W 61)

Yesterday evening Mrs. Arundel insisted on my going to the window, and looking at the glorious sky, as she called it. . . . And what was it? It was simply a very second-rate Turner, a Turner of a bad period. (W 62)

In this style Wilde continues: "No great artist sees things as they really are." The only answer to the question of "What we have to do, what at any rate it is our duty to do, is *to revive this old art of Lying*" (W 65, 68; emphasis added). For, after all: "The final revelation is that lying, the telling of beautiful untrue things, is the proper aim of art" (W 72).

IV

When Nietzsche composed his treatise "On Truth and Lie in an Extra-Moral Sense" in 1873, he had already published *The Birth of Tragedy out of the Spirit of Music* in 1872 and offered a lecture course "On Ancient Rhetoric" in the winter semester of 1872–73. Both texts are of importance for his language theory and his ideas about truth and lie in an aesthetic sense. In *The Birth of Tragedy,* he maintained the possibility of an absolute and unfalsified expression of truth in the medium of music, and claimed that in Dionysian art "nature cries to us with its true, undissembled voice," whereas in Apollonian art "pain is obliterated by lies from the features of nature" (FN 1:108). But in his lectures on ancient rhetoric delivered only shortly thereafter, such claims have disappeared.

Nietzsche begins these lectures with the observation that the "extraordinary development" of rhetoric in the ancient world "belongs to the greatest differences between the ancients and the moderns." He says about these differences that "the feeling for what is true in itself is much more developed" in the modern age, whereas "rhetoric arises among a people that still lives in mythic images and has not yet experienced the unqualified need for historical accuracy: these people would rather be persuaded than instructed" (N 415). Rhetoric also is "an essentially republican art: one must be accustomed to tolerating the most unusual opinions and points of view and even to taking a certain pleasure in their counterplay." Yet what is truly unique in Hellenistic life is its tendency "to perceive all matters of the intellect, of life's seriousness, of necessities, even of danger, as play" (N 415).

Nietzsche claims that what we call "rhetorical" as a means of a conscious art is in reality only a conscious development of the *"artistic means already found in language."* Our language is intrinsically artistic and rhetorical without our knowing it. In this part of his lectures, Nietzsche draws directly from the romantic theory of language, but puts his own stamp on this theory. According to him, there is no use in appealing to an "unrhetorical 'naturalness' of language" because "language itself is the result of nothing but rhetorical arts." Aristotle had called rhetoric that power which discovers and exhibits what is effective and impressive in a thing, but that is already "the essence of language" for Nietzsche. Language, just like rhetoric, is not related "to the true, the essence of things." Language does not intend to instruct, "but to convey to others a subjective impulse and its acceptance." The one who forms language "does not perceive things or events, but impulses of them." He does not render "sensations, but merely copies of sensations." A sensation "does not take in the thing in itself," but presents it only "externally through an image." Nietzsche says: "It is not things that pass over into consciousness, but the manner in which we relate to them, the πιθανόν, the power of persuasion. The full essence of things will never be grasped." This is the first important feature of language for Nietzsche: *"language is rhetoric* because it desires to convey only a δόξα, a personal opinion, not an επιστήμη, a firm knowledge" (N 425–28).

A second feature of language concerns tropes, the "non-literal significations" as Nietzsche calls them. All words are "in themselves and from the beginning" nothing but tropes. Words do not represent "that which truly takes place," but only a "sound image." What applies to words, however, also applies to language in general. "Language never expresses something completely but only displays a characteristic that appears to be prominent" (N 427).

From his notes for these lectures, Nietzsche dictated the text of his essay "On Truth and Lie in an Extra-Moral Sense"[16] in the summer of 1873, beginning the story with a fabulous framing:

> In some remote corner of the universe that is poured out in countless flickering solar systems, there was once a star on which clever animals invented knowledge. That was the most arrogant and the most untruthful moment in "world history"—yet indeed only a moment. After nature had taken a few breaths, the star froze over and the clever animals had to die. (FN 1:875)

In a language overloaded with metaphors and exotic images, Nietzsche attempts to show "how shadowy and fleeting, how purposeless and arbitrary the human intellect appears within nature." Although this intellect was "given only as a help to the most unfortunate, most delicate, most perishable creatures, in order to preserve them for a moment in existence," it always manages to bring up "the most flattering estimation of this faculty of knowledge." Dissimulation, even "deception, flattery, lying, and cheating," appear as the true essence of the intellect, which makes it hard to comprehend "how an honest and pure desire for truth could arise among men." This question is the focus of the text in its further development. With impressive images, Nietzsche describes how the human eye, "deeply immersed in delusions and phantasmagoria," glides "around the surface of things" and engages in "a groping game on the back of things." Nature conceals almost everything from the human being, "even about his own body," and locks him within his consciousness—"unmindful of the windings of his entrails, the swift flow of his bloodstream, and the intricate quiverings of his tissue"—then "thr[ows] away the key." Woe to the one who would attempt to "[peer] through a crack out of the room of consciousness" and would suddenly realize "that man is based on a lack of mercy, insatiable greed, murder, on the indifference that stems from ignorance, as if he were clinging to a tiger's back in dreams" (FN 1:876–77).

Considering this situation, Nietzsche asks "where in the world does the desire for truth originate?" For the conventions of language are hardly products of knowledge, a congruent designation of things, an adequate expression of reality, but rather "illusions" and "empty husks." Only convention, not truth, had been decisive in the genesis of language. Properly speaking, we are not at all entitled to say "the stone is hard," because "hard" is only known to us as a "subjective stimulation." Just as little are we entitled to "arrange things by gender" and to designate the tree as masculine and the plant as feminine (in German, nouns have a "gender": a tree is *der Baum,*" a plant is *die Pflanze,*" etc.). If we placed the various languages side by side, we would realize "that words are never concerned with truth, never with adequate expression; otherwise there would not be so many languages." The "thing in itself" is something toward which the "creator of language" is indifferent, something that for him is "not worthy of seeking." He "designates only the relations of things to men, and to express these relations he uses the boldest metaphors" (FN 1:878).

In any event, our language does not relate to things too well. We believe that we know something about the things themselves when we speak of trees, colors, snow, and flowers, although "what we have are just metaphors of things, which do not correspond at all to the original entities." On the whole, the origin or genesis of language is not a logical process, "and the whole material in and with which the man of truth, the scientist, the philosopher, works and builds, stems if not from a never-never land, in any case not from the essence of things" (FN 1:879).

As is obvious in these arguments, Nietzsche's critique of language is a critique of the language of philosophy and the claim to truth traditionally connected with this language. "What is truth?" he asks, and responds:

A mobile army of metaphors, metonyms, and anthropomorphisms, in short,
a sum of human relations which were poetically and rhetorically heightened,
transferred, and adorned, and after long use seem solid, canonical, and
binding. Truths are illusions about which it has been forgotten that they
are illusions, worn-out metaphors without sensory impact, coins which have
lost their image and now can be used only as metal, and no longer as coins.
(FN 1:880–81)

Nietzsche illustrates this idea with numerous examples. When an investigator operates on the basis of this language, he ultimately discovers "just the
metamorphosis of the world into man." Just as the astrologer observes "the
stars in the service of men and in connection with their joys and sorrows,"
so this investigator observes the whole world as the "infinitely refracted echo
of a primeval sound, man; as the reproduction and copy of an archetype,
man." Such an investigator forgets "that the original intuitive metaphors are
indeed metaphors and takes them for the things themselves." Philosophy
and science originate "only insofar as man forgets himself as a subject,
indeed as an *artistically creating* subject." If the human being could escape
"from the prior walls of this belief, then his high opinion of himself would
be dashed immediately" (FN 1:883).

If we tried to relate these bold statements to the theme of truth and lie in
an aesthetic sense, we might be inclined to say that Nietzsche locates lie on
the side of philosophy and science, and assigns truth to poetry and literature. The former disciplines are blamed for their unjustified use of language
as a stable and objective signification system, whereas poetry and literature are praised for their appropriate use of language—just as in Novalis's
"Monologue." We might also be inclined to say that by blaming philosophy
as lie and praising poetry as truth, Nietzsche accomplished a complete reversal of Plato—something Heidegger always attributed to him.[17]

That this is not a correct understanding of Nietzsche and his position in
this debate, however, becomes obvious in the concluding sections of his "On
Truth and Lie." In these sections, Nietzsche sets the mythico-poetic experience against philosophical-scientific thought as two irreducible forms of
orientation towards the world. Their relationship is not one of mutual destruction, but of alternation and oscillation, of interaction and reciprocity.
Nietzsche provides the image of ages

in which the rational man and the intuitive man stand side by side, one
in fear of intuition, the other with mockery for abstraction; the latter being just as unreasonable as the former is unartistic. Both desire to master
life; the one by managing to meet his main needs with foresight, prudence,
reliability; the other, as an "overjoyous" hero, by not seeking those needs
and considering only life, disguised as illusion and beauty, to be real.
(FN 1:889)

In the more favorable cases of this alternation, a culture can form and a function of art can be established in which, as in ancient Greece, "that dissimulation, that denial of poverty, that splendor of metaphorical intuitions, and in general, that immediacy of delusion accompanies all manifestations of such a life" (FN 1:889).

V

These reorientations in the treatment of truth and lie in an aesthetic context from the point of view of modern language theory did not occur without affecting both parties involved in this debate. At the beginning of the nineteenth century, the position opposed to the romantic conception of truth and lie was a strong Hegelianism that, on the basis of "absolute knowledge" and "comprehended history," condemned the romantic attitude as irresponsible arbitrariness and as "evil as such."[18] Today the philosophical side of debate between philosophy and poetry uses the much softer conception of hermeneutic truth and dialogical understanding in the style of Gadamer, or a consensus theory like that developed by Habermas. Habermas has been selected here because of his unyielding criticism of the authors I have enlisted on the side of beautiful deception in an aesthetic sense—Schlegel, Baudelaire, and Nietzsche—but also because of his more tolerant and compromising attitude on other occasions. He says, for instance, that contemporary philosophy no longer expects "unconditional validity or 'ultimate foundations,'" but works with "fallibility consciousness" and truth claims at the same time. That is, philosophy has adjusted to the likelihood that its theories will have to be revised: "It prefers a combination of strong propositions with weak status claims; this is so little totalitarian that there is no call for a totalizing critique of reason against it."[19] This is certainly not to be interpreted as a victory of the aesthetic point of view in the ongoing debate about truth and lie, but rather as a sign of a constant continuation and reshaping of this debate in different historical contexts.

NOTES

1. Aristotle 980a, 21–22, and 1448b, 1–3, cited from the 1831 Academia Borussica edition. Subsequent references will be made in the text with AR followed by page and line number.

2. *Kritische Friedrich Schlegel Ausgabe,* ed. Ernst Behler, with Jean-Jacques Anstett and Hans Eichner (Paderborn: Schöningh, 1958–), 1:502. Subsequent references will be made in the text with FS followed by volume and page number. All translations from German and French, throughout this essay, are my own unless otherwise noted.

3. *Kritische Studienausgabe,* ed. Giorgio Colli and Mazzino Montinari (Berlin: de

Gruyter, 1980), 7:450. Subsequent references will be made in the text with FN followed by volume and page number.

4. Nietzsche's lecture notes from the Basel period are edited in Volumes 1–5 in the Second Section of the *Kritische Gesamtausgabe*, ed. Giorgio Colli and Mazzino Montinari (Berlin: de Gruyter, 1982–1995). Volume 4 contains his lectures on rhetoric. Subsequent references will be made in the text with N followed by the page number. The translation is taken from Friedrich Nietzsche, *On Rhetoric and Language: With the full text of his lectures on rhetoric for the first time,* ed. and trans. Sander L. Gilman, Carole Blaire, and David J. Parent (New York: Oxford University Press, 1989).

5. St. Augustine dealt with this topic in two different treatises: *De mendacio* (395) and *Contra mendacium* (420).

6. Immanuel Kant, *Kants Werke, Akademie-Textausgabe,* ed. Wilhelm Dilthey et al. (1903; reprint, Berlin: Walter de Gruyter & Co., 1968), 4:430. Subsequent references will be made in the text with KA followed by volume and page number.

7. Madame de Staël, *De l'Allemagne,* ed. La Comtesse Jean de Pange with Simone Ballayé (Paris: Hachette, 1960), 4:324.

8. Benjamin Constant, *Ecrits et discours politiques,* ed. O. Pozzo di Borgo (Montreuil: Pauvert, 1964), 1:68–69.

9. August Wilhelm Schlegel, *Sämtliche Werke,* ed. Eduard Böcking (Leipzig: Weidmann, 1846), 7:119. Subsequent references will be made in the text with AWS followed by volume and page number.

10. August Wilhelm Schlegel, *Kritische Ausgabe der Vorlesungen,* ed. Ernst Behler and Frank Jolles (Paderborn: Schöningh, 1989–), 1:49.

11. Novalis, *Schriften Die Werke Friedrich von Hardenbergs,* ed. Richard Samuel, Hans-Joachim Mähl, and Gerhard Schulz (Stuttgart: Kohlhammer, 1960–1988), 2:672. Subsequent references will be made in the text with NO followed by volume and page number. The translation of "Monologue" is Alexander Gelley's, taken from *German Romantic Criticism,* ed. A. Leslie Willson, foreword by Ernst Behler (New York: Continuum, 1982), 62–83.

12. Schlegel develops this argument in his essay "On Incomprehensibility" (1800). The translation is Peter Firchow's, taken from Friedrich Schlegel, *Lucinde and the Fragments* (Minneapolis: University of Minnesota Press, 1971).

13. Søren Kierkegaard, *Concluding Unscientific Postscript,* trans. David F. Swenson and Walter Lowrie (Princeton University Press, 1968), 59. Subsequent references will be made in the text with K followed by the page number.

14. Baudelaire is quoted from Baudelaire, *Oeuvres complètes,* ed. Claude Pichois (Paris: Gallimard. Bibliothèque de la Pléiade, 1975), 1:525–43. Subsequent references will be made in the text with BAU followed by volume and page number. The translation is taken from Charles Baudelaire, *The Painter of Modern Life and Other Essays,* trans. Jonathan Mayne (London: Phaidon, 1964).

15. Oscar Wilde, *Essays by Oscar Wilde,* ed. Hesketh Pearson (London: Methuen, 1950), 33. Subsequent references will be made in the text with W followed by the page number.

16. FN 1:873–90. The translation is taken from Nietzsche, *On Rhetoric and Language.*

17. See especially Martin Heidegger, "Nietzsches Wort 'Gott ist tot,'" in *Holzwege* (Frankfurt: Klostermann, 1950), 205–64.

18. Hegel himself epitomizes this stance, especially in his *Phenomenology of Spirit*. See Emanuel Hirsch, "Die Beisetzung der Romantiker in Hegels Phänomenologie," in *Materialien zu Hegels "Phänomenologie des Geistes*," ed. Hans Friedrich Fulda and Dieter Henrich (Frankfurt: Suhrkamp, 1973), 245–75.

19. Jürgen Habermas, *Der philosophische Diskurs der Moderne* (Frankfurt: Suhrkamp 1985), 246–47. The translation is taken from Jürgen Habermas, *The Philosophical Discourse of Modernity*, trans. Frederick Lawrence (Cambridge, Mass.: MIT Press, 1987).

CHAPTER FIVE

Pictures of Poetry in Marot's *Épigrammes*

Stephen G. Nichols

Murray Krieger influenced many things that have come to play a significant role in my life. Not the least of these contributions was the vision that led to his founding of the School of Criticism and Theory at the University of California, Irvine, in 1976, one of those peripatetic institutions that distinguishes U. S. academia from its counterparts in other countries by embodying the American entrepreneurial spirit in the best sense of the term. Third in succession to Murray Krieger as Director of the SCT, I can appreciate the astute blend of pragmatics and theory that led Krieger to his vision of a place where theory and criticism could address issues of teaching and scholarship faced by its participants.

Equally important for me has been Murray Krieger's passionate involvement with the problem of ekphrasis, described by Krieger as "the poet's marriage of the visual and the verbal within the verbal art."[1] Like many others, I first got interested in the problem of ekphrasis after reading Krieger's essay, "*Ekphrasis* and the Still Movement of Poetry; or *Laokoön* Revisited."[2] Krieger subsequently described that essay as "the most easily written—and I think the most lyrical—critical essay I remember having written." The spell of the subject, "both maddeningly elusive and endlessly tempting," gripped me as few essays have ever done.[3] What *was* ekphrasis anyway? And why did it seem to arrogate to itself the effort of poetry to be picture?

Murray Krieger pursued his own obsession with ekphrasis to one kind of conclusion in his 1992 book, the culmination of over twenty years of meditation and a work that repays careful reading. I was led to contemplate the problem of the visual text in medieval manuscripts where paintings of ekphrastic passages raised the stakes of the game as real pictures strove to represent—ironically? parodically? mimetically?—their verbal homologues.[4] This research, in turn, led me further into the role of words as pictures in medieval manuscripts, a project that I undertook at Murray Krieger's invitation and that led to a research group and colloquium at the Humanities Research Institute at Irvine when Krieger was still director.[5]

By way of acknowledging my gratitude to Murray Krieger for his many acts of kindness, and for his vigorous intellectual leadership, I conceived this study as a continental counterpart to the poetic tradition in which Krieger has worked. It is, in any case, meant as testimony to his oeuvre rather than an extension of my own.

MARTIAL, MAROT, AND THE EPIGRAM AS EKPHRASIS

When, in 1537–1538, Clément Marot began to cultivate the genre of the epigram, he made no secret of his fascination with the example that the Latin poet, Martial, had set in his extensive cultivation of the genre—fourteen books varying in length from eighty-odd to over two hundred epigrams. Martial's epigrams typically contain between two and twelve lines, in keeping with the association of the genre's supposed origin as poetic rubrics incised on the stone bases of sculptures. Nothing constrained the epigrammarian to limit his work, however, and Martial sometimes wrote epigrams of over fifty lines. Even such deviations from conciseness, however, share with their briefer counterparts a vividly imaged subject matter, depicting, for example, virtuoso scenes of an extensive country estate. Such extensive poetic landscapes may serve as *xenia* or gifts to a host, or, as in the following case, an ideal description of one estate serving to complement its owner, Faustinus, while castigating Bassus, the stingy proprietor of another villa, in the mordant epigrammatic mode.

> Baiana nostri villa, Basse, Faustini
> non otiosis ordinata myrtetis
> viduaque platano tonsilique buxeto
> ingrata lati spatia detinet campi,
> sed rure vero barbaroque laetatur.
> Hic farta premitur angulo Ceres omni
> et multa fragrat testa senibus autumnis; . . .

> [Our friend Faustinus' Baian villa, Bassus, does not hold down unprofitable expanses of broad acreage laid out in idle myrtle plantations, unwed planes, and clipped boxwood, but rejoices in the true, rough countryside. Corn is tightly crammed in every corner and many a wine jar is fragrant with ancient vintages. . . .][6]

The association of epigram with picture, or highly imaged verbal representation, links the genre with ekphrasis, as suggested by the term "iconic epigram," referring to more highly imaged examples of the genre. This accords with the etymology of "epigram," a compound formed of the Greek *"gramma"* ("letter, writing," in the sense of "graphics"), and the Greek prefix "*epi*" ("on"). The principle of written or sketched figures on a surface—signs, letters, designs—inhabits the semantic field of the epigram, assuring that it can never stray far from some visual connotation or demonstration. Indeed, the very sense of the prefix "*epi*" suggests a meta-relationship with the sign to which it refers or on which it comments: "on the figure," "on the letter," where *grammata* convey the visual experience of graphemes whether or not inscribed on the plinth of a sculpture.

Martial makes the relationship between the epigram and the picture explicit in a number of poems. These may take the form of an oblique description, where poetry evokes by language's powers of indirection—a subtle critique of what painting *cannot* do—as in the following, lapidary couplet in which we divine the subject to be the description of a painting not by seeing the portrait before our eyes, but by allusion:

> Clarus fronde Iovis, Romani fama cothurni,
>   spirat Apellea redditus arte Memor.

> [Memor, illustrious in Jupiter's leaves, fame of the Roman buskin, breathes, recalled by Apelles' art.] [7]

This couplet also recalls the close association between epigram and spectacle or theater in Martial, who called his first efforts in this mode *De Spectaculis Liber* (now given as Book One of the *Epigrams*). The "*fronde Iovis*" above evoke the golden oak leaves worn by the emperor Domitian, Martial's patron, at the spectacles he founded in honor of Jupiter; "*cothurni*" evokes the high boots worn by the tragedian, Memor, on stage while acting; and Apelles was the mythical inventor of painting. This art of allusion, of metaphor connects the visual with the intelligible, the eye or mind's eye with memory, the material with the intellectual, the present with the past. It is fundamentally an art of transformation, linking disparate domains of inner life and perception with external or material stimuli in the space of writing which is simultaneously a space for the eye and the voice.

Breathing, *spirare*, is exactly what the painted portrait cannot do, however, and it is the iconic epigram that restores this essential element of the tragedian's art to Memor. While this and the next epigram may postulate a *paragone*, or contest between poetry and painting, there is at least the possibility that Martial proposes not agon, but partnership in the interest of improved communication. He coins an apposite metaphor for this fertile connection between epigram and painting: "*non tacita imagine*," "a speaking likeness," rendered even more explicit in the Latin context by his insertion of the verb "*respondet*" between "*non tacita*" and "*imagine*," giving us the lines:

> candida non tacita respondet imagine lygdos
>   et placido fulget vivus in ore decor.

> [The white lygdus [marble] matches [answers] with a speaking likeness, and living beauty shines in your face.] [8]

Poetry could also complement painting through the resemblance of portrait image and real person—the magic of pictorial representation that led Pietro Bembo to say of Raphael's painting of Castiglione that "it was so *naturale* that 'Tebaldeo does not resemble himself as closely as this resembles him.'"[9] The close link between painted likeness and human subject infused both with temporal vulnerability. This time, the example comes from Martial's own experience of portraiture:

> Dum mea Caecilio formatur imago Secundo
>   spirat et arguta picta tabella manu,
> i, liber, ad Geticam Peucen Histrumque iacentum:
>   haec loca perdomitis gentibus ille tenet.
> parva dabis caro sed dulcia dona sodali:
>   certior in nostro carmine vultus erit;
> casibus hic nullis, nullis delebilis annis
>   vivet, Apelleum cum morietur opus.

> [While my likeness is taking shape for Caecilius Secundus and the canvas, painted by a skilful hand, breathes, go, book, to Getic Peuce and prostrate Hister: these regions with their subjugated nations he rules. You will give my dear friend a small gift but a sweet one; my face will be seen more clearly in my poems. No accidents, no passage of years will efface it; it shall live when Apelles' work shall die.] [10]

Poetry, unlike painting, stands outside time. While this has been parsed as paradigmatic of the rivalry between painting and poetry, it may just as logically be construed as postulating a partnership between the verbal and the visual, where poetry mediates the temporal vulnerability of the body and its likeness. For Martial does not repudiate the painting, nor disdain its resemblance to himself, as Plotinus does, for instance, in Porphyry's famous anecdote of the philosopher's unwillingness to have his portrait sculpted.

> Plotinus objected so strongly to sitting for a painter or sculptor that he said to Amelius, who was urging him to allow a portrait of himself to be made, "Why really, is it not enough to have to carry the image in which nature has encased us, without your requesting me to agree to leave behind me a longer-lasting image of the image, as if it was something genuinely worth looking at?" [11]

Far from evincing such repugnance, Martial sends forth his book as a messenger across time and space proudly announcing the birth of the portrait: "*mea . . . formatur imago.*"

"*Certior in nostro carmine vultus erit*" does not mean that the poet's likeness will be seen more clearly or more accurately in the poems than in the painting, but rather that it will be seen more surely, more definitely, more deeply. And this for three reasons: space, time, and interiority. The imperative "*i, liber*" ("go, book") evokes the song's mobility, its capacity to move rapidly across space, for the same reason it may transcend time. Visual art is more spatially bound, either affixed to wall or panel or else carved in stone. Far more than poetry, the graphic and plastic arts depend upon material context. As Marot reminds us in the preface to his edition of François Villon, you can memorize a song, and recite it in any circumstance, as his aged Parisian informants did when they sang Villon's ballades for him, but you cannot memorize, let alone recite, a painting or sculpture.

Interiority, the capacity to represent the inner person, frames the last of the claims Martial makes for the ability of poetry to complement painting. What he implies in the epigram on his own portrait becomes explicit in Book 10.32 where Martial comments on a portrait of Marcus Antonius Primus (*"vultus"* ["mien," "visage"] links the two poems around the theme of outer appearance/inner qualities). Here the text stresses dissimilitude between portrait and subject, for the latter has grown old, so that the portrait no longer resembles—it is only a memory. The picture fails to catch the continuity between the younger subject and his present self, for the connection between them, the signature of personality, lies in the inner being. The poem, then, must portray the deeps, the psyche, in order to match the beauty of the physical being:

> Haec mihi quae colitur violis pictura rosisque,
> quos referat vultus, Caediciane, rogas?
> talis erat Marcus mediis Antonius annis
> Primus: in hoc iuvenem se videt ore senex.
> ars utinam mores animumque effingere posset!
> pulchrior in terris nulla tabella foret.

> [This picture which I decorate with violets and roses, do you ask whose face it recalls, Caedicianus? Such was Marcus Antonius Primus in middle life; in this countenance the old man sees his younger self. Would that art could represent his character and soul! No painting in the world would be more beautiful.]

What I am here calling the complementarity between the iconic epigram and painting, a link underlying Martial's development of the genre, has recently been adduced as a major factor in the development of portraiture in the Renaissance. In his Mellon Lectures for 1988 at the National Gallery in Washington, John Shearman argued that the greatest progress in Renaissance portraiture occurred between 1490 and 1530, precisely the period of Marot's birth and poetic formation.[12] What fueled this progress, Shearman argues, was first of all a greater role accorded to the spectator—the assumed presence of a viewer not as accident, but as a thematic of the painting itself. The second decisive change concerns the presence of poetry in the painting: not just any poetry, but most particularly epigram. Shearman even ascribes what he calls "the communicative idea" to this link between epigram and painting: "Why was portraiture so dramatically affected by *the commu-nicative idea?* . . . I think poets have something to do with it."[13] Well, yes, but whereas the connection may be new in painting, and more particularly in portraiture, it is far from new in poetry. For we have already seen how Mar-tial's iconic epigrams frequently apostrophize an interlocutor to whose view the poet phatically exposes the image portrayed in the poem.

This is not the place to engage a dialogue with Shearman's fascinating theses. I cite them by way of entry into our main concern, the role of pic-tures and poetry in Marot's epigrams, and to remind ourselves of the cul-tural horizon, particularly as concerns the visual arts, surrounding Marot during his formative years, and immediately preceding his adoption of this genre in 1537. Whereas Shearman insists on the link between art and epi-gram as one of *paragone* or agon—and that may well be the case for Re-naissance pictures—I want to suggest that it is the partnership or comple-mentarity that Marot, like Martial, perceived as the essence of interartistic wisdom. He pursued this goal from his very first epigram, a subtle allusion to Martial's epigram 7.84. But, as we shall see, Marot eschewed the more di-rect and simple comparison of painting and poem. Most frequently, in a vir-tuoso ekphrastic reversal, Marot's pictures are of poems, but poems trans-formed into graphic images, word paintings. Let us see how this works.

Marot opens his *Épigrammes* with a clear transformation of Martial's epi-gram 7.84, the comparison between his portrait and his "*carmina*" which I discussed above. Martial, we saw, sent his book off to bear a likeness more certain than that in the portrait taking shape under the hand of the painter. With his own "*i, liber,*" Marot dedicates the first epigram to the governor of Bretagne, Jehan de Laval, Seigneur de Chasteaubriant, whom he designates as "Prince Breton." Like Martial, Marot sends his book some distance to the ruler of subjugated lands:

> Ce Livre mien d'Épigrammes te donne,
> Prince Breton, & le te presentant
> Present te fays meilleur, que la personne
> De l'Ouvrier mesme, & fut il mieulx chantant:
> Car mort ne va les oeuvres abbatant:
> Et mortel est cestuy là, qui les dicte.
> Puis tien je suis des jours a tant, & tant:
> De m'y donner, ne seroit que redicte.[14]

Whereas Martial juxtaposes his portrait and his book by evoking the portrait process in the first line ("*Dum mea . . . formatur imago*"), Marot excises any reference to a painting from his poem. Marot juxtaposes book and *person*—the book presents the person better than the person himself, and the book is even a better musician. He thus plays upon the Renaissance topos, already quoted, of the picture which is a better likeness than the model himself. In other words, Marot evokes painting's power of depiction, but ascribes it to his epigrams.

The elision of painting is the more strongly marked by a systematic reference to and reworking of the other elements of Martial's poem, such as temporality, the image of the artist, and song. Martial figures the temporality of the artistic process by the first word, *"Dum,"* and last two, *"morietur opus"*; Marot refigures these by playing on *"donne"/"presentant"/"present"* so that the purely temporal Latin *"Dum"* becomes the equivocal French *"don"*: a present present, the gift of writing, and a better song than that sung by the *Ouvrier* in person. Marot uses the generic term, *ouvrier,* for the transforming artist, rather than a mode- or genre-specific term like "poet" or "painter"; he does so, I think, to signal the conflation of painting and poetry in his poem. That same conflation makes the poet both the subject of the poetic picture and its maker; in short, it makes the poem a self-portrait. Marot refers to himself in this dual role more than once in his *Épigrammes,* as for example in the second book, epigram 5, "À Françoys Daulphin de France": "C'est ung Clement, ung Marot, ung qui rithme: / Voicy l'ouvrier, l'art, la forge, & la lime" (ll. 4–5).

"Ce Livre mien d'Épigrammes," the "presenting present," a gift in the present but also immediately present to the eyes, figures both painting and poetry, it is poetry as picture, doing in *song*—"& fut il mieulx chantant"—what required picture *and* song in Martial. Whereas Martial sends his book away to represent him in the subjugated provinces while his portrait remains in Rome with his person of whom it is the momentary likeness, Marot can both give *his* book to Jehan de Laval in Brittany, and also, thanks to printing, keep a copy present with him in Lyon.

NOTES

1. Murray Krieger, *Ekphrasis: The Illusion of the Natural Sign* (Baltimore: Johns Hopkins University Press, 1992), 22.

2. Originally published in *The Poet as Critic,* ed. Frederick P. W. McDowell (Evanston, Ill.: Northwestern University Press, 1967), 3–26.

3. Krieger, *Ekphrasis,* 1.

4. See, for example, my "Ekphrasis, Iconoclasm, and Desire," in *Rethinking the Romance of the Rose: Text, Image, Reception,* ed. Kevin Brownlee and Sylvia Huot (Philadelphia: University of Pennsylvania Press, 1992), 133–66.

5. See my "On the Sociology of Medieval Manuscript Annotation," in *Annotation and its Texts,* ed. Stephen A. Barney (New York: Oxford University Press, 1991), 43–73.

6. Martial, *Epigrams,* ed. and trans. D. R. Shackleton Bailey (Cambridge, Mass.: Harvard University Press, 1993), 1:240 ff.

7. Martial, *Epigrams,* 1:119.

8. The epigram addresses Julia, daughter of Domitian, comparing her to a portrait sculpture, and reads in full:

Quis te Phidiaco formatum, Iulia, caelo,
    vel quis Palladiae non putet artis opus?
candida non tacita respondet imagine lygdos
    et placido fulget vivus in ore decor.
ludit Acidalio, sed non manus aspera, nodo,
    quem rapuit collo, parve Cupido, tuo.
ut Martis revocetur amor summique Tonantis,
    a te Iuon petat ceston et ipsa Venus.

[Julia, who would not think you molded by Phidias' chisel or the work of Pallas' artistry? The white lygdus matches with a speaking likeness, and living beauty shines in your face. Your hand plays, but not roughly, with the Acidalian knot that it snatched from little Cupid's neck. To win back Mars' love and the supreme Thunderer's, let Juno and Venus herself ask you for the girdle.] (1:613)

9. V. Golzio, *Raffaello nei documenti nelle testimonianze dei contemporanei e nella letteratura del suo secolo* (Vatican City: Spoleto, 1936), 43, quoted by John Shearman, *Only Connect: Art and the Spectator in the Italian Renaissance* (Princeton: Princeton University Press, 1992), 116.

10. Martial, *Epigrams*, 7:84.

11. *Porphyry on the Life of Plotinus and the Order of his Books*, in *Plotinus, Enneads I*, trans. A. H. Armstrong (Cambridge, Mass.: Harvard University Press, 1989), 3.

12. "The transformation of [visual art] . . . in the direction of increasing awareness of and response to the spectator's presence, is more pervasively repeated in the portrait, and more obviously: it strikes you at once when you walk into a gallery of Renaissance portraits. . . . *The pace and scope of the change in this genre [of portraiture] are greatest in the period 1490–1530*" (Shearman, *Only Connect*, 108, italics added).

13. Ibid.

14. Clément Marot, *Oeuvres Poétiques*, ed. Gérard Defaux (Paris: Classiques Garnier, 1993), 2:203. All further citations from Marot are taken from volume 2, and will be made parenthetically in the text.

CHAPTER SIX

Murray Krieger versus Paul de Man

Denis Donoghue

The yellow moon of words about the nightingale
In measureless measures, not a bird for me
But the name of a bird and the name of a nameless air
I have never—shall never hear. . . .

WALLACE STEVENS, "Autumn Refrain"

In the spring of 1981, at a conference to mark the transfer of the School of Criticism and Theory from the University of California at Irvine to Northwestern University, Murray Krieger delivered a lecture under the title: "'A Waking Dream': The Symbolic Alternative to Allegory." M. H. Abrams and Paul de Man were the official respondents to the lecture. Abrams's response has not been published, so far as I know. De Man's appears as "Murray Krieger: A Commentary" in *Romanticism and Contemporary Criticism,* a posthumous collection of his papers.[1] A revised version of Krieger's lecture was published in Morton W. Bloomfield's edited volume, *Allegory, Myth, and Symbol* (1981) and later in Krieger's *Words* about *Words* about *Words* (1988).[2] I shall rehearse the exchange between Krieger and de Man, not to adjudicate their differences but to extend the discussion a little further. It turns, as it must, on the question: how to read.

I

Krieger's aim was to salvage as much as possible of the heritage of symbolism from the damage he thought Paul de Man and other writers had inflicted on it. In that respect "'A Waking Dream'" was part of Krieger's larger project, to recuperate certain literary values by showing that they have taken due account of the considerations ranged against them. Properly interpreted, these values can then be regarded as worth retaining because they have acknowledged and subsumed the grounds of the attack. Organicism, for instance: in another book, Krieger proposes to show that, "built into the mystical dialectic of organicism, with its magical imposition of unity, is a negative thrust that would explode it." Would explode it, he means, if given complete freedom. The call for unity which is clear in the rhetoric of organic form, he says, "occurs only in the company of its opposite, the call for a *variety* that gives to any attempted unity a dynamics that threatens its stability."[3] The values of organicism deserve to be retained if they are willing to turn against themselves, experimentally, impelled by a scruple: it is as if they were ashamed of their totalizing impulse, but stopped short of simply rejecting it. In this spirit, Krieger would speak up for metaphor, if it were cooled a long age by metonymy; for epic, if it acknowledged the merit of the mock-heroic tradition; for sacred writing, if it at least recognized the rights of a profane motive; and for aesthetic unity, if it held itself susceptible to acts of play, as in Schiller, to the Sublime, as in Edmund Burke, and to the daemonic, as in Goethe.

In "'A Waking Dream,'" Krieger's point of departure was the traditional distinction between symbol and allegory as it appeared, however diversely, in Goethe, Schelling, and Coleridge and as it persisted, with a radical shift of emphasis, in Mallarmé, Symons, and Yeats. Appropriately, Krieger quoted the well-known passage in *The Statesman's Manual* in which Coleridge makes the distinction as sharp as it was ever to be in his ruminations:

> A symbol . . . is characterized by a translucence of the Special in the Individual or of the General in the Especial or of the Universal in the General. Above all by the translucence of the Eternal through and in the Temporal. It always partakes of the Reality which it renders intelligible; and while it enunciates the whole, abides itself as a living part in that Unity, of which it is the representative. . . . Now an Allegory is but a translation of abstract notions into a picture-language which is itself nothing but an abstraction from objects of the senses; the principal being more worthless even than its phantom proxy, both alike unsubstantial, and the former shapeless to boot.[4]

The context of Coleridge's sentences is an attack on Hume's atheism. Coleridge acclaims "the great PRINCIPLES of our religion, the sublime IDEAS spoken out everywhere in the Old and New Testament" (24). He contrasts scriptural history "with the histories of highest note in the present age"—he means Hume and Gibbon—"in its freedom from the hollowness of abstractions" (28). Coleridge then refers to "a system of symbols, harmonious in themselves and consubstantial with the truths, of which they are the *conductors*" (29). It is among the miseries of the present age, he claims, "that it recognizes no medium between *Literal* and *Metaphorical*":

> Faith is either to be buried in the dead letter, or its name and honors usurped by a counterfeit product of the mechanical understanding, which in the blindness of self-complacency confounds SYMBOLS with ALLEGORIES. (30)

Then he makes the distinction I have quoted.

I remark the religious context of the distinction in the hope of making sense of it. It is clear from "consubstantial with the truths, of which they are the *conductors*" that the crucial instance of a symbol is the birth of Christ, the force of the Incarnation, that union of the divine and the human, eternity and time, spirit and body. A symbol is what it is because it denotes the natural world—God's Book of Nature—and partakes of the Word of God. "The power delegated to nature is all in every part," Coleridge says, "and by a symbol I mean, not a metaphor or allegory or any other figure of speech or form of fancy, but an actual and essential part of that, the whole of which it represents" (79).

Krieger alludes to Coleridge's context by referring to "the monistic conception of metaphor" as "a romantic reversion to the sacramental union put forth in Christian theology," and again by quoting, from the *Biographia Literaria,* Coleridge's definition of the primary imagination as "a repetition in the finite mind of the eternal act of creation in the infinite I AM."[5] But Krieger confuses the issue, I think, when he says that "through the typological *figura,* the unredeemed sequence of chronological time can be redeemed after all into the divine pattern, that eternal, spatial order which exchanges history for eschatology" (277). "Pattern" and "spatial" in that sentence are neither necessary nor desirable. The redemption of historical time does not entail recourse to a spatial figure. Eternity is not a supernatural mode of space.

This error—as I am bound to regard it—has serious consequences. It forces Krieger to define in static, spatial terms forces which, being temporal, require temporal description. He interprets each of these forces by transposing it into a spatial category, as if only there could it be significant. He defines form as "the imposition of spatial elements on a temporal ground without denying the figurative character of the word *spatial* and the merely illusionary escape from a temporal awareness that is never overcome" (280–81). Myth is "the shape that the imagination imposes on the flow of experience to make it conform to itself" (272). I don't see why a shape is especially conformable to the imagination, or why Krieger continues with this talk of spatial elements. Why not deem a myth to be a story, offered to its recipients as true, and giving them reasons why they should live according to its import? It is a narrative, or a group of narratives, issuing from the life of a community and returning to that life—it is not a shape. I recognize that we have a richer vocabulary to describe an entity in space than a force in time, but we gain nothing by confounding the latter with the former. There is no merit in transposing into the spatial category such terms as myth, form, sacrament, *figura,* and metaphor.

Krieger finds the modern attack on symbol and the correspondingly high valuation of allegory most comprehensively deployed in Paul de Man's "The Rhetoric of Temporality," and he quotes from that essay part of the following:

Whether it occurs in the form of an ethical conflict, as in *La Nouvelle Héloise,* or as an allegorization of the geographical site, as in Wordsworth, the prevalence of allegory always corresponds to the unveiling of an authentically temporal destiny. This unveiling takes place in a subject that has sought refuge against the impact of time in a natural world to which, in truth, it bears no resemblance. . . . Whereas the symbol postulates the possibility of an identity or identification, allegory designates primarily a distance in relation to its own origin, and, renouncing the nostalgia and the desire to coincide, it establishes its language in the void of this temporal difference. In so doing, it prevents the self from an illusory identification with the non-self, which is now fully, though painfully, recognized as a non-self.[6]

It follows that de Man, to avoid convicting romantic poets of bad faith and mystification, must argue that the crucial relation in their poetry is not between mind and the natural world but between mind and time. They must be shown to be allegorists, not symbolists, insofar as they know themselves and their genuine life in time. This is de Man's aim in several essays.

Krieger deals with this critical situation by claiming, in effect, that romantic poets and their readers may honorably deal with symbols, provided they know the risk they run, chiefly the risk of self-delusion:

> I want us to earn a chance to retain some of the symbolist's ambitious hopes for what man, as fiction-making creature, can accomplish in language, without falling prey to the ontologizing impulse that symbolist theory has previously encouraged. To do so we must balance a wariness about projecting our myths onto reality with an acknowledgement that we can entertain the dream of symbolic union, provided it does not come trailing clouds of metaphysical glory. Within the aesthetic frame of a fictional verbal play, the poem can present us with a form that creates the illusion of simultaneity, though even as we attend it we remain aware of its illusionary nature. (285)

"Dream" and "illusion" keep the stakes pretty low, unless Krieger has in mind only the sense in which everything in language is fictive. But there is a difference between a fiction and an illusion; we are in thrall to our illusions, but not to the fictions we make. I don't think, incidentally, that Krieger has given up the ontologizing impulse.

Krieger takes, as an example of such saving knowledge—"we remain aware of its illusionary nature"—the last stanzas of Keats's "Ode to a Nightingale":

> Thou wast not born for death, immortal Bird!
>   No hungry generations tread thee down;
> The voice I hear this passing night was heard
>   In ancient days by emperor and clown:
> Perhaps the self-same song that found a path
>   Through the sad heart of Ruth, when, sick for home,
>   She stood in tears amid the alien corn;
>   The same that oft-times hath

> Charm'd magic casements, opening on the foam
>   Of perilous seas, in faery lands forlorn.
>
> Forlorn! the very word is like a bell
>   To toll me back from thee to my sole self!
> Adieu! the fancy cannot cheat so well
>   As she is fam'd to do, deceiving elf.
> Adieu! adieu! thy plaintive anthem fades
>   Past the near meadows, over the still stream,
>   Up the hill-side; and now 'tis buried deep
>   In the next valley-glades:
> Was it a vision, or a waking dream?
>   Fled is that music:—Do I wake or sleep?

Keats's speaker, as Krieger says, wakes up from the momentary trance, "his all-unifying fancy," to return to his sole self:

> Yet the final words of his poem ("Do I wake or sleep?") suggest that the final moment of demystification is not necessarily privileged as the only authentic reality. . . . The perspective that sees the fancy as cheating is itself not a final reality, and the magic of the fancy is not altogether dispelled. Even more, the experience itself is still cherished, even in the aftermath of loss. The struggle in the speaker between the poet's willed visionary blindness that has permitted the fancy and the mortal's dull, perplexed brain that has resisted it has not relaxed: once again—or rather still—the struggle between myth and history. The music has fled, we learn in the opening of the final line, though its continuing effects lead to the uncertainty about the present reflected in the question that concludes the poem ("Do I wake or sleep?"). (287–88)

Krieger implies that the poet who exercises his "fancy" is not in bad faith, provided he wakes up from the trance and acknowledges that he has indeed been dreaming. The redemptive force is—it is my word, not Krieger's—irony. Irony as a higher degree of knowledge recovers the lower degree by exceeding it. When the poet brings irony to bear upon his dream, he retains the dream as a valid experience, not a naiveté. What de Man calls "the fallen world of our facticity"[7] is not the whole world or the whole story.

II

De Man's response to Krieger is strange. He begins by praising the New Critics—including Krieger among them—for letting the efficacy of their technical procedures, "as they developed in close contact with the points of resistance they encountered in the understanding of texts, reach beyond and even turn against the limits of their own ideologies."[8] But then he scolds Krieger for preferring one trope to another—symbol to allegory—as if de

Man himself had not spent much of his energy overturning that preference. In Krieger's terms, according to de Man's reading of them, "allegory is equated with a thematic assertion of finitude, defeat, and mortality of which symbol is the aesthetic sublimation and redemption." Krieger "thus recovers the fragmentation of time and of the self in the beautiful song of the severed head, reconciles the clear-eyed skepticism of knowledge with the fervor of vision, the language of fusion with that of separation, the gesture of conceding with that of asserting or countering" (183).

The test case, according to de Man, is Krieger's reading of the last two lines of the poem:

> Was it a vision, or a waking dream?
> Fled is that music:—Do I wake or sleep?

De Man comments:

> Guided by the apparent symmetry of the two or constructions (a vision *or* a waking dream; wake or sleep), Krieger can suspend the uncertainty of the wake/sleep opposition and make it into a stable cognition by stressing the symbolic complementarity of "a vision" with "a waking dream"—in which the "second alternative" is not "wholly a denial of the first"; it is a cliché, but not an unreasonable one, to call a waking dream a vision. (184)

The past of recollection ("Was it . . .") and the present of writing or thinking ("Do I . . .") can be brought together, de Man concedes, "because sleeping relates to waking as vision relates to waking dream, that is to say, in the mode of the symbol" (184). De Man doesn't offer to refute Krieger's general argument or to deny him the pleasure of his synthesis. He has already engaged some of these issues in "Hypogram and Inscription," his extended essay on Michael Riffaterre.[9] He does not want to go over that ground again, so he leaves Krieger's hoped-for synthesis without further comment. But he remarks that Descartes points out, in the first two Meditations, that when we dream, we always dream that we are awake. De Man says: "Unlike reverie or day-dream, dream and wake (or sleep) are mutually exclusive, not symbolically complementary" (185). But de Man's main question is not whether or not Krieger's synthesis is valid, but whether or not Keats's ode can be invoked in support of it.

De Man concentrates on the word "Forlorn!" which leads to the last two lines of the poem:

> This moment in the text, and this moment alone, occurs as an actual present in the only material present of the ode, the actual moment of its inscription when Keats writes the word "forlorn" and interrupts himself to reflect on its arbitrary sound. At that precise moment, is it possible to say whether Keats, in the present of that moment, is awake or asleep? Thematically speaking, it is the very moment at which the subject in the text states that it awakens; textually speaking, however, it is also the moment at which this

same subject starts to dream—for as we also all know since Freud, such plays of the letter are also the work of the dream, accessible to us only within a system in which the difference between waking and dreaming cannot be decided and can, henceforth, not be assimilated to a symbolic reconciliation of opposites. The actual inclusion, in the texture of the lyric, of an alien piece of metalanguage makes the "Ode to a Nightingale" one of the very poems, the very allegory, of the non-symbolic, nonaesthetic character of poetic language. (186–87)

Very odd. Insofar as I understand it, it comes to this. Krieger takes the apparent symmetry of the questions—was it A or B? Do I wake or sleep?—as proof of Keats's eventually standing aside from the rhetoric of his symbolism to the extent of questioning its status. By doing so, he earns the right to use the song of the nightingale as a symbol. De Man answers, in effect: No, because the symmetry of the questions is specious, there is no ascertainable difference between each of the states in the pairings; vision or waking dream; dream or waking. There is no place, not a crevice, into which Keats's ostensibly later knowledge can insert itself. "Forlorn" breaks the unity of tone it claims.

But surely the moment at which Keats steps outside the rhetoric of his meditation and withdraws the word "forlorn" from it is not dream-work but the work of wide-awake self-scrutiny. Plays of the letter may take place in dreams, but they also occur—and are acted upon—in waking consciousness. In the Ode, the difference between waking and dreaming can be decided: dream-work may play with the word "forlorn" but it does not run to a comparison between that word and a bell tolling Keats back from the nightingale to his sole self. That is an act of syntax which the dream can't perform. Dreams have images, but no syntax. Hazlitt says, in his essay "On Dreams," that the difference between sleeping and waking

> seems to be that in the latter we have a greater range of conscious recollections, a larger discourse of reason, and associate ideas in longer trains and more as they are connected with one another in the order of nature; whereas in the former, any two impressions, that meet or are alike, join company, and then are parted again, without notice, like the froth from the wave.[10]

There is enough difference, then, to justify the symmetry of the questions. David Bromwich says, with good reason, that it does not matter whether Keats wakes or sleeps, "because he is free to renew his journey, and to return again,"[11] but this does not support de Man's claim that the question is specious because its terms cannot be distinguished. They can be distinguished well enough.

The symbolic reconciliation of opposites which Krieger proposes to show seems to be intact. "Forlorn" is not an alien piece of metalanguage but the moment in which Keats separates himself from the rhetoric of his trance. In the essay on Riffaterre, de Man claims that the question "Was it a vision or a waking dream?" "is destined to remain unanswered."[12] Not necessarily; any reader is free to think that, on balance, Keats's experience was more a waking dream than a vision, or vice versa. But the question is not opaque, whether it is answered or not. Translated into prose, it might be phrased: was it a vision, "something apparently seen otherwise than by ordinary sight," as the OED has it, though with concentrated attention; or was it a casual, disordered reverie, a loose association of images, from which I have now returned to my sober senses?

I think Krieger is right, therefore, to maintain that Keats has found a place for irony, the later knowledge. Several places, I would say: not only the one surrounding "Forlorn!" but also the one between the past tense of "Was" and the interrogative present of "Do I . . . ?" and the places on each side of the interpolated sentence, "Fled is that music." The oddity of that sentence makes a further space: "music," not bird, and "Fled" with its implication of flying away from danger. These are acts of alert discrimination, not words of trance. As in Keats's "Sleep and Poetry,"

> The visions all are fled—the car is fled
> Into the light of heaven (ll. 155–56)

because they can't face the "sense of real things" come "doubly strong."

De Man's last words in the reply to Krieger quoted above are memorably gruff, when he refers to the "Ode to a Nightingale" as "one of the very poems, the very allegory, of the non-symbolic, nonaesthetic character of poetic language." In his early writings, de Man hovered between describing poetic language in this way and in virtually the opposite way. In "Criticism and Crisis"—a lecture he gave at the University of Texas in the spring of 1967—he spoke with dismay of Husserl's claim for European supremacy and of the pathos of such a claim "at a moment when Europe was about to destroy itself as center in the name of its unwarranted claim to be the center." Then he went on to talk about literary criticism:

> Similarly, demystifying critics are in fact asserting the privileged status of literature as an authentic language, but withdrawing from the implications by cutting themselves off from the source from which they receive their insight.
>
> For the statement about language, that sign and meaning can never coincide, is what is precisely taken for granted in the kind of language we call literary. Literature, unlike everyday language, begins on the far side of this knowledge; it is the only form of language free from the fallacy of unmediated expression.[13]

But in the Gauss Seminar at Princeton, still in the spring of 1967, and while repeating that "unmediated expression is a philosophical impossibility," de Man denied the privilege he had accorded, at Texas, to literature:

Literature, presumably, is a form of language, and one can argue that all other art forms, including music, are in fact protoliterary languages. This was, in fact, Mallarmé's thesis in his Oxford lecture, as it is Lévi-Strauss's when he states that the language of music, as a language without speaker, comes closest to being the kind of metalanguage of which the linguists are dreaming. If the radical position suggested by Lévi-Strauss is to stand, if the question of structure can only be asked from a point of view that is not that of a subject using a privileged language, then it becomes imperative to show that literature constitutes no exception, that its language is nowise privileged in terms of unity and truth over everyday forms of language. The task of structuralist literary critics then becomes quite clear: in order to eliminate the constitutive subject, they have to show that the discrepancy between sign and meaning (*signifiant* and *signifié*) prevails in literature in the same manner as in everyday language.[14]

I cannot explain how literature, merely by moving from Austin to Princeton, lost the privilege of being free from the fallacy of unmediated expression.

But it is clear that de Man, en route in 1967 from structuralism to deconstruction, was determined to go far to seek disquietude. By the time he had written "The Rhetoric of Temporality," he had read or reread Benjamin's *Ursprung des deutschen Trauerspiels,* and the repudiation of symbol in favor of allegory, in "The Rhetoric of Temporality," is taken directly from Benjamin's book. Benjamin, who had his own reasons for hating time and history, resented the attempt of certain modern writers to "redeem the time" or to show daily life under a possible blessing of miracle, Incarnation, or some other transfiguring value. If you want to transform the lives people have to live, he implied, you must do so by direct political action or by exemplary action, as in Brecht's theater. Hence his hatred of the enhancing tropes, especially of symbol and myth. (Fredric Jameson hates them for the same reason.) Benjamin's method was to deride any literary or dramatic form that appeared to alleviate the malady of the quotidian. Tragedy was the main culprit. The dialogue between Lear and Cordelia near the end of the play is apparently designed to make the audience feel that the gouging of Gloucester's eyes is not the whole story; that suffering, as in the crucifixion of Christ, may be suffused with a redemptive aura of value and meaning. Benjamin rejected the consolation prize and countered Tragedy with the *Trauerspiel,* which—like the plays of Webster, Tourneur, and Middleton—left the fragments of time entirely unredeemed. Benjamin writes:

Whereas in the symbol destruction is idealized and the transfigured face of nature is fleetingly revealed in the light of redemption, in allegory the observer is confronted with the *facies hippocratica* of history as a petrified, primordial landscape. . . . Allegories are, in the realm of thoughts, what ruins are in the realm of things.[15]

That is the gist of de Man's attack on symbolism: allegories are honest because they don't pretend to offer semblances of unity of being; they don't give even a fleeting intimation of redemption; they show time for what it is, mere facticity. It is not surprising that de Man was gruff with Krieger's attempt to retain the glow of symbolism.

When he replied to Krieger's lecture, de Man was already moving away from the trope of metaphor as the essential poetic figure, since it entailed sundry mystifications of likeness, reference, creativity, constitutive power, ontology, and epistemology. I think this accounts for the impression, in his reply to Krieger, that talk of metaphor had ceased to interest him. He was already abandoning Aristotle's theory of the primacy of metaphor and endorsing Vico's claim that language begins in the trope that "gives sense and passion to insensate things."[16] This is the speech act of positing or summoning, apostrophe, prosopopoeia, the act by which I call someone or something into existence as a subject. Keats heard a nightingale and was charmed by its song, but in the poem he does not describe what he heard, he summons a nightingale—type of all nightingales from all ages—to appear. In the essay on Riffaterre, de Man writes, agreeably enough, of "the delicate and ever-suspended balance between reference and play that is the condition for aesthetic pleasure," but the reference to reference soon drops away, and he writes of "the epistemological tension that produces prosopopoeia, the master trope of poetic discourse." Indeed, "prosopopoeia, as the trope of address, is the very figure of the reader and of reading."[17] The particular finesse of prosopopoeia is that it achieves the uncanny effect of making the invisible appear to be visible; it produces an hallucination, or rather an hallucinatory effect. Repeating a few sentences from the reply to Krieger, de Man goes on to produce a quandary dismal enough for any devotee of Benjamin:

> How then is one to decide on the distinction between hallucination and perception since, in hallucination, the difference between I see and I think that I see has been one-sidedly resolved in the direction of apperception? Consciousness has become consciousness only of itself. In that sense, any consciousness, including perception, is hallucinatory: one never "has" a hallucination the way one has a sore foot from kicking the proverbial stone. Just as the hypothesis of dreaming undoes the certainty of sleep, the hypothesis, or the figure, of hallucination undoes sense certainty. This means, in linguistic terms, that it is impossible to say whether prosopopoeia is plausible because of the empirical existence of dreams and hallucinations or whether one believes that such a thing as dreams and hallucinations exist because language permits the figure of prosopopoeia. The question "Was it a vision, or a waking dream?" is destined to remain unanswered. Prosopopoeia undoes the distinction between reference and signification on which all semiotic systems, including Riffaterre's, depend.[18]

But on second reading this may not be as dismal as it seemed. When Hardy, in a series of love poems, belatedly calls upon his dead wife to come forth, of course she does not obey, as Lazarus obeyed Christ. But in a fictive sense she appears to appear. If we think of this appearance as a semblance rather than an hallucination, we take the harm out of de Man's conclusion. Semblances are all that works of art and literature offer to give. The "Ode to a Nightingale" doesn't produce a nightingale or a song. We see nothing, hear nothing. But we have semblances of things seen and heard.

III

My disagreement with Krieger's essay "'A Waking Dream'" begins with its first paragraph:

> The war between the poets and the philosophers, out of which Western liter-ary theory began, is with us still. Though it has taken many forms, it is there now, stimulating yet new varieties of dispute. As a war, it continues to par-take of the oppositional force of the Platonic dialectic, forcing us to choose which of the two ways we will accept as a path of knowledge, or which of the two we shall reject for having no valid claim to lead us there.[19]

I do not think that is the best way of reading. Suppose it were not a question of knowledge but of—as I hold—action and experience, as in Kenneth Burke's *A Grammar of Motives:*

> To consider language as a means of information or knowledge is to consider it epistemologically, semantically, in terms of "science." To consider it as a mode of *action* is to consider it in terms of "poetry." For a poem is an act, the symbolic act of the poet who made it—an act of such a nature that surviving as a structure or object, it enables us as readers to re-enact it.[20]

The written or printed poem is like a musical score: it permits us to act it out, follow its action. If we read a poem as symbolic action, we retain its qualities in temporal form. Form itself becomes a temporal sequence involving, in Burke's terms, "the creation of an appetite in the mind of the auditor, and the adequate satisfying of that appetite."[21] One of his examples is the for-mal perfection of Shakespeare's presentation of the Ghost to Hamlet, a choice instance of the auditor's desires excited, thwarted, sidestepped, but in good time richly satisfied.

The first merit of this approach to reading is that it does not start a war between poets and philosophers about knowledge. Or between poets and scientists on the same issue. If the realm of literature is action and its con-tent is real or imagined experience, such wars are unnecessary. Novelists may use the work of physicists, as Pynchon does in *Gravity's Rainbow,* but they do not compete with physicists. To each his own labor. A dispute would break out only if novelist or physicist claimed to run the whole show. It is not likely to happen. Meanwhile, current disputes about the allegedly social constitution of knowledge are matters in which a poet may take a lay interest, but they are not a poet's problem in any consideration of craft or profession.

Even if a statement is made in a poem or a novel, it does not come up for judgment with respect to its truth or falsity but only with respect to its relation to the feelings involved at that point. I. A. Richards's old theory, according to which statements in a work of literature are not statements but pseudo-statements, is not much valued nowadays, but it should be taken seriously, provided we agree that a pseudo-statement is a statement the truth or falsity of which is not, in its particular context, a consideration. If I were to say, in conversation or in print, that " 'tis better to be vile than vile esteemed," I should be hooted for committing a falsehood and the further sins of vanity and self-pity. But the sentence is thoroughly appropriate as the first line of a sonnet by Shakespeare, since the implied context there makes it a feasible thing for the speaker to say. The statement is not true, according to reputable ethics and moral doctrine, but it is true to the life of the implied speaker.

Or take Sidney's sonnet:

> With how sad steps, Oh Moon, thou climb'st the skies!
> How silently, and with how wan a face!
> What, may it be that even in heavenly place
> That busy archer his sharp arrows tries?
> Sure, if that long-with-love-acquainted eyes
> Can judge of love, thou feel'st a lover's case,
> I read it in thy looks; thy languished grace,
> To me, that feel the like, thy state descries.
> Then, even of fellowship, Oh Moon, tell me,
> Is constant love deemed there but want of wit?
> Are beauties there as proud as here they be?
> Do they above love to be loved, and yet
> Those lovers scorn whom that love doth possess?
> Do they call virtue there ungratefulness?

The first line is untrue, the moon does not climb the skies with sad steps. But the speaker, a bruised sad lover, might well call upon the moon, in fellowship, to respond to his complaint. The poem is a symbolic act in the mode of apostrophe or prosopopoeia; it summons the moon as a subject, gives it a face, and speaks to it. The moon is, as we say, a symbol of the transience of love, of the conviction that new Love, as in the "Ode to a Nightingale," cannot pine at Beauty's lustrous eyes "beyond to-morrow." As a symbol, is it vulnerable to an analysis such as de Man's? I don't think so. I can't speak for Krieger, but in his terms I would find the symbol justified by the fact that after the first quatrain, in which Sidney's speaker addresses the moon as victim of love and Cupid's arrows, he gives the moon—with the steadying words "acquainted" and "judge"—a different role. The moon is no longer a mere victim but an adjudicator, a witness qualified to report on lunar conventions and dispositions.

The question of knowledge, true or false, does not arise in reading Sidney's sonnet or Shakespeare's: what arises is a question of feeling, action, experience, and the values they adumbrate. Nor does the question of knowledge arise in the "Ode to a Nightingale." I agree with Helen Vendler that art in this ode—by which she means the song of the nightingale—"has no conceptual or moral content." I assume she is referring to the song and not to the poem when she says that "ravishingly beautiful and entirely natural, it is a stream of invention, pure sound, in no way mimetic, on which we as listeners project our own feelings of ecstasy or grief."[22] The song is pure expression, expressing in itself nothing but sensation. But Keats's speaker, too, projects his feelings upon it. Krieger says:

> Indeed, the bird seems to function for the enraptured speaker as a metonymic metaphor. The magic of the speaker's momentary indulgence leads him to identify the single, mortal bird with its voice and song and to make the voice and song identical with those of the distant past. All nightingales become one bird because the songs are one song, heard but unseen. On the strength of this transfer Keats treats the bird itself as immortal, in contrast to his own mortality and that of the historical or mythological personages who earlier heard the same bird (voice, song). Humanity's individual lives are tied together by the bird once it has been turned into the all-unifying metonymic metaphor, so that history across the ages has been turned into the instantaneous vision of myth. Thanks to a repetition so complete that it achieves the identity of eternal recurrence (de Man's objections notwithstanding), time is redeemed.[23]

Metonymic metaphor is evidently Krieger's name for the metaphor that knows it is a metaphor, or rather for the use of metaphor which accommodates this knowledge. I do not find any problem in reconciling the nightingale's song as pure expression with the song as that into which Keats's speaker projects his feelings and desires. But I do not see how Krieger is justified in collapsing the differences between "the identity of eternal recurrence" and "the instantaneous vision of myth." Again he is thinking of myth as the spatial culmination of history, as if the redemption of time were necessarily to be achieved out of time or beyond it.

My main disagreement with Krieger is, I hope, clear. He makes the question of symbol and allegory an epistemological issue; I want to make it—or keep it—a question of action, suffering, and experience. I concede that he has Coleridge's authority on his side. Coleridge, too, made the symbol an epistemological issue, so that the crucial question was the relation between knowledge and faith. But I argue that a symbol is not an object as if seen in space; it denotes an action or a multitude of cognate actions. The force of

Keats's nightingale is not semantic, it is a symbol by virtue of the feelings we (you, I, anyone) project upon it. It is not a constituent of knowledge but of desire. In this respect I think it significant that when Arthur Symons formulated the theory of Symbolism, in the light of the diverse practices of Nerval, Villiers de L'Isle Adam, Rimbaud, Verlaine, Mallarmé, and Laforgue, he placed it in a world beyond knowledge. Or at least beyond any mode that passed for knowledge. "The forces which mould the thought of men change," he said,

> or men's resistance to them slackens; with the change of men's thought comes a change of literature, alike in its inmost essence and in its outward form: after the world has starved its soul long enough in the contemplation and the re-arrangement of material things, comes the turn of the soul; and with it comes the literature of which I write in this volume, a literature in which the visible world is no longer a reality, and the unseen world no longer a dream.[24]

Only in such a world, in which Coleridge's epistemological doctrine of the symbol was abandoned, could poems of *symbolisme* have been achieved. *Symbolisme* is a poetry that has released itself from the Incarnation by giving each word its autonomy as a word, independent of its old duty in the mundane world. In a world such as Symons intuits, words are not burdened with the duty of reference; there is no longer an empirical world to claim such priority. As a result, words are set free to act not as signs pointing beyond themselves and beyond the poem, but as presences in relation to other presences. They are like sounds in music or pieces in a board game; nothing in themselves but everything in their relation to their fellows. Questions of ontology and epistemology do not arise. The relation between one word and another in a symbolist poem is an event of kinship or difference, marked by internal affiliations, acoustic, promiscuous, self-delighting.

I see more clearly now where I differ from Krieger. He wants to keep symbols close to knowledge; I want to keep them close to desire. I agree with David Lloyd that a symbol "functions as a means to a narrative organization of desire rather than a mode of mimetic representation."[25] Lloyd has in view the relation between Yeats's symbols and the political state they summon into existence:

> Both nationalist poetry and nationalist violence have the same end: to organize the incoherent desires of the population towards the goal of popular unity, which is the essential prerequisite of an effective political struggle for national liberation. The narrative of symbolism is one which progressively leads its subjects on by way of symbols which are consubstantial with the nation which they represent.[26]

If a symbol is predicated on desire rather than on knowledge, it is invulnerable: if it ceases to organize the desires in question, it ceases to be a symbol and must be replaced by a more effective one. But so long as it does its work, I don't see how it could be refuted by allegory or by any other figure.

NOTES

1. Paul de Man, *Romanticism and Contemporary Criticism: The Gauss Seminars and Other Papers,* ed. E. S. Burt, Kevin Newmark, and Andrzej Warminski (Baltimore: Johns Hopkins University Press, 1993), 181–87.

2. Morton W. Bloomfield, ed., *Allegory, Myth, and Symbol,* Harvard English Studies 9 (Cambridge, Mass.: Harvard University Press, 1981), 1–22. Murray Krieger, *Words* about *Words* about *Words: Theory, Criticism, and the Literary Text* (Baltimore: Johns Hopkins University Press, 1988), 271–88.

3. Murray Krieger, *A Reopening of Closure: Organicism Against Itself* (New York: Columbia University Press, 1989), 40–41.

4. R. J. White, ed., *The Collected Works of Samuel Taylor Coleridge: Lay Sermons,* Bollingen Series, vol. 75 (Princeton: Princeton University Press, 1972), 30. Further citations will be made parenthetically in the text.

5. Krieger, *Words* about *Words* about *Words,* 276, 277. Further citations will be made parenthetically in the text.

6. Paul de Man, *Blindness and Insight: Essays in the Rhetoric of Contemporary Criticism,* 2d ed., revised (Minneapolis: University of Minnesota Press, 1983), 206–7.

7. De Man, *Blindness and Insight,* 13.

8. De Man, *Romanticism and Contemporary Criticism,* 182. Further citations will be made parenthetically in the text.

9. Paul de Man, *The Resistance to Theory* (Minneapolis: University of Minnesota Press, 1993), 27–53.

10. William Hazlitt, *Works,* 12:20–21, quoted in David Bromwich, *Hazlitt: The Mind of a Critic* (New York: Oxford University Press, 1983), 385.

11. Bromwich, *Hazlitt,* 386.

12. De Man, *Resistance to Theory,* 50.

13. De Man, *Blindness and Insight,* 16–17.

14. De Man, *Romanticism and Contemporary Criticism,* 9, 12–13.

15. Walter Benjamin, *The Origin of German Tragic Drama,* trans. John Osborne (London: New Left Books, 1977), 166, 178.

16. Giambattista Vico, *The New Science* (New York: Doubleday, 1961), 87, quoted in Cynthia Chase, *Decomposing Figures: Rhetorical Readings in the Romantic Tradition* (Baltimore: Johns Hopkins University Press, 1986), 215.

17. De Man, *Resistance to Theory,* 36, 48, 45.

18. Ibid., 49–50.

19. Krieger, *Words* about *Words* about *Words,* 271.

20. Kenneth Burke, *A Grammar of Motives,* in *A Grammar of Motives and A Rhetoric of Motives* (Cleveland and New York: World Publishing Company, 1962), 447.

21. Kenneth Burke, *Counter-Statement* (Chicago: University of Chicago Press, 1957), 31.

22. Helen Vendler, *The Odes of John Keats* (Cambridge, Mass.: Harvard University Press, 1983), 95.

23. Krieger, *Words* about *Words* about *Words,* 286.

24. Arthur Symons, *The Symbolist Movement in Literature* (New York: E. P. Dutton, 1958), 2–3.

25. David Lloyd, *Anomalous States: Irish Writing and the Post-Colonial Moment* (Durham: Duke University Press, 1993), 85.

26. Ibid., 70–71.

CHAPTER SEVEN

Organicism in Literature and History: From (Murray Krieger's) Poetics to (Jules Michelet's) Politics

David Carroll

Consult naturalists, consult physiology. Try for once to learn what organic unity *is. Only one people has it—the French.*
JULES MICHELET, *La France devant l'Europe* (1871)

One people! One homeland! One France! . . . Without unity, we will perish.
MICHELET, *Le Peuple* (1846)

Converted into a hegemonic instrument, literary organicism can be uncritically analogized in order to serve as a justification for nationalism, for ethnocentrism even to the extreme of racism. . . . [But] I have yet to be persuaded that the organic metaphor is necessarily *dangerous in being applied to literary texts by other critics who, as secular skeptics, retain an awareness of the figurative, and even fictive, character of that application.*
MURRAY KRIEGER, *A Reopening of Closure: Organicism Against Itself*

I. LITERARY SPECIFICITY AND THE POETICS OF THE "WELL CRACKED URN"

Either as a general theory of literature with deep roots within literary history, or as a metaphor associated with a particular way of reading literature which reached its height decades ago, literary organicism has certainly not had many defenders in recent years. It no longer seems to be of even historical interest, and when it is evoked, it is most likely to be attacked and dismissed as the expression of the elitist, Eurocentric, gendered values of the traditional literary academy, a remnant from another, less progressive era. Organicism has gone the way of other theories arguing for the specificity of literature and defending the integrity of the individual literary text, at a time when political and cultural issues seem to be of much more pressing concern. Those who regret that important movements within the recent history of literary criticism and theory are dismissed in this way might see here another sign of the theoretical narrowness and ideological rigidity of the politicized contemporary academic world, another indication that it is no longer fashionable or permissible to do any form of literary criticism that is primarily or exclusively oriented toward literature.

A certain number of these critics have made it clear that they feel that cultural criticism, postcolonial studies, gender analysis, and gay and lesbian studies have followed in the wake of structuralist, poststructuralist, new historicist, and deconstructionist theories and modes of analysis not only to displace true literary analysis but also to attack and destroy literature itself. They bemoan the fact that there seems to be little if any place in the academy today for the kind of close reading and complicated, nuanced poetic analysis once advocated and practiced by the best literary organicists—no place, even in literature departments, to do literature rather than history or sociology or politics. Some would even argue that literary studies have simply ceased being literary at all, and thus no longer have any justification for continuing to exist.

I should state immediately that I do not share this stark view of literary studies. I might agree that in the desire to open literary studies up to larger cultural problems and to deal seriously with non-canonical texts—which had been ignored for much too long—new, more politicized orthodoxies have replaced previously dominant, more formalist or textualist orthodoxies. I would not concur, however, with those who see this phenomenon as the sign of the impending death of literature or literary studies. On the contrary, I have confidence that responsible, legitimate criticism of the limitations and excesses of these orthodoxies—which is far different from rejecting the different cultural and historicist theories and movements in their entirety—will have and is already having positive, critical effects.

There is of course no going back—and who would want to if one could?—to a mythical time when literature was allegedly literature and nothing else. For there never existed a time "before theory" when theory had not yet disrupted literature with its own, extraliterary concerns; when history, politics, and theory, with their focus either on problems of class, gender, culture, and/or ethnicity, on the one hand, or "abstract" philosophical concerns, on the other, had not complicated and in part displaced a more formalist literary concern with tropes, narrative structures, and rhetorical effects. This does not mean, however, that such literary concerns should themselves ever become irrelevant. Critical discourse, if it is to remain critical, and regardless of whether it is more literary or historical or political in nature, cannot afford to plunge headlong "back to the future," into a world where literature was (and is once again) privileged without question, dictating its rules to itself and to other fields. But, for the same reasons, critical discourse can also not afford to leap "forward into the past," where literature will cease (already ceases) to exist except as an expression of culture, gender, ethnicity, or class, and where it is originally and/or in the last instance determined by some form—which one?—of history, politics, or ethnic or sexual identity.

In fact, the issues which emerge out of the constantly changing field called literary studies have always been literary and extraliterary at the same time. Within even the most self-enclosed literary theory or practice, extra- or what I call paraliterary elements and forces can always be found pushing not just literary critics but literature as well outside and beyond literature. *The question* of literary specificity, as a question, inevitably leads to the question of the "outside" of literature, an outside, however, that is also, at least in part, "within" literature. This means, therefore, that literature has as much to say *about* the outside and potentially does as much *in* or *to* the outside— whether philosophical, political, historical, cultural, gendered, or sexual— as any other field. But what literature says and does and how it says and does it may very well not be the same as the activities and practices of other fields and disciplines, assuming that we still have solid grounds for distinguishing among them all. And it is this difference above all others that makes a difference in how we understand both the inside and outside, both the specifically literary and the paraliterary dimensions of literature.

One of the purposes of the present essay is to argue against the notion that we should or must choose between "doing literature" and "doing history or politics," between, on the one hand, defending the integrity of the literary field at all costs against invasions from its historical-political neighbors, and, on the other hand, surrendering its integrity and relative autonomy to them without a struggle. For various historical and theoretical reasons, the alternative facing us today, I would insist, is *obviously not* the one presented by Walter Benjamin in his much-quoted essay of 1936, "The Work of Art in the Age of Mechanical Reproduction": that is, the stark choice between the aestheticization of politics and the politicization of art.[1]

Clearly, for Benjamin and many others who opposed the rise of fascism and its form of the aestheticization of politics, the politicization of art as an aesthetic position and some form of communism as a political position seemed virtually unavoidable. But despite the sympathy one has to have for Benjamin's militant opposition to fascism, the alternative he proposed cannot be accepted, nor can the terms of the opposition itself. This in no way implies, however, that the aestheticization of the political—or at least the aesthetic basis and function of different forms of nationalist politics—constitutes a problem that has already been resolved and thus is no longer worth investigating. It simply means that a critical investigation of the problem cannot rely on politics, aesthetics, or poetics alone for a solution.

For the sake of argument, let us say that a literary critic interested in the relations of aesthetics and politics in general chooses to study the literary and aesthetic dimensions of the politics of a group of French extremist nationalist and fascist writers and critics. These writers are certainly not representative of all French writers, just as their particular views on literature and politics are not representative of literature and politics in general. In studying them, the critic discovers that a certain form of literary organicism is at the heart of both their antiromantic aesthetics and their militantly antirepublican, nationalist politics. By analyzing the effects of their application of the metaphor of literary organicism to politics in a nationalist and even fascist context, the critic necessarily emphasizes what could be called the totalitarian implications of the organic metaphor. Alternative views of the functions and goals of literature and politics are not pursued, so that the particular effects of literary and political extremisms may be better understood.

By analyzing in detail and insisting on the literary-aesthetic presuppositions of particular forms of extremist politics, might not such analyses be understood as attributing to art and literature the ultimate responsibility for political extremism? Might not the critic be accused of giving in to the temptation to attack literature "in itself" for supporting or encouraging a reactionary politics, and thus of forgetting or denying that literature also provides means for resisting and undermining the totalizing tendencies of certain organic forms of political extremism and of literature itself? Could he not be accused of saying, or at least implying, not only that literature in its organicist forms implies some form of totalization but also that literature in itself is essentially totalitarian or fascist? Because of his focus on the dogmatic application of organic literary models to politics, might he not even be seen as an enemy of literature and art, an antiliterary literary critic, a critic with the not-so-secret agenda of attacking and destroying literature? If so, should he not be considered a traitor to his field, to the national literature he has chosen to study and to literature and art in general, someone whose real agenda is to help bring about the end of literature and the end of literary studies as we know them?

I have formulated these questions in their most extreme (and absurd) form—which does not mean that critics and theorists threatened by recent theoretical emphases and developments have not already formulated them this way—in order to highlight certain aspects of the kind of attacks being leveled today against so-called "non-literary" literary studies. Because of such polemical attacks, it is important to stress, for example, that there is a crucial difference between the analysis of how a certain poetics or aesthetics was used as a model for politics in a specific extremist nationalist or fascist literary context, and the general argument or even implication that organic forms of art and literature are in their essence totalitarian and do not in any circumstance provide resources for a (para)aesthetic or (para)literary resistance to totalitarianism.

A second purpose of this essay, therefore, is to insist on the dangers of generalizing the totalizing implications of literary organicism or any other theory of literature that insists on literary specificity or closure. It is also to indicate the limitations of any abstract criticism or condemnation of the organic model in itself which does not undertake a thorough critical investigation of how the model or metaphor is applied in various extraliterary fields, and the specific effects of such applications.

In the search for alternatives to Benjamin's alternative of either the "aestheticizing of politics" or the "politicizing of art," it seems to me necessary to read not just critics and theorists who directly address the problem of extremist politics, but also those who are more concerned with the question of the specificity of literature than with the political determination of literature or its political effects. These would, however, have to be theorists for whom literary specificity remains a *question* rather than an issue that can be determined either by literary-formalist or historical-political means alone. I consider Murray Krieger to be one of the most important of such theorists, for he has repeatedly shown why the question of literature (or, for him, more precisely, the question of poetry or the poetic) is radically different from the question of either history or politics, and why it is not a question that historical theses can entirely explain or political forces completely determine, even in the last instance. Furthermore, he has also argued that it is precisely this difference or distance from history and politics that gives literature its critical force and provides it with ways of resisting, complicating, and recasting accepted notions of history and politics.

I would want to add to such a defense of literature only that the differences between literature and history or politics are also to be found *within* history and politics themselves, and are produced by the literary and/or aesthetic premises, functions, and effects of the discourses and practices constituting both fields. They divide these fields internally and complicate them, making the ends they attempt to realize and the closures they attempt to impose problematic. And literature, by being situated always in part outside itself and the field it constitutes, takes on an extraliterary function and thus complicates its own relation to itself and to its own internal, specifically literary practices and ends. I would go even further, and say that it is precisely its differences with (or distance from) politics that link literature to politics, but in ways that are not exclusively or even primarily political.

The insistence and tenacity with which Murray Krieger has returned to the complex question of the specificity of literature demonstrate not only the centrality of the question of literature for him, but also what he himself acknowledges is the open, unfinished, constantly changing nature of his own responses to the question.

> As I look back over the many years and books to the start of my career, now four decades ago, I hope my argument has grown and changed, or at least that it has thickened with qualifications, so that it rests on very different grounds from those from which it emerged originally. Still, how should I respond if one were to turn the words of my earliest title against me now and

charge me with being, after all these years and books, a renewed apologist for poetry? Guilty.[2]

Krieger obviously takes some pride in repeatedly returning to the scene of the "crime" of defending literature against its attackers, often using the very terms of the attackers as part of his defense. But his constantly reevaluated and reformulated "apologies for poetry," and the pleasure he takes in admitting his "guilt" for this crime, also reveal that he is anything but repentant for repeatedly committing the same crime—even if each time with different critical weapons and on slightly different theoretical grounds.

What makes Krieger's apology for poetry so sophisticated and powerful is that it is directed as much toward the cracks in the poetic as toward the wall certain poets and literary theorists try to construct around poetry in order to distinguish the poetic from the non-poetic and keep poetry from being swallowed up by history and politics. The specificity of poetry and thus its difference from ideology are, for Krieger, paradoxically the very reasons why poetry also spills over into the ideological:

> The poetic act represents the failure of the period ideology to sustain the enclosure it would enforce. Instead the poetic act probes to find the fissures of disbelief and slips in to explore and exploit them. . . . And what had been a secure structure of linguistic hegemony is shaken and left tottering—or crumbled. Yet, unlike ideology, the poem itself stands up despite all its underminings, only strengthened by the cracks in its surfaces and depths. The well wrought urn should rather be thought of as the well cracked urn, its substance flowing through it until one cannot tell what is inside from what is outside: the world becomes its language and its language becomes the world.[3]

The more perfectly wrought the urn, the less it reflects or supports ideology, and thus paradoxically the more cracked it is, the more it spills over into ideology, the more insistently and effectively it questions and complicates the ideological in general, standing up on its own, even if insecurely, on a ground it has helped shake or even undermine.

Krieger's "apology for poetry," therefore, is an apology not for poetic closure but for what within poetic closure resists closure and opens poetry, *as poetry,* to what it is not. It is a defense of what in organicism is not organic but nonetheless unthinkable outside of a relation to the organic.

> These essays are not intended as a last-ditch attempt to defend a now-outmoded aesthetic. . . . I do not want to offer once more to theory the metaphor of organicism as if we can take it seriously as an analogy for the work of art. But I do mean to suggest that the aesthetic and philosophical tradition we associate with organicism has had lurking within it tendencies that would break open the closed structure we have usually attributed to it. . . . I want to look into those tendencies in hopes of finding in them their

own resistance. . . . I intend to offer a version that is also a subversion of organicism. (1)

Being a subversion from within, Krieger's apology for organicism is all the more effective in thwarting those attacks from the outside that simply want to do away with all closure, a strategy as dogmatic as the one that would seek to impose closure and transport it from the aesthetic to the political realms.

Krieger has at times expressed impatience with the politicizing (and policing) of literature, but his impatience has never taken the form of a rejection of historical or political questions or issues. For example, he criticizes those who end up "analogizing . . . the text to a body politic," those who every time they come across a unifying principle in literature consider it "as not only totalizing but also totalitarian," who treat closure itself, in all its forms, as "a disease in need of post-modernist therapy" (4). His impatience and criticism are thus directed primarily at the way in which the attack on all forms of closure "slides easily—perhaps at times too easily—from the metaphysical-political realm . . . to the linguistic . . . to the aesthetic" (4). But he also admits, and this seems to me to be crucial, that arguments defending closure—and thus certain dogmatic forms of literary organicism— tend to slide from one realm to the other just as easily, due to what he calls "the structural similarity between arguments for and arguments against closure" (4–5). Krieger thus shows that the argument against closure (and most often also against literary specificity) "derives from the application of the political analogy" to literature, while "the aesthetics of unity" and thus the defense of (a certain form of) literature "derives from its analogizing of aesthetic perception to the perception of the whole objects we act upon in everyday life" (5). Unquestioned analogizing seems to be the problem, more than a belief in or an enmity toward closure and the organic in themselves. It is what links certain acritical apologies for organicism with the most sweeping and dismissive attacks against it.

It is not as if the different perspectives and fields are totally cut off from each other, or as if aesthetic organicism has no relation to political organicism. It is rather that in spite of links, one cannot simply replace one with the other or impose one model on the other. The politicization of art and the aestheticization of politics make the same mistake in applying to one field the specific models, procedures, and ends of the other, and thus deriving or determining one field from the other. The relative specificity of each field, both the literary and the political, is lost in the process.

With Krieger's caveats against facile analogizing in mind, and because the questions of literary specificity and of the role of art and literature in history and politics continue to concern me, I want to raise in my own way the issue of organicism once more, not this time in the literary field per se but rather in the field of history and politics. Because my intent is to avoid "unquestioned analogizing" in Krieger's sense, the point of my analysis has nothing to do with attempts to capture either the aesthetic or literary truth of history and politics, or the historical or political truth of art and literature. What interests me is rather the hybrid nature of what I consider to be a simultaneously aesthetic and political question, one that cannot be completely relegated to or exclusively derived from either field. I also want to follow Krieger in his defense of what could be called an "open" or even postmodern organicism, by which I mean an organicism in which the moment of totalizing is never final or definitive. Rather than eliminating or transcending differences, such an organicism provides a way to link differences to each other without resolving the conflicts and tensions they produce.

II. ORGANICISM, FOR AND AGAINST ITSELF

The work of the nineteenth-century French romantic historian, Jules Michelet—the most "literary" of nineteenth-century historians and for that reason perhaps the most commented upon by literary critics—comes to mind immediately as an example of a developed historical application of organicism, or, better, an example of the use of organicism as the defining element of history. It would be difficult to miss this aspect of Michelet's work, for he repeatedly and triumphantly proclaims his own organicism as his greatest contribution to history. However, rather than constituting the basis for an antirepublican, elitist, totalitarian political position—as it did, for example, for extremist nationalists at the end of the nineteenth century—organicism grounds Michelet's radical, populist republicanism as much as his unquestioning nationalism. His historical work, and the organicism on which it relies, in fact provide a model for national unity which has important political implications for both the extremist nationalist antirepublican right and the democratic left. The problem of the contradictory nature of Michelet's political legacy in turn sheds light on the *literary* question of organicism as well.

A recent article by Lionel Gossman, "Jules Michelet: histoire nationale, biographie, autobiographie," provides an important critical perspective on the literary dimensions of Michelet's historiography, and an analysis of what could be called the positive, even critical effects of his organicism. Gossman argues that Michelet's organic view of the nation represents his most original contribution to historiography and that it is anything but restrictive or dogmatic:

> Michelet's new conception of the nation as a living organism, as *bios* and
> soul, has had consequences almost as revolutionary for historical conscious-
> ness and historiography as the project of Jean-Jacques Rousseau's *Confessions*
> had for the modern consciousness of self and autobiography. For whoever

accepts it, everything is from then on linked to everything else and nothing can be isolated from the whole.[4]

Gossman shows how the organic metaphor in Michelet not only provides a model for thinking the nation and for writing its history, but also greatly expands the scope of history beyond political and diplomatic history to include every aspect of life.

Organicism in Michelet is thus, at least initially, a way of moving history from an exclusive concern with great events, and the kings, queens, and military heroes allegedly responsible for them, to an appreciation of everyday life and the voices of those silenced by the history of great events. Under the banner of organicism, Michelet opens history up to those groups, classes, forces, and subjects which traditionally had no place in history. The concept or metaphor of organicism also provides him with ways to link these various elements together, or allows him to argue that they are already linked together.

In a letter written in December of 1833, Michelet describes the advantages of his own organic view of history and the historiographical practices it supports, in comparison with the views and practices of other schools of history:

> The picturesque school of history has been superficial; it has said nothing about interior life and has spoken neither about art, nor law, nor religion, nor even about geography, which more than anything else it considers necessary to its point of view. The philosophical school has been dry and boring. . . . They have neither the heart nor the feeling for art. They do not realize that all this lives and moves, that all these elements—philosophy, religion, art, law, literature—engender themselves, one after the other. . . . Before me, no one spoke of geography as an historian; no one attempted the history of art in the Middle Ages. I except neither the Germans nor the author of *Notre-Dame de Paris*. He circled around monuments. Me, I showed how this vegetation of stone germinated and grew.[5]

The historical enterprise of Michelet thus potentially touches all aspects of economic, political, geographic, and cultural life, none of which in principle is more important than any other because all are elements of the same national organism and are engendered by and grow in connection with all the others. It should be noted that a certain "feeling for art" has an important role to play in understanding the way all aspects of history "live" and "move," how even monuments constitute an integral part of the germination and growth of "the vegetation" which is the national culture, the life of the nation itself.

Michelet's primary concern, and the principal subject of his histories, is of course the French nation, whose "life" provides the underlying principle of continuity in all of Michelet's histories. Michelet repeatedly argues that he was the first (and only) historian to portray the nation as a "living person," which means at the very least that all history for him is biography, the narrative of the life of this collective and, he claims, organic subject. In Michelet's organicism, not only is everything linked, but, as Gossman shows, every part stands for every other part and is in a synecdochal relation with the whole as well: Michelet's is an "idea of the nation as *bios,* as an enormous living body, of which each member, linked organically with all others and with the totality, is like the reflection of and key to the whole" (42). From the perspective of Michelet's organicism, no detail is too small, no subject too insignificant, no force too disruptive, no heterogeneity too divisive to be ignored by the totality or to be rejected by it out of hand, because each is a part of the functioning of the totality and in this sense each reflects it. Each "I" is in itself a potential or actual "we"; each part, in itself, is a miniaturized version of the whole. And as Gossman shows, the narrative of the life of the collective, living person called the nation—its "biography"—is inseparable from and reflected in the narrative of Michelet's own life—his *autobiography.* Michelet's organicism thus provides him with the means for unifying and totalizing all elements of the nation's and his own life. The organic metaphor provides an apparently solid ground for personification, for the depiction of the nation as a living person dependent on the diversified elements and forces which both constitute and disrupt its organic totality.

Examples abound in Michelet's work of what could be called the common application of the organic metaphor. In an early work, *Introduction à l'histoire universelle* (1831), he gives an idealized description of the political harmony of Europe using the image of a living organism: "Modern Europe is a very complex organism whose unity, whose soul and life, is not in one or another predominant part but in their mutual relation and arrangement, in their profound meshing together, in their intimate harmony" (*OC* 2:238). When the organic metaphor is applied to Europe, its linguistic, cultural, religious, and ethnic diversity and the political conflicts inevitably produced by it appear to Michelet's eyes (even if only ideally) as the harmonious functions of a single, living organism. It is certainly not politics per se that could bring about such harmony, because the politics of Europe are for him competitive, divisive, and destructive. What is needed to make a complex but harmonious totality out of different countries with different and conflicting interests is not the external political repression of differences, but rather the total organic transformation and transcendence of political differences from within each national unity.

Michelet's organicism is, however, uncompromising. In the preface to his monumental *Histoire de France,* he argues that organicism dictates a specific general task to the historian: to uncover the basis for the unity in all things. Either the historian will penetrate the secrets of the unity of life or he will fail as an historian; either he will capture the organic whole or he will capture nothing:

Life has a sovereign and very demanding condition. It is truly life only inasmuch as it is complete. Its organs are all interconnected and act only together. Our functions are linked together, and each one supposes all the others. If one were to lack, then nothing would work anymore. . . . Thus, all or nothing. . . . My historical problem . . . presented itself as *the resurrection of integral life*, not on its surfaces but on the level of its profound, interior organisms. No wise man had even dreamed of this. Luckily, I wasn't a wise man. (*OC* 4:11–12)

It is in fact not the wise, objective scientist, but the intuitive, "instinctual" poet, capable of penetrating the surfaces of history and life, who senses what is not visible to the eye alone. The poet-historian must always have one eye on the way superficial, political unity works, on how material conditions create closure and a sense of totalization. He must also, however, have his other eye on what complicates surface unity and thereby indicates the existence of a higher form of spiritual unity, not determined by geography, race, or the politics of ideologies, parties, and politicians. Michelet's admission of a deficiency in wisdom, of a lack of logical, deductive philosophical or political reasoning, in fact represents what he also feels is his greatest gift as an historian and "poet."

Michelet presents life both in terms of its unity at any one moment and in terms of the continuity among what appear to be the diverse moments of existence: "True life has a completely different sign, its continuity. Born in a burst, it continues on and grows placidly, slowly, *uno tenore*. Its unity is not that of a little play in five acts but . . . the harmonic identity of the soul" (*OC* 4:12). Life itself thus provides the model for both the unity and the continuity of history, of the collective histories of various peoples and of the particular histories of individuals. The history that narrates life itself is not the "little play" staged to amuse and divert the audience, but the total, organic poetic work. The historian is in this sense not just the biographer of the collective "person" called the nation; he is also in some sense the biographer of life itself, the "poet" able to penetrate and resurrect the deep organic unity of *bios* in all its forms.

Just as personification is perhaps the dominant trope in Michelet's histories, personhood is the summit of life for him, for self-creation is ultimately the determining element of Michelet's organicism, and only a person can have a life that is self-created, not merely unified and continuous. The organicity of life and history is progressive and hierarchical. It consists of the negation and transcendence of material determinants such as race into higher spiritual unities through the process of constant self-creation. This for Michelet is the path nations had to take:

Race, the strong and dominant element in barbaric times, before the great work of nations, is less sensible, is feeble, almost erased to the extent that each nation elaborates and personifies itself. . . . It is the powerful work of

> self on self by which France, through its own progress, will transform all
> brute elements. . . . France made France, and the fatal element of race
> seems to me secondary. France is the daughter of her freedom. (*OC* 4 : 13)

France made itself; the French people, as the model for all peoples, transformed itself from a mixture of different races into a unified people, an autonomous, self-conscious, creative and self-created, spiritual person. France
created itself freely, as the poet creates the poem, through a transformation
of "brute elements," but through the process of creation the poet is also
transformed by his own creation. The freedom to make oneself, and the *process* of self-creation, therefore constitute the bases of a truly organic unity,
one that cannot be imposed from the outside but arises only out of the *internal* transformation of disparate parts into a functioning unity.

Organicism also supports Michelet's antiracial or antiracist position.
Michelet attacks those historians who evoke the racial (or racist) foundations for national history because he is an *antimaterialist* organicist, for whom
race, geography, and climate are the primary material determinants that
must be negated and transcended. If the diversity of races constituting
a people represents for him its greatest strength, it does so only if that diversity is successfully unified, if the many become one. And according to
Michelet, only the spirit unifies: "Matter wants dispersion, spirit wants unity.
Essentially divisible matter aspires to disunion, discord. Material unity is
nonsense. In politics, it is tyranny. Spirit alone has the right to unify, alone
it includes" (*OC* 4 : 328). On the one hand, race is a principle of division and
destruction when it constitutes the principal or exclusive determinant of
a nation or a people. On the other hand, the mixture of races is constitutive and constructive when different races become part of a unified, organic
whole, when race has been transcended, and a free, self-created people born.
The political unification of a people on the basis of race, ethnicity, or class
alone is always for Michelet a form of tyranny, even when it is carried out
in the name of the Revolution. Unification must come from below and not
be imposed from above; it must arise out of and manifest the diversity constituting it which Michelet claims strictly political totalizations necessarily
destroy.

Unification in Michelet's terms is thus not organic unity, but only its ex-
terior form. This is why unification can produce disunity and disharmony.
For example, in his *Histoire de la Révolution française,* Michelet stresses the importance of unity for a people, even arguing that it is a question of life or
death: "The unity of the homeland, the indivisibility of the Republic, is the
holy and sacred word of 1793. . . . *No life outside of unity.* For organized beings, to be divided is to perish." But he also distinguishes the "sublime idea
of true Unity" of the people in the Revolution from both "the false royal
unity that for so long covered over a real disunion" and the "feeble federal

unity of the United States and Switzerland which is nothing more than con-
sensual discord" (*OC* 1 : 195). In fact, the "idea of true Unity" will, except at
a very limited number of moments in history, remain just that—a sublime
idea. This idea is repeatedly contrasted with the false, feeble, and often tyran-
nical political unities—even those produced by the Revolution—that are
in fact disguised forms of disunion.

In terms of class differences, the historical product of the mixing of classes
is anything but positive, for it has produced a "bastard" class—the middle
class. Though it might pretend to be universal, the middle class in reality
lacks an identity of its own: "There has been between classes not union and
association but rapid and vulgar mixture [*mélange*]. . . . This class of all
classes, this bastard mixture which was made so quickly and which is weak-
ening already, will it be productive? I doubt it. The mule is sterile."[6] Steril-
ity is the sign of an organism that doesn't work and can't (re)produce, of an
artificial, forced mixture without its own integrity or unity. Organicism demands unity, but not just any unity and not at any price. Certainly not at the
price of the negation of the productive potential of the various elements—
in this instance, the different social classes—that contrast with each other
and are in conflict. In Michelet's organicism, as in all organicisms, distinctions have to be constantly made between artificial, material mixtures and
true organic (spiritual) unities. Unity as such cannot be generalized.

Michelet's most developed discussion of the two opposed tendencies
within any organic unity or process of unification—whether historical, political, or aesthetic—occurs in *Le Peuple,* and is focused on "the man of genius." Michelet evokes this highly charged romantic ideal of the literary and
scientific visionary in order to demonstrate how the dialectic of division and
unification actually works, as a dialectic of criticism and complication, on
the one hand, and of spontaneous intuition and simplification on the other.

> [The genius is] the man who, in acquiring the gifts of the critic, retains the
> gifts of the simple man. These two men, opposed everywhere else, are rec-
> onciled in him. At the moment when his interior critique seems to have
> pushed him toward infinite division, the simple man in him maintains the
> present unity for him. He always conserves the feeling for life and keeps it
> indivisible. But even though the genius has in him these two powers, his love
> of living harmony and the tender respect for life are so strong that he would
> sacrifice research and science itself if they could be obtained only by means
> of dismemberment. Of the two men that are in him, he would leave the one
> who divides; the simple man would remain. (184)

The genius would not be a genius if he were simply simple, if all he had to
do was affirm and slavishly imitate the harmony that already existed outside
him and/or in him. And he certainly would not be a genius if he were simply a critic, a man of distinctions and divisions. The choice of the simple

man is thus at the same time the choice of the complex man, that is, the choice of the *unity* that binds the critic and the simple man together. The respect for unity is for a unity made out of division, a unity that always risks being torn apart by the very elements that constitute it and create the demand for it.

If the mule (or the bourgeoisie) is sterile, the genius represents creativity and productivity in their highest form because he embodies the reconciliation of all sexual, generational, cultural, and class differences: "He is in some sense man and woman, child and adult, barbarian and civilized, people and aristocrat. . . . He alone is complete; also he alone can engender" (187). The art of the genius is to have made his works and himself into the perfect work of art, into the ultimate figure of dialectical synthesis and production, the natural product that also serves as the model for art: "If perfection is not of this world, the man who approaches it the most closely is in all appearances harmonic and fertile man. . . . This overabundance of gifts, this fecundity, this lasting creation, each is apparently the sign that we should find there the plenitude of nature and the model of art" (187). The genius is not just the origin of the organic work of art; he is also the most complete and elevated example of art, a masterpiece (*chef-d'oeuvre*) in himself.

The genius is also, therefore, or at least for Michelet he should be, the model for society in general: "The art of the social, the most complicated of all, should look very carefully to see if this masterpiece of God, in which rich diversity is in harmony in a fertile unity, cannot shed some light on the object of its own pursuits" (187). Michelet's organicism is thus essentially aesthetic, and as such it serves as a model for the art of the social and the political as well. It, and not politics or the application of political principles, is the fundamental model for the active, internal unification of diversity and for the creation and production of works modeled after such a procedure. In the political realm, these organic works of art have a particular name: "The world [is] harmonically divided into these great and beautiful systems that are called nations" (219). Michelet is thus an aesthetic organicist before being a specifically *French* nationalist, in the sense that the *nation-form* itself is for him the highest form of political art, the organic form that maintains diversity in harmony. In his eyes, the privilege of the French is based on their mastery of the *art* of the creation of the nation-form and therefore their mastery of their own self-creation.

Michelet's ultimate poetic-political credo for both the individual and for the people is: "Be yourself." For what threatens a people more than anything else is *imitation* of the other. Imitation destroys the imagination and all possibility of creativity. It brings into the living organism material that is already formed, dead, foreign—material that cannot be successfully appropriated and made an active, integral part of the organism:

One takes from a neighboring people something that in him is living. One appropriates it as well as one can, in spite of the repugnance of a organism that was not made for it. But it is a foreign body that you thus allow into your flesh; it's an inert and dead thing, it's death that you adopt. What can be said if this thing is not only foreign and different but enemy[?] (224)

The difference between imitation and assimilation is quite slight. Being yourself means assimilating but not imitating others; being a living "poetic" organism means appropriating everything that can be made a living part of the organism and rejecting and expelling out of the organism everything which remains a foreign body and thus would ultimately threaten the very life of the organism into which it is forced.

This is not an argument for ethnic or cultural purity or purification, however, for Michelet throughout his work argues that the strength of the French comes precisely from the diversity of their ethnic and racial origins, from the fact that the French have been able to assimilate "others" into themselves and continually remake themselves and remain one. Still, such an exclusion of the foreign, no matter on what level it occurs, does of course present a problem. For even if ethnic, racial, cultural, and religious diversity are crucial for the formation of a people, there is always a moment when the foreign must be confronted and rejected, when the internal demands of the living organism must expel every foreign body that interrupts or complicates its life and the smooth functioning of its internal organs. The very organic model that depends on diversity and complexity thus also provides the basis for an argument against them.

If the choice is presented as being one between life and death, the living organism must always choose its own life over the death represented by the foreign, just as it chooses its own internal functioning over the imitation of others. Here it is not even a question of hastily analogizing aesthetic perception to the perception of sociopolitical objects, but rather a contradiction built into the model or metaphor of organicism itself. Organicism always reaches its limit at precisely the point where the living, self-created organism functions the most smoothly and completes itself, thus closing itself off to everything that is not itself and that cannot be incorporated into what it has become. In this sense organicism is always "against itself" by having to be at some point—at the moment of the realization or completion of unity—against everything that is determined to be foreign to the unity the living organism has achieved. It thus has to be against elements, no matter what their origin or nature, which could, in principle, have been the very components that might have been actively linked together to constitute organic unity, or at least that would have been able to lose their foreignness by being assimilated into the national (or poetic) organism.

Michelet's organicism—that is, his use of the metaphor of a living organism to characterize the nation—reaches its limit when he must defend the national organism itself against the disruption caused by the foreign. At such moments, his nationalist organicism clearly offers support for extremist defenses of the nation, based on religious, cultural, political, or even racial grounds. At the same time, it offers the model of a people that is formed *by itself* but *out of* "foreign" elements, and thus not determined by any material factors, certainly not by race.

Michelet's organicism is thus constituted by an irresolvable tension between the incorporation and the rejection of the foreign. Near the end of his life, and after France's humiliating defeat in the Franco-Prussian war, Michelet attacked Germany's annexation of Alsace-Lorraine in *La France devant l'Europe*, on both racial and linguistic grounds. In this attack, he evokes the special status of the French people, whom he characterizes as the most linguistically, culturally, and racially diversified, *and thus* the most perfectly unified, of peoples. "There is one thing that is extremely ancient and specific to this country; it is the singular perfection with which the fusion of races was accomplished in it, the exchange and marriage of diverse populations" (*OC* 20:705). The "singular perfection" of organic unity clearly arises only out of such diversity and the resulting exchanges and marriages necessary to fuse the various populations together. A country that has no need of such fusion is one that is paradoxically *inorganic*, precisely because its unification depends exclusively on geographical, political, or racial factors. It may perhaps constitute a "natural" or material totality, but its unity, by not being sufficiently "aesthetic," that is, self-made, cannot be considered truly *organic*.

Michelet claims that the French are the "only people" to possess such perfect organic unity, and because of that, they are the one people, the only national organism, that cannot afford to lose any of its members. The French people is "the least dismemberable, the one from whom, its circulation being rapid and perfect, a member cannot be separated" (*OC* 20:705). This applies especially to its members that have a different ethnic, linguistic, or cultural formation than the peoples constituting the majority of the organism. To remove such members violently, and implant them or graft them onto another organism that is not yet formed, represents for Michelet the height of folly: "To pull out Alsace and Lorraine from a living body, from the strongest organic unity that ever was, to extract these intestines from us with a knife in order to stuff them into a body like Germany which is still being formed, is a strange form of surgery" (*OC* 20:706). Such transplants cannot take, because they weaken and even destroy the body from which the members are taken as well as the body into which they are grafted or "stuffed," as if into a sausage. In other words, the identity of the parts can only come from the organism in which they function. Assimilation is necessary for the formation, growth, and perfection of the organism, while both the surgical removal of any of its members and the violent, artificial graft-ings of new members bring about its deformation and demise. The line between assimilation and grafting is very fine and can never be determined outside of the play of elements and forces that constitute the organism in the first place.

Michelet repeatedly insists that, even if parts cannot be removed from the whole without causing serious damage to its unity, at the same time the process of unification is never completely accomplished. Unity as such, were it to be achieved, would signal the end of the harmonious union based on diversity:

> Union always advances in this way without the risk of ever achieving unity. . . . If the impossible happened and all diversity ceased to be, if unity were achieved, every nation singing the same note, the concert would be over. . . . The monotonous and barbaric world could then die, without even a regret. (*Le Peuple,* 220)

This metaphor of the concert works as a way of describing both relations among different nations and the relations of various peoples and groups within each nation. In each case, their death comes only when organic unity and closure are in fact achieved. The moments during the Revolutions of 1789 and 1830 in which, Michelet claims, all social, political, and regional divisions were overcome and the organic unity of the people spontaneously manifested itself on the historical scene, did not and in fact could not be perpetuated in history. Organic unities serve in his work as ideals to be pursued in the future, not models to be *applied* to the present (or the future).[7]

What Michelet is proposing for the nation is a totalizing process without totalization, a historical-political, nationalist organicism without closure. And this is perhaps another reason why his nationalism has two very different, even opposed historical implications. As an applied organicism that stresses the organic integrity of each nation as opposed to every other nation, it gives support to extremist forms of nationalism. As an unfinished, incomplete, self-contradictory organicism that keeps the nation open to what it is not, it leads in an entirely different direction. Extremist nationalisms and opponents of nationalism can both find support for their positions in Michelet, but only if they read him selectively. Read in terms of the conflicting tendencies found in his nationalist organicism, his organicism should perhaps also be considered a (nationalist) organicism against itself.

Murray Krieger argues that in the most critical expressions of literary organicism, from Aristotle to the present, the elements that most risk undermining the principle of organic unity are neither excluded nor admitted only reluctantly into the organism constituted by the poem. Rather, the critical organicist welcomes these elements into the poem and makes the struggle to incorporate or assimilate them central to its organic unity itself. What Krieger claims is the case for Aristotelian poetics would certainly apply to Michelet's nationalist historiography as well: "Greatness for him [Aristotle] may well be measured by the intensity of the struggle, by the resistance of the obstacles to an easy system of probability, by the difficulty with which unity—and hence poetic beauty—is achieved."[8] And as we have seen, at the very moment it is allegedly "achieved," true, dynamic organic unity is in a sense lost, for when the process of unification ends, so does organic unity. To achieve it is always to lose it.

If, as Krieger also argues, the explanations and justifications of how and where the poetic or political system completes itself are inevitably based on aesthetic mystifications—mystifications of the Poem or, in Michelet's case, of the People—it is also true that opposing forces of resistance to unity can be found underlying and resisting such mystifications. In terms of the necessarily unfinished nature of the contradictory dynamics constituting an "organicism [that works] against itself"—regardless of whether the metaphor of organic unity refers to a literary, historical, or political entity—all claims to aesthetic (or historical) closure can be seen as potentially "self-undermining." The unity of the poem (and the people) can be argued thus to constitute a "restless and, hence, endangered oneness"—in spite of all poetic and political (ideological) arguments to the contrary.[9] Krieger's organicism, one of the most radical and critical of organicisms—and perhaps the only defensible form of organicism today—affirms and at the same time breaks with the organic tradition whose apology it writes. Looking back on Michelet from the critical perspective on organicism Krieger delineates allows us to see all the more clearly in Michelet a militant nationalist who nevertheless preferred "restless and endangered oneness" to determinable unity, an organicist for whom closure was more a problem than a solution.

Krieger defends literary organicism only by opening it up to the diversity that *originally* and, in his interpretation, *finally* constitutes it. He defends literature by insisting on literature's resistance to ideology and what I would now call an organicism that is exclusively *for itself*. In fact, he makes the analysis and support of that resistance the primary obligation of the literary critic: "It is up to the critic to respond to the obligation to dwell upon that resistance [to ideological closure] as a special feature of literature."[10] I would argue that the same obligation should be carried over into the study of history and politics, where the critic should dwell on what in history, as well as literature, resists organic closure and the ideological and aesthetic ideologies that support it.

Meeting this obligation is perhaps never more necessary than when the critic is confronted with a form of history such as Michelet's, which borrows organic models, strategies, and practices from literature and attempts to assimilate them into, rather than simply apply them to, history and politics. In doing so, history makes the poetics (not the politics) of the people its central concern, and invites the literary critic as well as the historian to investigate the different ways literature and history both support and resist the aesthetic and political closures and mystifications characteristic of ideology.

NOTES

1. Benjamin's concluding remarks in the essay are the following: "Mankind, which in Homer's time was an object of contemplation for the Olympian gods, now is one for itself. Its self-alienation has reached such a degree that it can experience its own destruction as an aesthetic pleasure of the first order. This is the situation of politics which Fascism is rendering aesthetic. Communism responds by politicizing art" ("The Work of Art in the Age of Mechanical Reproduction," in *Illuminations,* trans. Harry Zohn [New York: Schocken, 1968], 242).

2. Murray Krieger, *The Institution of Theory* (Baltimore: Johns Hopkins University Press, 1994), 91–92.

3. Murray Krieger, *A Reopening of Closure: Organicism Against Itself* (New York: Columbia University Press, 1989), 29. Further citations will be made parenthetically in the text.

4. Lionel Gossman, "Jules Michelet: histoire nationale, biographie, autobiographie," *Littérature* 102 (May 1996): 29–54, quotation from 36, my translation. Further citations will be made parenthetically in the text.

5. Jules Michelet, *Oeuvres complètes,* ed. Paul Viallaneix, 20 vols. (Paris: Flammarion, 1971–87), 4:8, my translation. Further citations will be made in the text as *OC.*

6. Jules Michelet, *Le Peuple,* ed. Paul Viallaneix (Paris: Flammarion, 1974), 162–63, my translation. Further citations will be made parenthetically in the text.

7. In his *Histoire de la Révolution française,* Michelet characterizes what for him is the culmination of the French Revolution, the Fête de la Fédération, as the total transcendence of history, for in a single moment all material limitations, even space and time themselves, were negated and a new creation produced, a new spiritual people born:

> Where are the ancient differences of place and race, those geographic oppositions which are so strong, so decisive? Everything disappeared, geography is killed. No more mountains, no more rivers, no more obstacles between men. . . . The two material conditions to which life is subjected, time and space, perished. . . . A strange *vita nuova* begins for France, one that is eminently spiritual and that makes its Revolution a kind of dream, at times delightful, at times terrible.

But if the Revolution in one moment spectacularly accomplishes the end of all of history, that moment cannot be sustained in or as history. Revolution thus has the characteristics of an intense aesthetic experience of immanence; it is a dream that is at the same time beautiful and frightening in its power and scope. (Quotation from Jules Michelet, *Histoire de la Révolution française,* ed. Gérard Walter, 2 vols. [Paris: Gallimard, 1952], 1:406.)

8. Krieger, *Reopening of Closure,* 38.

9. Ibid., 42, 52.

10. Krieger, *Institution of Theory,* 47.

CHAPTER EIGHT

Of Wisdom and Competence

Wesley Morris

I

I remember two demonstrations, two strategies of interpretation, that characterized literary criticism in the modern/postmodern age. The modernist approach was epitomized by Murray Krieger's brilliant reading of John Donne's "The Canonization." Postmodernism was equally well represented by Geoffrey Hartman's startling elucidation of W. B. Yeats's "Leda and the Swan." I was witness to Krieger's readings of Donne; Hartman's display was reported to me. Nonetheless, the two have remained bound together in my mind for the more than three decades that followed my entry into literary theory in the 1960s. Curiously, both interpretations rest on distinct perceptions of the singlemost important modernist metaphor: the ontological suggestiveness of the image of a "center." For Krieger, the poetic process is constitutive of a verbal structure organized by a central metaphor or complex of metaphors. The poem slows our progress as readers and thickens into "corporeality," into the uniqueness of an aesthetic experience. Hartman's approach is deconstructive of centers; the ontology of the poem's closed structure unravels in an atomic breakdown of metaphoric organization into metonymic seriality.

Krieger's interpretation of "The Canonization" focuses, appropriately, on the poem's central stanza, where the image of a "miraculous" transformation appears in the poem's complex metaphoric structure.

Call us what you will, wee are made such by love;
　　Call her one, mee another flye.
We'are Tapers too, and at our own cost die,
　　And wee in us find the' Eagle and the Dove,

> The Phoenix ridle hath more wit
> By us, we two being one, are it.
> So to one neutral thing both sexes fit,
>   Wee dye and rise the same, and prove
>   Mysterious by this love.[1]

The poet's images move us from the trivial to the profound. We link the disparate items: "flye" and "Tapers" to "Eagle and Dove," then to "Phoenix." The "flye," of course, is a moth drawn to the heat of the candle by an irresistible desire that is self-destructive, and so, too, the candle consumes itself in its own burning. The "Eagle and Dove" are traditional masculine and feminine symbols joined here grammatically and figuratively and linked to the self-destructive flame of the "flye" and the "Taper," both in the momentariness of the passion of lovemaking and in the figurative union of two into one. Thus self-consuming desire is overwritten as sexual passion, and the lover and his mistress "die," joined as one in orgasmic pleasure, only to rise again to reawakened desire, like the legendary "Phoenix" whose five-hundred-year cycle of life and fiery death lends "mystery," mythic status, to all who "dye and rise the same," that is, to all lovers at all times.

The fourth stanza builds upon the extravagant claims of the third, elevating the lovers to the status of "legendary" figures, far above mere history ("Chronicle"), and rejecting the too-earthly image of "tombes" as unfit to preserve in remembrance their "mysterious" remains, electing instead those archetypal love poems, Renaissance "sonnets," which will sing in praise of the lovers just as "hymns" sing eternal praise to holy saints. Poetry, therefore, is a fitting monument to love's passion, "As well a well wrought urne becomes / The greatest ashes, as halfe-acre tombes." And the profane lovers are linked irrevocably to the sacred stature of the blessed and immortal saints.

If the thrust of Krieger's reading of "The Canonization" is toward closure, self-referentiality, and "contextualism" in the sense of organic form, Hartman's reading of Yeats's outrageous sonnet deconstructs the organic. Here the sonnet, with its rigid boundaries and demand for economy and closure, is broken open by another sort of extravagance. The traditional 4-4-6 stanza form is designed to present a problem or perhaps ask a question in the initial octave, only to resolve the problem or answer the question in the final sestet. But Yeats violates this tradition, and the poem cracks in two in line eleven:

> And Agamemnon dead.
>   Being so caught up,[2]

It is as though another line, a fifteenth, were struggling to enter the tightly guarded domain of fourteen. The sestet is almost, but not quite, a septet.

The close rhyme scheme of the last stanza—e-f-g / e-f-g: "there," "tower," "up" / "air," "power," "drop"—has an extra, upstart non-rhyme: "dead." The hard midline period stop disrupts both traditional rhythms and rhymes that would lead us to a powerful closure. What is at stake here?

The poem's first stanza depicts a rape, and what issues from that violent event is a narrative of destruction and death. The questions raised in the second stanza are never answered, merely repeated in the final two lines. They are diminished by the vividness of "And Agamemnon dead." This half line reveals the consequences of that originary violence; it is a remarkable expression that collapses upon itself, repeats itself through the assonance of "Agamemnon dead," doubling the sounds: "A . . . a . . . n . . . n . . . d . . . d," tripling the "And" which initiates the phrase. Mythic meaningfulness, or even the eventfulness of legend/history, explode into echoing "linking" words prophesying unending conjunctions, limitless supplementation: "and . . . and . . . and. . . ." Here the age of the postmodern has penetrated (violently?) the Idealism of the age of the modern.

II

There seemed a polarity in these two demonstrations during the emerging of postmodernism; that emergence was a triumph of various structuralisms over formalism, but a struggle for hegemony had radicalized critical methodologies into apparent oppositions. The differences between these two readings of poetry, like many cultural distinctions, had been legitimized by the era, by political and ethical confrontations driving theory in the 1970s and 1980s toward undecidables. In time, postmodernism revealed itself to be an extension of modernism, indeed, a valuable corrective. The postmodern era arose Phoenix-like from the dying embers of what modernism had become.

The political climate of the times redirected early-twentieth-century modernism's slide into avant-garde aestheticism by turning formalism away from modernist political ineffectuality and social unconcern. During the 1960s, modernism was purged of its Romantic sense of loss, its celebration of heroic failure and egocentric quests for subjectivity; in this reincarnation modernism had to abandon its self-indulgent obsession with the present moment. Postmodernism was one of the forces that enabled a neomodernism, but in so doing postmodernism failed to pursue the central ethical interest of authentic modernism: the belief that the primary obligation of all generations is what comes after the "now." In the extremity of its attack on the sacred "presence" of modernist formalism, the postmodern lost sight of its own time.

This postmodern reformation emerged against a background of shared phobic reactions. In the beginning, modernism had struggled to write itself out of history. The "drag" of the past, the illusions of memory, it seemed to modernists, threatened the purity of modernism's vision and the transcendental suggestiveness of its principal expressive device: the symbol. Postmodernism took up a similar antihistoricism, protecting the freeplay of its communicative device: the sign. At the heart of this retreat from history in both movements is modernism's failure to coexist with, and postmodernism's oversimplification of, technology. Technology is a specific way of knowing the world, a mastery of how things work rather than what things are. Technology orients thought toward pragmatism and functionalism and away from ontology and history; it diverts knowledge and wisdom toward information and competence. Postmodernism largely accepted the modernist reading that branded technology (from industrialization to artificial intelligence to genetic engineering) as dehumanizing. Modernism abhorred it; postmodernism embraced it. Both granted technology far too much force in the construction of social relationships.

In its countermove against technology, modernism gathered its finest images from nineteenth-century biology, from the humanization of form, from the mystique of organic life represented in the developmental marvels of the human body vitalized by a desire for wholeness. The consequent images of a unique and total individuality asserted modernism's uncompromising polarity to "the machine." On the other hand, postmodernism conceived of itself as coordinated with the invasion of the totalized modernist body by molecular chemistry; with the demystification, if not outright erasure, of the grandeur and mystique of the organic. Genetic codes and highly organized and controlled interactions of amino acids and paired bases revised the modernist imagination by demythologizing "life." Postmodern biology radically decentralized the modernist "subject," miniaturizing and distributing the productive and reproductive work of the modernist "whole" individual across a galaxy of billions of infinitely iterable cells managed and regulated by non-organic executive codes. The body was reimagined as a special kind of machine (a cyborg), and desire was rewritten as language itself or cultural encoding (a Symbolic Order).

Each biology produced its own specialized images or overdetermined buzz words. Modernism reveled in the suggestiveness of origins, growth, fulfillment, closure, independence, freedom, subjectivity, and identity. Postmodernism celebrated structure, repetition, clone, model, simulation, power relations, and difference. The language of modernism was insistently referential despite its protests to the contrary; the dream of the modern was a revelation of foundational organic being. The language of the postmodern was equally referential, regardless of Saussurian convention and arbitration; the project of postmodernism was a description of the ethical world.

Postmodernism drew part of its strength in this ethical reform project from an early-twentieth-century attack on formalism initially orchestrated by Marxian theorists. This Marxian critique was expressed in political terms, convicting modernism of abandoning its foundation in social engagement, of retreating from ethical responsibility and social commitment. Hampered by a plethora of internecine squabbles, and confronted by the powerful mythology of bourgeois individualism, Marxism had to fight its battles on too many fronts and failed to stem the modernist drift into formalist aestheticism. Marxism offered an alternative world but could not bring about a full swing of the theoretical pendulum. Nevertheless, it gave impetus to structuralism and, therefore, eventually to poststructuralism, which retained significant elements of the Marxian agenda. Yet to differentiate itself from the modern in the worldwide political crises of the 1960s, postmodernism, unlike Marxism, engaged its enemy in the language of form and not politics; postmodernism focused its assault on what it presumed to be modernism's strength. Unfortunately, postmodernism's antiformalist strategy irrevocably bound it to the very formalism it would destroy.

Modernism's strength, of course, was its greatest vulnerability. The humanist appeal of the organic metaphor proved to be dehumanizing, for the moderns troped their master tropes, creating a metaphor of metaphorics, articulating the rule that poetry is always about poetry rather than about the human condition. Organic form situated the aesthetic before the ethical and transformed originality and individuality into the banal. Errant modernism rarefied its formalist metaphors not only beyond experience and time but also outside the reach of language. Modernist metaphor was offered as an image of transcendental order, as liberation from a priori values and as therapy for a middle-class neurosis produced by a perceived collapse of traditional cultural values. By the time that Krieger, through what he called a new historicism, and other neomoderns initiated a return to modernism's post-Romantic, liberationist, one might even say democratic or revolutionary roots, formalism had become reactionary, characterized (somewhat unfairly, certainly, but effectively) as an elitist harangue against difference and a racist and sexist justification of identity, an apology for bourgeois resistance to cultural and political reform. What began as a radical challenge to the status quo, as a critique of certain Enlightenment repressions and exploitations, became an escapist disengagement from the world, a translation of the language of culture into the language of metaphysics. Each metaphor of this modernist paradigm echoed a Conradian cry of horror at the slightest touch of reality, as if "the real" contaminated the formal purity of the modernist dream.

But have we not simply learned to read modernism this way because postmodernism desired to write itself as the end of the modern? Is not the extremity of this metaphysics of the modernist metaphor a product of retrospective scapegoating? Must we read the dictum that poetry is about poetry narrowly, as a retreat from reality? These are difficult questions; for the moment it will suffice to note that modernism does not bear all the guilt, although it was certainly complicit in its own deformation. What is clear is that the deconstruction of modernist formalism, in the almost obsessive dismemberment of the organic metaphor, was an unforeseen trap for the postmodern. Blinded to the historical position of modernism by its own refusal of history, postmodernism also lost sight of its social and political grounding. It deconstructed modern formalism with a powerful critique that, ironically, imprisoned postmodernism within the same socially irresponsible formal logic that it shared with misdirected modernism. Deconstruction, so central to postmodern interpretation, hardened into an unproductive symbiosis with the modern.

Postmodernism, proposing its difference from the modern, argued that our recognition of an antimetaphysics embedded in all grand metaphysical schemata derived from our learning to read the postmodern way. Modernist aestheticism, according to this exposé, had blinded modernist thought to its unacknowledged metaphysical assumptions. Hence, quintessentially nonmetaphysical postmodernism established itself as "prior" to the modern, as a reality of the nonmetaphysical which was "already" embedded in the classical, Greek "origins" of modern Western thought, as a repressed vision "always" ready to reveal itself in the Western philosophies which derived from that originary tradition, especially in the modernist illusion of having escaped metaphysics. Yet this "always already" principle also lifts itself out of time and history into the banal, into the very "sameness" for which postmodernism condemned modernism. Deconstruction, despite its militant vitality and command of Western academia, declined into a rote practice, into repetitious critiques unveiling infinite identical aporias, into the emptiness of "and . . . and . . . and. . . ." All language was about all language and, much as with deviant, ivory tower modernism, nothing could be said about actual lived experience. Exposing the fallacious logic of modernist metaphysical metaphors to Nietzschean scorn also deconstructed the timeless first principle of postmodernism, *différance*, allowing us a not so gentle fall back into time where we discover that historical differences are the only ones we have available to us. History appears to be the true counter to metaphysics.

III

The distinction between modernism and postmodernism is a genuinely historical one. Modernism can be understood only as that which gave rise to postmodernism, and modernism itself must be read as a moment in a history firmly grounded in what we know to be human experience. Of course, the term "modernism" is variously defined. In discourses of philosophy and history, the modern has its origins at least as far back as the Renaissance. But literary modernism is more recent, and it is that more limited perspective that reveals itself in literary imagination, in metaphor.

Literary modernism emerges at the moment of the decline of the image of production and the fetishism of the product, in the age of the decline of individualism. In effect, literary modernism arose on a platform of intense antimodernism, on what was to be read as the crisis of the "self." The production-oriented industrial phase of capitalism, in order to develop highly centralized (monopolistic) institutions, had initiated a reformation of social relations, specifically an uprooting of labor; this produced a complete transformation of the "self" registered bodily, psychologically, and culturally (metaphorically). The strategy required the shift of metaphoric "centers" from local communities to independent "subjects" liberated from identity-conferring bonds with tradition or culture. Workers became mobile in order to go to the factories; labor-intensive production required relocation and urbanization. The metaphor of organic self-realization established a tradition-free individuality and translated readily into a fluid and plentiful workforce. The family and community were partly replaced by wage-alliances between worker and industry; in the words of an old union protest song, the newly discovered subject "owed his soul to the company store" and not to church, community, or home.

Such a strategy, of course, created unexpected difficulties. The organic metaphor suggested independence, self-centered wholeness, as in the Romantic image of the oak fully contained in the tiny acorn. Yet the uprooting and transplanting of the newly discovered organic individual was not problem-free. Uprooting was not always ecologically (socially) sound, for it removed the individual from its native environment without regard to its ability to adapt to new conditions. The projected allegiance of worker to industry was derailed by social bondings arranged according to economic class rather than community, and this gave vital strength to the oppositional strategies of labor unions. In the most highly industrialized nations, however, class identity was held in check by modernism itself, by the very image of individuality and subjectivity that defined bourgeois ideology. The rapid expansion of the middle class absorbed (in fact or fantasy) much of the potentially oppositional working class. At the same time, individualism deepened the inner life of the isolated subject. The metaphor that gave rise to the image of a liberating (bourgeois) individualism came to represent a lacking or "hollowness" at the center of alienated modern being. Desire as a force for both production and material consumption defined the modern self. Problematical individualism was ready for another transformation; modernism was generating the postmodern.

Production-centered individualism had produced very specific metaphoric expressions. The traditional distinction between human and non-human rested on an ancient dichotomy of the human and the monstrous which was always troubled by the metaphor of a half-human beast that transgressed primal boundaries, the terror of the Sphinx. The Western myths of

Oedipus and Eden, as well as Renaissance humanism and the Enlightenment, all persistently tested and reaffirmed the differences that defined the
realm of the human. The image of Bottom, a man with the head of an ass
cavorting across the stage of Shakespeare's festival comedy, *A Midsummer
Night's Dream,* unmistakably marked the limits between the human and the
nonhuman by heightening the differences between reason and magic, culture and nature, or the sacred and the profane. Shakespeare explained away
the dream by associating it with the poet's imagination, with the very idea of
the play itself:

> The poet's eye, in a fine frenzy rolling,
> Doth glance from heaven to earth, from earth to heaven.
> And as imagination bodies forth
> The forms of things unknown, the poet's pen
> Turns them to shapes, and gives to airy nothing
> A local habitation and a name.[3]

The airy nothingness of Bottom's difference, however, lost resonance
in the industrialized urban world of centralized productivity. A new metaphorics arose, coordinated with the emergence of a new technology and an
older mechanization; modernist human difference was determined by the
otherness of the machine and not the animal. Modernism's reaction to the
machine deepened the mystery of the individual, exploited the irrationality of unconscious drives, and resisted every form of materiality in the name
of insubstantial subjectivity. Ironically, that which had formerly been excluded from the realm of the human (the image of Bottom with the head
of an ass—the monstrous, the magical, the natural, the irrational) was now
located deep within the unique individuality of the modern subject: in the
imagination, as Shakespeare had it, but also in the destructive figures of the
human unconscious.

This radical self-centering weakened class identity as well as the traditional sense of community, and it spread across a wide economic panorama.
The portrait of modern loneliness ranged from the figure of a frightened
bourgeois socialite like T. S. Eliot's J. Alfred Prufrock to the "realistic" images of powerless women workers in sweatshops, underpaid laborers on assembly lines, and miners suffering from black lung disease. Scenes of urban
decay dominated the wasteland sensibilities of moderns who clung to the
tenuous self in weak protest against the modern industrial monster which
threatened to transform organic form into mechanical action. The dislocated organic individual drawn to the industrial centers away from native local cultures had become too much of a replaceable part of a larger and dehumanizing mechanical process.

This social decentralization and alienation underwent a rapid and widespread intensification during the modern period, but even as this crisis of

the self was playing itself out in modern literary metaphors, another decentering was under way. A post–World War I globalization was grounded in internationalization, which constituted a second-phase decentralization of industry itself, a redeployment that depended on technological development, on a move beyond the metaphorical oppositions of human versus machine. Modernism, of course, saw technology as a mere component of industrialization, but an emerging postmodernism understood that the new technology was a departure from machine culture as well as production-oriented capitalism. New metaphors would have to be developed to imagine this next reorganization of society and subjectivity. The actual heavy-work phases of manufacturing could be exported to areas of high unemployment and, therefore, of low wages and taxes. The sweatshops and mines were exported to third worlds where they were operated unseen. The assembly of final products could be relocated according to demands of marketing advantage, rather than in urban centers where production and consumption were locally managed. Industry itself, and not just its products, gradually became "portable," to borrow a term from Dickens's inimitable Wemmick. What made this possible, of course, were extraordinary developments in modes of rapid transportation and, particularly, communication. Industry no longer followed the centralizing model of locating itself near sources of raw materials or major shipping ports, and this allowed for repeated renegotiations of favorable economic contracts with local communities, negotiations driven by the ever present leverage of industrial free agency.

We need not see this decentralization of industrial production only in terms of physically moving a factory. Downsizing, mergers, takeovers, restructurings, and robotic manufacture also undermined collective labor power's goal of driving up wages and reforming working conditions. The era of labor unions ended. In the process, the emphasis on production with its metaphoric translation of the individual's organic self-productivity into labor value underwent a radical change. The old individual, with its centralized ego—its dualistic image of public and private, outer mask and inner essence—was reconstructed into a figure of multiple personalities, a schizophrenic plurality. The inner self was projected onto the surface mask and lost its mysterious essence. The new social drama staged not six characters in search of an author but one character with six or more emanations in need not of authorial direction but of games to play. Like Tom Stoppard's brilliant revision of Shakespeare's hapless Rosencrantz and Guildenstern, identity was to be determined by a role performed either competently or poorly. This critical alteration rested on a necessary loss of the power of remembering: in this postmodern revision of Shakespeare's claim that all the world is a stage, Rosencrantz and Guildenstern cannot remember where they were before the curtain rose, before the text, or even which identity is which.

Here we become aware of a shift from the metaphorics of creativity to the metaphorics of performance, from images of production to images of distribution. As both producer and consumer in this postmodern economic biosphere, the individual was forced to demonstrate an aptitude for learning and forgetting, for quickly adapting to new systems, for unhesitatingly changing identities as one might change hats according to the season or roles according to the script. The old image of wholeness was replaced by the image of schizoid disorders. Disorders became the order of the day. The metaphors of organic individuality which emphasized origins, presence, interiority, developmental subjectivity, coherent identity, historicism, responsibility, and judgment, all factors of memory and constituent of wisdom, gave way to orders of information, agency, plurality, and competence. Identity became a function of linking, of incessantly logging on/off; the "I" which centered gave way to the "and" which dispersed.

IV

Thus postmodernism represented a second order of decentering consequent upon modernism's decentering of community through the creation of an image of the self-centered modern subject. Until postmodernism, metaphor had situated subjectivity in relation to familiar reality, a movement designed to stabilize subjectivity. Yet this positioning of the subject was also capable of destabilizing reality. Metaphor *might* be subversive. It rested on the power of recognition or remembering, on a measure of change, development, or difference. Modernism deepened the image of subjectivity. Only the modern subject could decide to make it new; only a coherent self that recalls what has been the case could have the wisdom to make decisions for change. Postmodernism, on the other hand, in deconstructing the organic subject, substituted competence for wisdom, performance for decision-making. It read metaphor as repression of difference, insofar as difference was understood to be a rule rather than a reality. Postmodern metaphors situated subjectivity as belatedness, a play where characters had no past and recalled nothing. As with Stoppard's Rosencrantz and Guildenstern, improvisation within the rules, within the "text," was all there was of being alive.

It is clear now that modernism, despite its resounding rejection of tradition and history, was wedded to remembering. That which was new differentiated itself as a decision to be new, to depart from or project beyond the familiar. Metaphor lent itself to such action. Aristotle observed simply that metaphor was the talent of seeing sameness where others saw only difference; we might say this is the ability to recognize the new within the familiar. Metaphor disappears if it enters the familiar. There is in this a genius for change, a challenge to see the traditional in new ways, to choose to reform that which no longer addresses human needs. This is not to say that metaphor is revolutionary; difference is not always progressive and any change in the way we imagine familiar reality is subject to social ratification. But it is to argue that the force of metaphor is timely, and, consequently, there is a story of metaphor.

Krieger's reading of Donne, therefore, rests on a narrative of metaphoric strategies stretching from the Renaissance to the period marked by the modern/postmodern engagement. On the way to the emergence of modernism there is another very instructive moment worthy of notice, a specific critique of metaphor articulated by Dr. Johnson against what he called metaphysical conceit, the violent linking of heterogeneous ideas very much like those found in Donne's "The Canonization." A critique of this poem in Dr. Johnson's terms would accuse the poet of violating the decorum of that which is deemed "real," those metaphysically legitimized orders of difference that define familiar identities. More importantly, reading Dr. Johnson calls attention to the curious fact that the suppression of difference in metaphoric linkings can also be said to expose certain suppressions of speech and imagination by the legitimation of culturally sanctioned differences, by the rules of difference policed by the "truth" of the age. Such rules of difference rest on foundational assumptions about what things are, as well as what they are worth; Dr. Johnson's observations emerge out of familiar Enlightenment principles, from within the historical context of a specific ontology and ethics under the direction of Cartesian rules for clarity and distinctness, that which instinctively abhors ambiguity and paradox.

Yet one age's clarity is another's confusion, and the rules for linking or differentiating are historically unstable. Donne, and his contemporary "metaphysicals," appeared to be opening a door which Dr. Johnson perceived as dangerous on a cosmic as well as a social level, but which, for all its metaphysical implications, was historically located in its own context of cultural demands for specific images of clarity and distinctness, for familiar reality. Such a perception of writing as potentially subversive or repressive, as a powerful weapon for *either* the suppression *or* the affirmation of difference, has steadily maintained its force in Western thought from Plato to Lévi-Strauss, perhaps bolstered by an endemic Western weakness for metaphysics, but more immediately visible as a companion to the history of various cultural coercions of difference. It is this that lends a particularly sharp edge to Donne's poem, seen as an expression close to blasphemy, defying proper order by mingling the sacred and the profane. Yet Donne's poem is unseemly, not seamless. We understand Donne's poetic tropes to be openly outrageous, deliberately designed to evoke an appreciative outburst of laughter from his audience, perhaps a smiling, a clucking of tongues. It is a play of wit, as he named it himself, and this constitutes his defense against theological outrage, against even Dr. Johnson's critique. Donne did not challenge convention in his linking of lovers and saints; rather he affirmed the socially proper hierarchy of the great chain of being by means of the too-obvious, self-identified play of his foregrounded illegitimate linkings.

For the modern reader the stakes were different; the self-consuming artifice of Donne's wit (as well as the rationalist superiority of Dr. Johnson's critique) moved to a new register. Twentieth-century modernism, reflecting Matthew Arnold's powerful antimodernism, was troubled by a culture perceived to be devoid of beliefs, by a sense of fragmentation in human concerns, miscommunication in human desires, and deeply felt alienations from primary life sources. The thrust of modernist metaphor was toward the production of new orders that would shore up the fragmented world of the new age. Donne's influence on late-modern poetry, therefore, was not in his wit (moderns were driven by Arnoldian seriousness, not by laughter, a weakness readily exploited by postmodern gaiety), but rather in the formal extremities of his connectives, in the metaphoric technique which suggested that radical heterogeneities could be contained in a poetic illusion of a different order. Robert Penn Warren called this the necessity of "making peace with Mercutio," the necessity for the modern poet to embrace oppositional irony as a defense against the potentially destructive forces of modernist skepticism.[4] In fact, this constituted a preemptive strike against postmodernism and the paratactic freeplay of "ands." The modern poet, Warren asserted, must have the courage of her metaphors. This courage was another sort of metaphysical conceit, an arrogance of linking, a daring of heterogeneity in the facing of recalcitrant reality or fragmented human experience, even against the self-deconstructive nature of language itself, while asserting, with clamoring skepticism and sometimes blatant irony, an impossible fiction of momentary harmony and unity—the merest "idea of order," according to Wallace Stevens.[5]

Perhaps this explains the force of modern characters like Eliot's J. Alfred Prufrock, who talk and talk against the impossibility of self-expression, who talk and talk of things, and others, and ideas, and visions, and revisions in a futile quest for the single image or word or metaphor that will contain and order the resistant multiplicity of modern experience.

> After the sunsets and the dooryards and the sprinkled streets,
> After the novels, after the teacups, after the skirts that trail along the floor—
> And this, and so much more?—
> It is impossible to say just what I mean![6]

Prufrock endlessly names things until expression breaks down; it is a quest to overcome the power of "and," the deconstructive force of parataxis. The distance from Donne to this modernism is at once monumental and trivial. Donne's wit self-consciously deconstructs itself within the coercive rules of his relatively stable cultural images. Metaphoric joinings in modernism, on

the other hand, rest on a background of highly conventional images of fragmentation, images of difference read as apocalyptic signs of cultural and
ethical entropy: we need only recall Yeats's powerful modernist image: "And
what rough beast, its hour come round at last, / Slouches towards Bethle-
hem to be born?"[7]

To be sure, metaphysical conceit often functions as ersatz metaphysics;
but as metaphoric expression it comes always trailing clouds of difference,
not only the difference that has been suppressed in the metaphoric linking
but also a difference in the orders metaphorically substituted for convention.
Are all metaphors the same? Perhaps Eliot thought, in the spirit of "The
Canonization," in an Arnoldian reading of Donne, that he could ontothe-
ologize metaphor in his image of the "wheel" which "may turn and still /
Be forever still"[8]—the point of intersection between timelessness and time.
But this is, at best, merely the evanescent glow of an unattainable unity, a
Kantian pure idea which translates poorly as Crocean or Husserlian "expression." It is a sublime moment searching for a correlative real object
which can present an image of the Idea. For Eliot there was always Prufrock,
always the retreat from the "overwhelming question." Stevens, more the
modernist antimetaphysician, consciously rewrote metaphysics as aesthetics; for Stevens the poet is a metaphysician in the dark strumming supreme
fictions on a blue guitar, or is one among a modernist (or is it postmodernist?) band of pagan dancers celebrating in rhythmic harmonies an old
chaos of the sun.[9] Yeats retreated to his tower, which both protected him
from the modern apocalypse where the "best lack all conviction, while the
worst / Are full of passionate intensity,"[10] and also provided him with the
uncommitted yet critical perspective of the culturally disengaged avant-
garde artist. There is more difference than identity in this little panorama
of modernism.

So it is that Krieger emphasizes in Donne's metaphorical junctures not
identity (the "now" or static presence) so much as movement, a shift (across
a contradiction) from denial to affirmation located in the slide from random
lists to virtual unities, the effect of which is a sleight of hand, the pen quicker
than the eye. The suppression of differences resides beyond metaphor as
the idea of order; what we perceive in the poem itself is the process by
means of which we reach that idea. Krieger asks us to imagine that by line 6
of stanza 3 in Donne's "Canonization" ("we two, being one"), identity has
been suggested. By line 8 of that stanza, the idea of a scholastic "proof" has
been placed into circulation. Thus in stanza 4 all differences are linked under the idea that certain culturally specific laws of non-contradiction, of difference (the sacred and profane), have been temporarily (that is, tempo-
rally) suspended, united in the metaphoric structure of the poem.

Metaphor facilitates thought. Reality is imagined in the mind's intercourse with materiality; thought interacts with sensation in order to make

sense, to constitute an idea of order. Metaphor is a deception of the eye very much like the illusion of motion made from the misperception of a successive series of still images, or it is the sensation of infinite colors shaded out of an impoverished palette of red, green, and blue pixels projected on a glowing screen. These are, one might argue, flaws of the mind, blindnesses, specific inabilities to see clearly what is right before our eyes, but such limitations enrich reality by allowing us to give shape, color, and texture to our world. Metaphor is the product of this same faulty "rage for order"; [11] it is a manner of speaking, a request for legitimation by means of familiarization. Cognition rests on re-cognition, and the world we inhabit comes always with some assembly required. Like peripheral vision, reality is fuzzy around the edges, faintly demarked at the borders of recognition, and it is from these extremes that revisions arise. These alterations in the fabric of life range between near affirmation and total revolution, and cognition is always personal no matter how invested we are in the commonality of reality. Metaphor reconfigures systems and tweaks worlds; it cannot do otherwise, for the very act of metaphorizing disrupts proper differences.

The sweeping charge of ontotheologism hurled by postmodernism against metaphor simply rarefies metaphor into identity with itself. It is, perhaps, the fate of modernism to be so misread, to be troped as a one-dimensional suppression of differences. Yet Krieger's reading of Donne rests on the principle that identity cannot present itself without difference. Metaphor inscribes identity within difference, just as postmodernism would have it. Warren's "irony of Mercutio," and Krieger's insistence on corporeality, locate the affective force of metaphor in the making and unmaking of realities, and with each constitutive motion there is a concomitant repositioning of the perceptive subject. Metaphor fixes identity as a temporary point of view or judgment; it defines the self as engaged with reality, in a posture of critique or affirmation. Modernism, therefore, maintains a significant difference from postmodernism by representing difference in a double sense. Familiar differences are subjected to unifying metaphoric linking, yet they remain visible within the metaphoric process even while the new order differs from the reality we already inhabit. Identity always differs from an original difference, and metaphor is always a differing from difference.

The familiar reality of modernism rested on sanctioned dichotomies of self and other, inner and outer, experience and expression, the present and the past. Modern metaphor sought resolution of these conflicts in presence, poetry, inwardness, and subjectivity, in the repression of the "ands" which exposed the links of irreducible dualisms. Erasing "ands" collapsed oppositions into the poetic subject itself. Hartman's reading of Yeats with its deconstructive multiplication of "ands," like all postmodern critique, was situated historically within this modernism, as a reminder that the reality of difference was the ground of metaphoric linking. Lying within modernism, the postmodern woke modernism from its dogmatic slumber by shifting modern metaphor away from a lexicon of privileged symbols to a grammar of incessant conjunctions, from nouns to connectives, from words to phrases. But with this single task accomplished in the blink of an eye, postmodernism was left with no further windmills to charge, and the postmodern passed quickly into decline.

Yet modernism remains as an unfinished project. Without simply turning back, modernism is forced to retrace the history of its emergence in order to rediscover its future. That past is rooted in narratives of liberation; and, problematical as that source now appears, it nonetheless grounds the modernist project in its original ethical and political commitments. Postmodernism provided no platform for making moral choices, for commitment to action and beliefs; it relegated judgment, and, hence, justice, to the playfulness of Borges's Chinese novelist whose labyrinthine narrative of forking paths followed all possible plot divisions.[12] Modernists were better served in this domain by the romantic Frost, whose wandering everyman pauses to reflect on life decisions that make "all the difference."[13] Differences do not occur naturally; that which makes a difference is a matter of choosing, and choice occurs within time narrated as cultural history. At the level of play, Borges's image of infinite divisibility is no less liberating than Frost's stereotypical, lonely New Englander's individualism, yet it is Frost's image that makes choice a project for good or ill.

Judgment returns us always to the problematics of the subject. Modernist metaphor sought to represent the nature of this subjectivity, the image of an animal able to make promises, as Nietzsche ironically phrased it.[14] It was a project that modernists thought both philosophy and ethics had failed to take up. The idea of choice for modernists was harsh; it depicted a lonely decision-maker undirected by a priori determinations. The full weight of responsibility came to rest on this individual, a powerful deterrent to haste and thoughtlessness. For all of its sentimentality, this idea of choice is not reactionary. Choice is a project for the future just as it is the consequence of experience, of remembering, and such a conception of choice demands something like the modernist individuality, a perspective which does not reside at the still point of the turning wheel but rather at the site of contact between ideas of order and sensations, the locus of reality.

V

In *Absalom, Absalom!* William Faulkner's incomparable Rosa Coldfield tells of her youth, and of the South, and the Civil War, and of what remains of past events which still cause her shame and deep pain. As she tells her story she digresses for a moment in order to instruct her listener on the nature of remembering, a reflex action which she defines as neither story nor event.

Once there was—Do you mark how the wisteria, sun-impacted on this wall here, distills and penetrates this room as though (light-unimpeded) by secret and attritive progress from mote to mote of obscurity's myriad components? That is the substance of remembering—sense, sight, smell: the muscles with which we see and hear and feel—not mind, not thought: there is no such thing as memory: the brain recalls just what the muscles grope for: no more, no less: and its resultant sum is usually incorrect and false and worthy only of the name of dream. —See how the sleeping outflung hand, touching the bedside candle, remembers pain, springs back and free while mind and brain sleep on and only make of this adjacent heat some trashy myth or reality's escape: or that same sleeping hand, in sensuous marriage with some dulcet surface, is transformed by that same sleeping brain and mind into that same figment-stuff warped out of all experience. Ay, grief goes, fades; we know that—but ask the tear ducts if they have forgotten how to weep.[15]

It is the body and not the mind that remembers pain and pleasure. The mind can only warp experience into myth, dreams, mere ideas or stories *"for which,"* as Rosa says, *"three words are three too many, and three thousand words that many words too less"* (166). Everything that is or has been or will be *can* be told, but life is remembered as pleasure and pain, not as event or tale. Memory is empty, but remembering is the lingering of experience, the tempering of sense as though pleasure and pain have written a message in a script burned into flesh. We say something is beautiful or ugly, kind or careless, good or evil as we say something is hot or cold, soft or harsh. Whatever stories we tell of good and evil, with whatever words we name specific differences, there is always the sense of pleasures and pains, the remembering of sensations which give corporeal foundations to our thoughts and expressions.

Why do we say that a phrase "makes sense"? Oddly, philosophy divided "sense" and "reference," making "sense" a function of language, of grammar, of grammatology, thereby casting "reference" outside the boundaries of "sense." But where? Into "nonsense"? But "sense" cannot be removed from sensation, from the world that envelops the body, from pleasure and pain. A phrase "makes sense" because it appeals to the body for validation—not the validity of logic, or mathematics, or cognition, or even authenticity or truth, but rather the validity signaled by the recognition of a human response. The power of ideas is in what touches us.

Modernism once agonized over this dissociation of sensibilities, at the division of feelings and thoughts, but modernism also thoughtlessly set about the destruction of the body while in pursuit of mind and consciousness. The end of mimesis was in the metaphysics of the subject. Postmodernism did not differ from modernism in this. To be sure, the postmodern also abandoned the mind, slowly, since it had to await the inhospitality of Derrida to rid it of Lévi-Strauss's uninvited guest, but this merely rewrote the solitary confinement of solipsism as the prison house of language. The denial of remembering is one of the conditions of the move from wisdom to competence, for wisdom is remembering in Faulkner's intuition of it. Wisdom decides what matters. This is not to say that we judge merely on vague feelings; rather, remembering our pleasures and pains locates wisdom at the level of lived experience, at the intersection of thought and consequences, in the play of recognition (what it *feels* like, not what it *is*) and concern (obligation, not fear).

In contemporary science fiction the image of disembodied intelligence — of body snatchers always cold, always cruel — rises to trouble our dreams. And we hear of the utopia of cyberspace, which is no space at all, devoid of sensations, a treasure of competencies that will do our remembering for us. Whether or not it will one day feed the hungry is yet to be proved. Knowledge is power, but one wonders if food and guns, starvation and dying, are therefore altogether archaic. Perhaps this doubt has always tugged at the sleeves of modernism, for we cannot read the dominant figures of modernist consciousness without acknowledging the eccentric challenges to the modern by those who profess to be realists, even materialists. And can we not see in Krieger's reading of Donne, in the metaphor of corporeality and the profanation of the sacred, can we not feel here the remembering of the body, of that which makes sense? In that dimension of the modern where form turns upon itself and calls attention to the process of composition, to making, to the act of writing, here something other than the rarefied subjectivity of self-consciousness appears. It is a reminder to remember, barely discernible in the ontic extravagance of New Critical theorizing, but a call for recognition of the world's body nonetheless. Mark Seltzer calls this "the becoming visible of writing" and sees in it a sociology as well as an ontology.[16] Perhaps it is more accurately a politics and ethics. Seltzer finds it in realism; but it is not only there, for even in its total submersion into consciousness, the mind of modernism could not altogether forget the body.

The form of Faulkner's *Absalom, Absalom!* is an imitation of conversation, of storytelling. In the latter half of the novel much of this conversation takes place at night, in the dark, where seemingly disembodied voices float freely on the cold air. Yet here and there, often enough, the reader is reminded of the sensation of that coldness and of the intertwined acts of composition which comprise the story, the writing of the novel itself. Much of the dialogue centers on a legendary and mysterious murder that took place in Mississippi at the end of the Civil War. The narrators search for explanations, motives, and evidence, yet they have very little that is concrete. They have only stories, tales, mere words. Most of the narration comes from those born long after the events took place; no extended piece of narrative, except for that of Rosa Coldfield, comes from an eyewitness. It is she alone who can remember, but she cannot even testify to the reality of the body of the murdered man in the casket she helped carry to the site of its burial.

The conspicuous absence of the body in this story again draws us into the realm of language, into the patching together of bits of narration, the incessant linking of narrative "ands." Yet here also we are reminded on occasion, often enough, that at issue is the question of passions that underscore the questions of guilt or innocence, the matter of justice. Versions of the crime are constructed to make sense to the narrators, to evoke feelings of love and hatred that constitute the ground for making judgments, for revealing a "wrong" that otherwise can have no voice. These can only be sensed as grief and sorrow, joy and anger, within the range of possible sensations that give substance to all human concerns, good and evil.

Lest we forget this grounding as we are swept up into the play of story-telling, of language itself, Faulkner inserts a disruption into the narrative, the figure of a document, a letter presumably written by the murdered man to his fiancée (although these identities are deliberately left in doubt). It is not, however, the contents of the letter, what it says, or the remarkable play of its words, but the object itself that causes us to pause, for it is quintessentially a "becoming visible of writing." This is how the letter begins:

> *You will notice how I insult neither of us by claiming this to be a voice from the defeated even, let alone from the dead. In fact, if I were a philosopher I should deduce and derive a curious and apt commentary on the times and augur of the future from this letter which you now hold in your hands—a sheet of notepaper with, as you can see, the best of French watermarks dated seventy years ago, salvaged (stolen if you will) from the gutted mansion of a ruined aristocrat; and written upon in the best of stove polish manufactured not twelve months ago in a New England factory.* (129)

The description reinforces the general thematics of this novel about the defeat of the South, but, more importantly, the letter trivializes postmodern absence. The letter makes writing sensational, an object we hold in our hands as we read. It presses against our palms and weighs on our muscles as we hold the book wherein this letter resides. It is an eternal presentation which does not make reality but rather guarantees that realities have been made, for such an object testifies in the place of an otherwise silent world occupied by bodies and electrified by sensations.

Just as the mind filters stimuli, words arrange experiences: sometimes into the familiar, directed by the coercive power of culturally legitimized differences everywhere present in language, and sometimes into improprieties wherein one begs to differ from familiar differences. So this filter gives us reality, that which is named and ordered, produced by the mind, constituted within language, and recognized by consciousness. Yet it is always merely "myth" or "*figment-stuff warped out of all experience.*" And we understand this, need this, and regret it. The search for explanations, for evidence to convict, that motivates the telling of these linked stories of murder and hatred, love and honor, and the racism that ignites violence, has not been advanced very far by this letter, yet we now understand that these stories arise out of recognizable human concerns, sensational needs, inseparably merged with bodies as expressions of that which truly matters. The letter is a metaphor binding together that which postmodernism, by extending modernism, sought to divide: the elemental and immaterial alphabet that signifies insensible difference, and the material being of ink (or stove polish) and paper, visible manifestations of difference in plain black and white. This letter gives sensational representation to the thematic racial differences between black and white in the novel, differences that even when they cannot be seen still constitute a motive for murder and a revelation of violence in the social realities that lie at the heart of Faulkner's fictional exploration of the American South.

There is here an insistence on materiality in all language, a remembering of what is always before the text, the body that is reflected in the mirror image which even the power of the symbolic order cannot erase. It is not the ontic suggestiveness of all this that is significant, however. Sensation is the voice of the world's body speaking through our bodies. It is something like the brute materiality which sparked Sartrean nausea, or that which asks us to attend to its presence, to "listen" with all of our faculties of perception. We recognize sensation even in the absence of phrases; in pauses or silences of written texts we "sense" what might be said or what must be said just as powerfully as we hear the voice of one whose breath brushes our ears.

Modernism, stimulated by postmodernism, may bring us back to this realization someday. We find such a move in the philosophizing of a quintessential postmodernist like Lyotard, in the remarkable recuperation of Kant that grounds his politics in *The Differend*. It is a prelude to Lyotard's appropriation of Levinasian ethics, that interface between self and other that constitutes the basis of human judgment and, for Lyotard, the condition of rendering justice. Listen to this reading of Kant's "Transcendental Aesthetic," which shows itself as a remarkable (metaphoric?) linking of modern and postmodern. Here is a true engagement with the material world which speaks to us:

> An unknown addressor speaks matter . . . to an addressee receptive to this idiom, and who therefore understands it, at least in the sense by which he or she is affected by it. What does the matter-phrase talk about, what is its referent? It does not yet have one. It is a sentimental phrase, the referential function is minor in it. What is important is its conative function, as Jakobson would have said.[17]

A conversation wherein matter speaks? Yes, a message that registers on our sensations, an ontology that does not know its referent, but which necessitates the enlightening of a reality. Everything that "is" asks us to articulate our perceptions of it; we feel the presentation of the other, a cry, a demand to be recognized. So we must listen to our sensations and name and rename our worlds. An order of linkings, a conjunction of "ands," a ratification of differences is constructed which forms a familiar reality. This reality arises out of Lyotard's second phase of the conversation that matters. The addressee, the subject that receives the sensational message, then becomes the addressor, the naming subject:

> This subject . . . addresses the phrase of space-time, the form phrase, to the unknown addressor of the first phrase, who thereby becomes an addressee. This phrase, as opposed to the matter phrase, is endowed with a referential function.[18]

This response closes our engagement with the world that matters, the base for any reality, and is finally marked not by ontological counters but by political and ethical obligations. That which is conjoined by "ands" is ratified, sanctioned, and coerced into the reality we know and recognize. Yet what kind of a world can be built into that which we call "reality," that which will coerce differences and render judgments? How will we differ from difference should we encounter injustice, should we sense pain that calls for recognition and relief? These questions temper all language, philosophical and poetic. Here metaphor operates to differ from difference, not as a guarantee of the good, but as a reminder of our most fundamental human engagement with the corporeal substance of our world, a remembering that is located at the level of pleasure and pain, joy and sorrow, celebration and regret. The poem that asserts itself as an image of presence, in Krieger's terms, does not detach itself from what matters but turns us back to that sensational response which obligates us to justify reality. Can we say that justice is sentimental? Yes, as we say that justice invokes experience, wisdom and not competence. Knowledge rests on sensation, on the recognition and acknowledgment of consequences and responsibilities, not at the point of intersection between timelessness and time, but at the juncture of thought and concern.

NOTES

1. John Donne, "The Canonization," in *The Norton Anthology of English Literature,* 3d ed. (New York: W. W. Norton, 1974), 1:1185–86.

2. William Butler Yeats, "Leda and the Swan," in *The Collected Poems of W. B. Yeats* (New York: Macmillan, 1956), 211.

3. William Shakespeare, *A Midsummer Night's Dream,* in *The Complete Works of William Shakespeare,* vol. 1 (New York: Doubleday, 1956), 5.1.12–17.

4. Robert Penn Warren, "Pure and Impure Poetry," in *Critical Theory Since Plato,* ed. Hazard Adams (New York: Harcourt, Brace, Jovanovich, Inc., 1971), 983.

5. Wallace Stevens, "The Idea of Order at Key West," in *The Collected Poems of Wallace Stevens* (New York: Alfred A. Knopf, 1969), 128–30.

6. T. S. Eliot, "The Love Song of J. Alfred Prufrock," in *T. S. Eliot: The Complete Poems and Plays* (New York: Harcourt, 1952), 3–7, quotation from lines 101–4.

7. William Butler Yeats, "The Second Coming," in *Collected Poems,* 184–85.

8. T. S. Eliot, *Murder in the Cathedral,* in *Complete Poems and Plays,* 183.

9. Wallace Stevens, "The Man with the Blue Guitar" and "Sunday Morning," in *Collected Poems,* 165, 66.

10. Yeats, "The Second Coming."

11. Stevens, "The Idea of Order at Key West."

12. Jorge Luis Borges, "The Garden of the Forking Paths," in *Labyrinths* (New York: New Directions, 1964), 19–29.

13. Robert Frost, "The Road Not Taken," in *The Complete Poems of Robert Frost* (New York: Holt, Rinehart, and Winston, 1964), 131.

14. Friedrich Nietzsche, *The Genealogy of Morals,* in *The Birth of Tragedy and The Genealogy of Morals,* trans. Francis Golffing (New York: Doubleday, 1955), 189.

15. William Faulkner, *Absalom, Absalom!* (New York: Modern Library, 1964), 143. Further citations will be made parenthetically in the text.

16. Mark Selzer, "Statistical persons," *Diacritics* 17, no. 3 (Fall 1987): 92.

17. Jean-François Lyotard, *The Differend: Phrases in Dispute,* trans. George Van Den Abbeele (Minneapolis: University of Minnesota Press, 1988), 62.

18. Ibid.

CHAPTER NINE

What Is Literary Anthropology? The Difference between Explanatory and Exploratory Fictions

Wolfgang Iser

What is literary anthropology? Before even attempting to answer such a question, one needs to focus on the aims and methods of anthropology itself. As long as the process of hominization constitutes its objective, the evaluation of fossils is of paramount concern. These factual remains call for inferences, and these inferences have always been theory-laden, with evolution being the dominant explanatory model in modern times.

Theoretical implications were always a subconscious undercurrent in anthropology, though for a long time they did not attract any particular attention, since they were taken for facts, or even realities, not very different in quality from those that can be observed. Evolution, however, does not present itself to observation, and equally ungraspable—inevitably, in the evolutionary context—is the origin of humankind, which has given rise to all kinds of theories. But although anthropology has been a theory-laden enterprise right from its inception, a critical inspection of the explanatory procedures employed is only of recent vintage.

The methodological scrutiny to which Darwinian anthropology has been subjected has resulted—according to different standpoints—in a departmentalization of what had once seemed self-contained. We still have ethnography, which is basically what the practitioners of anthropology are concerned with, but we now also have philosophical, social, cultural, and historical anthropology, distinguished by their respective objectives and by their methodological presuppositions. Even ethnography has changed its focus, no longer dwelling exclusively on origins of hominization, but also and especially on what happened after the hominids had launched themselves. Clifford Geertz made it his overriding concern to understand "what ethnography is, or more exactly *what doing ethnography is*,"[1] which he identified as a study of human culture becoming self-reflexive.

Consequently, "doing ethnography" is basically a two-tiered undertaking: it makes culture the prime focus of anthropology, and simultaneously initiates a self-monitoring of all the operations involved in this study. Why should culture be so central? Because, as Geertz maintains, it is not something "added on, so to speak, to a finished or virtually finished animal," but is "ingredient, and centrally ingredient, in the production of the animal itself," which leads him to the conclusion that "[w]ithout men, no culture, certainly; but equally, and more significantly, without culture, no men."[2]

This is a common view, shared by a great many influential anthropologists today, irrespective of whether they regard the production of culture as a reparation undertaken by a "creature of deficiency," as Arnold Gehlen has it, or as a result of the cortex expanding owing to the erect posture of humans, as André Leroi-Gourhan suggests, or as arising out of resentment to be coped with when humans find themselves displaced from center to periphery, as Eric Gans so cogently argues.[3] Whichever explanatory hypothesis one might be inclined to favor, all of them are unanimous in conceiving of culture as the capstone to the rise of humankind. Furthermore, these divergent approaches share a common perspective. They view culture as a response to challenges, and the response as a revelation of what humans are. This double-sidedness of culture, as a product and as a record of human manifestations, has repercussions on humans themselves, insofar as they are molded by what they have externalized. As Geertz puts it, "men," in the final analysis, "every last one of them, are cultural artifacts."[4]

What remains noteworthy in these various theories of culture advanced by anthropologists is the fact that almost all of them end up by discussing the role of the arts in the setup of culture. Sometimes one gets the impression that the prominence accorded to the arts brings a hidden teleology out into the open. And even when they do not figure as the epitome of culture, artistic elements nevertheless emerge as important concomitant features right from the observable beginnings of humankind, providing indispensable "support" for the effort to meet challenges. According to Leroi-Gourhan, the tool as the externalization of the human hand was early on studded with ornaments, indicating a "style, which is a matter of ethnic figurative value," and which accompanies "the mechanical function and the material solutions to the problem of functional approximation." Without such figurative representations, the balance of the various aspects of toolmaking would be disturbed, putting the very use of the tool into jeopardy.[5] The figural clothing of the mechanical function symbolizes a relatedness to that use, and without it the tool may not be "forged" into its operable form. Thus ornamentation represents the way in which the producer relates to the product, indicating that it has been made. Whether the arts in general are considered the apex of culture or whether a functional aesthetics appears indispensable to humankind's externalization of its capabilities, the arts embody an ineluctable component of culture. And as culture has become—albeit only recently—the central concern of anthropology, literature as an integral feature of culture is bound to have an anthropological dimension of its own.

Unfolding such a dimension entails a glance at the methodological problems that have to be faced in "doing ethnography," not least because literary anthropology gains salience when viewed as part of a constellation of more general anthropological concerns. If culture is the outgrowth of the unfinished animal, how is one to conceptualize such a continually changing performative activity? The latter does not seem to be any sort of entity, and thus eludes definition, for it cannot be identified with any of its ingredients. Geertz writes:

> One [way] is to imagine that culture is a self-contained "superorganic" reality with forces and purposes of its own; that is, to reify it. Another is to claim that it consists in the brute pattern of behavioral events we observe in fact to occur in some identifiable community or other; that is, to reduce it. But though both these confusions still exist, and doubtless will be always with us, the main source of theoretical muddlement in contemporary anthropology is a view which developed in reaction to them and is right now very widely held—namely, that, to quote Ward Goodenough, perhaps its leading proponent, "culture [is located] in the minds and hearts of men."[6]

Consequently, all umbrella concepts for defining culture have to be discarded, because all of them furnish, in Geertz's terms, nothing but "thin description."[7] These generalizing concepts, however, are to a large extent still the tools of the trade, in spite of the fact that "evolution" is no longer taken as a blanket explanation of everything that happens in the reciprocal interaction between humans and the culture they keep producing.

The methodological predicament of anthropology, however, consists of a virtually insoluble problem. On the one hand the ethnographical approach—based on field work—has to draw controlled inferences, either from the fossils found or the observations made, in order to establish a fact, as evinced by Leroi-Gourhan's reference to "the concept of tools . . . being a 'secretion' of the anthropoid's body and brain."[8] On the other hand, such generalizations are indispensable to the filling of gaps even if there is no evidence for their validity. The plausible suggestion that the tool is an externalization of what the human hand is able to perform implies a great many presupposed combinations relating to the way in which muscular power is translated into the functioning of the tool, and the way in which hand and brain must interconnect in order to produce the desired effect. Although there is no tangible evidence for these generalizations, which are necessary to make the fossils speak, there is also no reason to dispute such conclusions, since they appear to be perfectly acceptable.

But what is acceptable as an explanatory concept is not yet the reality for which many successful explanations are so frequently taken. Whenever such a concept is taken for reality, the result is reification, which makes self-monitoring of these explanatory activities all the more pertinent, so that their basically heuristic character will never be eclipsed. Such an awareness is bound to qualify the methodological guidelines of anthropological research as fictions by nature. Geertz fully acknowledges this when he assesses his own methodological framework called "thick description":

> In short, anthropological writings are themselves interpretations, and second and third order ones to boot. (By definition, only a "native" makes first order ones: it's *his* culture.) They are, thus, fictions; fictions, in the sense that they are "something made," "something fashioned"—the original meaning of *fictiō*—not that they are false, unfactual, or merely "as if" thought experiments. To construct actor-oriented descriptions of the involvements of a Berber chieftain, a Jewish merchant, and a French soldier with one another in 1912 Morocco is clearly an imaginative act, not all that different from constructing similar descriptions of, say, the involvements with one another of a provincial French doctor, his silly, adulterous wife, and her feckless lover in nineteenth century France. In the latter case, the actors are represented as not having existed and the events as not having happened, while in the former they are represented as actual, or as having been so. This is a difference of no mean importance; indeed, precisely the one Madame Bovary has difficulty grasping. But the importance does not lie in the fact that her story was created while Cohen's was only noted. The conditions of their creation, and the point of it (to say nothing of the manner and quality) differ. But the one is as much a *fictiō*—"a making"—as the other.[9]

Fictions, it seems, allow us to map out an actor-oriented scenario which holds true for both the network of thick description and literature; such scenarios are enactments designed for finding things out. Fictions, however, are not independent of those things that have to be found out, and this fact is somewhat obscured when the difference between explanatory fictions and literary fictions is ignored. The constellation between a Berber chieftain, a Jewish merchant, and a French soldier refers to an actual occurrence, whereas the one in Flaubert's novel has no such reference. Obviously, the fiction is put to different uses in the two cases, and that changes the very function the fiction is meant to perform.

Thick description starts out from reading signs emitted by the chieftain, the merchant, and the soldier in their social interaction, which Geertz uses in order to illustrate his procedure. Reading signs is a matter not so much of grasping what they represent as of spotlighting what they imply. There is always a gap between what is manifest and what is implied in either saying or doing something. Thick description is, therefore, first and foremost, an unfolding of the implications of the manifest, which thus becomes all the more richly orchestrated.

By revealing the observable manifestations, thick description establishes a semiotic web of interacting features, which we are given to read. Reading culture appears to be the only way of gaining access to it. There are no universals to be invoked, there are no frameworks to be superimposed, and there are no constants of human nature to be appealed to if we want to explain human behavior. Instead, culture arises out of human responses to a challenging environment; it is an assembly of "extragenetic, outside-the-skin control mechanisms,"[10] which are subject to change, otherwise humans would imprison themselves in the products of their reactions.

When reading culture is of paramount concern (and this is the way thick description realizes itself), then scenarios of reading can only be basically fictional. These fictional scenarios not only reflect the avoidance of thin description, which is a superimposition of concepts on what one is given to observe; they also facilitate a "treatise in cultural theory"[11] insofar as such a theory seeks to find out the implications of the human actions and interactions that inform the "actor's act" from which—as the only given—inferences are to be drawn. These fictional scenarios are, as Geertz maintains, made up; however, they are not "'as if' thought experiments," because the established semiotic web refers to an indisputable reality. In other words, the fictional construct of reading, though made up, has a specific use, which again confirms that a fiction is always defined by its use. How does this fictional reading of culture operate, bearing in mind that the very many "outside-the-skin control mechanisms" are the direct offshoot of human responses to entropy? If culture as an outgrowth of human reactions is built into the void, the fictional scenario of reading such human achievement can only proceed in terms of recursive looping. Human interaction with its environment realizes itself through a feedback system.

This feedback system develops as an interchange between input and output, in the course of which a projection is corrected insofar as it has failed to square with what it has targeted. Consequently, a dual correction occurs: the feedforward returns as an altered feedback loop, which in turn feeds into a revised input. Thus, recursive looping adjusts "future conduct to past performance."[12] Geertz maintains that such an interaction is already operative in intracerebral processes, and for corroboration he enlists the support of neurophysiologists by quoting some of their findings:

> The working of the central nervous system is a hierarchic affair in which functions at the higher levels do not deal directly with the ultimate structural units, such as neurons or motor units, but operate by activating lower patterns that have their own relatively autonomous structural unity. The same is true for the sensory input, which does not project itself down to the last final path of motor neurons, but operates by affecting, distorting, and

somehow modifying the pre-existing, preformed patterns of central coordi-
nation, which, in turn, then confer their distortions upon the lower patterns
of effection and so on. . . . The structure of the input does not produce the
structure of the output, but merely modifies intrinsic nervous activities that
have a structural organization of their own.[13]

In this respect Leroi-Gourhan concurs with Geertz, by demonstrating the
extent to which the feedforward of hand and brain starts up feedback loops
which continually fine-tune the development of the tools and machinery
that allow humans to cope with a challenging environment. Leroi-Gourhan
and Geertz are equally in agreement that the human brain itself, like the
nervous system as a whole, operates recursively, thus anticipating what Varela
has meanwhile established on grounds of biological evidence.[14] There are
levels of recursive looping between body and brain, between human plasticity and the artificial habitat built into the void, and between the patterns
of social behavior in human interaction. If culture is the product of recursive looping, the very recursion makes the human being into a creation of
culture. If both human being and culture arise out of recursive looping, recursion provides an explanation for the physical evolution of humans, for
the functioning of the brain, for the structure of social organization, and
finally for the changes of cultural patterns themselves.

Is recursion, then, not only one of the "outside-the-skin control mechanisms" but also a substantive ingredient of humans, or even an umbrella for
them both, and hence much more than a pattern that structures the operations of the fictional scenario made up for reading the semiotic web?
Geertz himself answers this question:

We live, as one writer has neatly put it, in an "information gap." Between
what our body tells us and what we have to know in order to function, there
is a vacuum we must fill ourselves, and we fill it with information (or misin-
formation) provided by our culture. The boundary between what is innately
controlled and what is culturally controlled in human behavior is an ill-
defined and wavering one.[15]

This "information gap" points to a vital feature of culture. As Jurij Lotman
once remarked, culture is an all-encompassing mechanism instituted by humankind for converting entropy into information in order to ensure survival.[16] What remains eclipsed in such a process, however, is the turning
point at which entropy is transmuted into information, hence the "information gap" that is sealed off from penetration.

The consequences of such a vacuum are threefold. First, culture keeps
emerging out of this constitutive emptiness, which implies that there are no
discernible origins of culture, and any presumption to know such origins is
bound to turn into mythology. If culture is a continuously emerging phe-

nomenon, then it does not arise out of anything given, but rather out of a transformation of what is given.

Second, the vacuum may also be conceived as the mark that "an incomplete, an unfinished, animal"[17] imprints on what it spins out of itself. Therefore culture evolves in unending recursions that make human beings—owing to their incompleteness and plasticity—into cultural artifacts.

Third, convincing as such a process may seem, it is in the final analysis nothing but a plausible explanatory framework, and hence itself a fiction designed to cope with the "information gap." The very fact that Geertz qualifies the explanatory schemata operative in anthropology as fictions acknowledges the fact that origins are unplumbable, and that we "live" in this "information gap."

Although fictions are made up, they are for Geertz neither untrue nor merely "as if" constructions, because they relate to human beings and the habitat that this "unfinished creature" keeps generating—both of which are indisputable givens. The fiction has to provide an explanatory framework, which in turn will prod the imagination into action, in order that we may conceive what is beyond knowing. For this reason, as Geertz maintains, there is "the need for theory to stay rather closer to the ground than tends to be the case in the sciences more able to give themselves over to imaginative abstraction."[18] Thus the theory itself bears the inscription of the gap, the negotiation of which requires an extension beyond what remains ungraspable if at least an imaginary solution is to be obtained.

Dealing cognitively with human beings—who have made themselves into what they are both socially and culturally—appears to require a transgression of epistemological boundaries, since only fictions can bring the unknowable within reach. Fictions, as Francis Bacon observed, "give some shadow of satisfaction to the mind . . . in those points wherein the nature of things doth deny it."[19] If there is only a fictional completion of this incomplete and unfinished creature, any description of the latter is bound to entail a fictional scenario of reading, as humanity cannot be subsumed under any pre-existing frame of reference.

This is most brilliantly demonstrated by Eric Gans, who has cast the whole human development, from an "originary scene"[20] to postmodernism,[21] as a supreme fiction. In his cogently argued "Generative Anthropology," fiction is taken as dual by nature; it is a hypothesis for conceiving the "originary scene" out of which humankind has evolved, and it is the overall explanatory pattern for all the vicissitudes of human culture ensuing therefrom.[22] Gans breaks away from ethnographical research altogether, and instead advances a breathtaking construct of culture. In one sense, however, this construct meets a requirement for theories of culture that Geertz had already postulated, namely that such a theory should fit not only past realities, but also the realities to come.[23] This is one of the reasons why Gans tries to draw out the implications inherent in the basic constellation of the "originary scene" so as to accommodate the welter of occurrences between the inception of humankind and the present. The construct necessary for such an all-encompassing accommodation is bound to be fictional in nature, and thus the function of fiction changes again in this generative anthropology.

The minimal hypothesis is not merely a scenario that, for instance,

> could describe a hunting scene in which the band of hunters, armed with primitive weapons, face each other around the body of their victim. . . . At best such a scenario can be of heuristic value . . . but there is always a danger that such a persuasive model is nothing more than a myth of origin in a modern guise. The minimal hypothesis does not suffer from this weakness because it is constructed by working backward from its necessary result— that is, the act of representation—rather than forward from a conjectured prehuman state. (99)

If the details of the scene are fairly irrelevant, what is important is the act of representation, which makes the "hands reaching out toward the object hesitate in mid-course through the fear of each that he will fall victim to the reprisals of the others. This hesitation turns the gesture of appropriation into a gesture of designation, and the locus of the body into the original scene of representation" (14). The abrogation of appetitive satisfaction effected by the ostensive gesture towards what is in the center converts the originary scene into an originary event, which leads Gans to the conclusion that "man's origin was revolutionary, not evolutionary" (38). Such a statement means no less than that humankind sprang into existence by means of fiction, or, perhaps more aptly, the act of representation as a deferral of conflict proves to be an explanatory fiction for the differentiation of humankind from the animal kingdom: "In our anthropology, man is not distinguished from the animals by his propensity to economic activity but by his use of representation" (88).

The act of representation, however, is marked by a duality. As long as it is motivated by fear of conflict—a conflict to be avoided by the gesture of designation—the act of representation appears to point to a fictionalizing capability inherent in the human makeup itself. As long as it is taken to effect the initial deferral of appetitive satisfaction, which opens up a difference between the individual and the appetitive object as well as a difference between the individuals themselves, the act of representation appears to be a basic explanatory pattern of this generative anthropology. Again the question poses itself: do fictions generate differences, or are they just vehicles of explanation for what remains cognitively inexplicable? If the act of representation is basically a deferral of conflict, what in actual fact does it then represent? It cannot be the conflict, which it suspends; at best it represents absence. But how could absence—by nature intangible—be represented? Even if an absence were made present, it requires a clothing of sorts, otherwise the presence of an absence could not be perceived. Consequently, the act of representation, which creates an absence by means of deferral, simultaneously gives a fictional clothing to that absence by making the center into the appearance of the inaccessible.

If the prevention of conflict by means of the temporarily aborted gesture defines this gesture as one of representation, then the next question is: how does this representation come to life? The answer is: through the aesthetic images, formed by every individual facing the object from whose appropriation all of them are barred. The abrogation of appetitive satisfaction transforms the object into an object of desire, indicating the impossibility of appropriating it:

> Esthetic contemplation is inevitably accompanied by desire. But the specifically esthetic moment is the contemplation itself, in which not the "private" image of desired satisfaction but the "public" image of the desire-object is perceived. The desire that attaches to esthetic contemplation, however it may distort this public configuration, returns to it as its guarantee, its formally objective correlative, in a characteristic oscillation of imaginary content. (31)

The image of desire is first of all imaginary, and as representation—effecting the deferral of a real presence for the sake of avoiding conflict—it highlights the status of desire as unfulfilled satisfaction. Thus every individual entertains such an image, through which the inaccessibility of the central object translates itself into the mind. This is an initial step towards turning the representation of absence into productivity. The image that each individual has may be totally different from the others'; however, impenetrable as these differences may be, the awareness prevails that every individual is bound to have an image. If having images is something shared, a nascent sense of togetherness begins to emerge; a group is established. Representation of absence mobilizes the imaginary, which transforms the interdiction into a feeling of collectivity.

The originary event as a construct is not meant to mark the beginning of human evolution; it is, however, viewed as a mainspring of culture in all its diversifications and ramifications, from the ostensive gesture as the nascent institution of language through changing tribal organizations to the rich variations of the arts. Thus the originary event figures as a sort of retrospective projection of the productive process that is to be observed in culture and that unfolds human history as a rhythmic alternation between restriction and derestriction. For this reason the originary event is not conceived in cognitive terms as a myth of origin, but as a blank. It is a fiction, "because the origin of representation is an event that . . . is nonconstructible" (101). However, "if representation is not in itself an irrational activity incapable of the thematic expression of truth, why then does there exist a set of representations called 'culture' that can express whatever truth they possess only through fictions, which is to say, through *lies?*" (126). And the answer is as follows: "representation as such is rational because it reproduces the worldly on an unworldly scene, creates an unreal model that does not disturb its real referent. Culture is irrational because it presents this act of representation that defers the real as a worldly act of adequation between man and reality" (126–27).

It is the "nonconstructibility" of what underlies culture that makes culture unfold in a series of fictions, by means of which humans keep eliminating the difference between themselves and the reality they are exposed to. Hence the "irrationality" of culture, in the sense that its developments are unpredictable, because the act of representation, in deferring "the real as a worldly act of adequation between man and reality," points to the fact that such a deferral is an occupation of the blank—an occupation which is the very root of culture. It is this occupation, however, that disestablishes the equilibrium achieved through the deferral, and so a new conflict is bound to arise. The constitutive and "nonconstructible" blank of culture, visualized in terms of an originary event, not only defies conceptualization, but also drives the unfolding of culture as an ever new attempt to defer the newly arisen conflict. The originary conflict between appetitive appropriation and the interdiction of its satisfaction can never be resolved once and for all, because the act of representation in itself only produces changing fictions. If the heart of culture is the deferral of violence through representation, by substituting the sign for the real, then the real is bound to bounce back on the scene, thus creating a new conflict, to be averted once more by means of representation.

Culture is the offshoot of a generative anthropology insofar as its basic constellation of the originary event contains a blank that cannot be eliminated and continually invites occupation. This blank is created by the sign, since the "being of the object is not present in the sign, yet the sign reveals the object to the imagination. But what is revealed in the sign itself is the interdiction that separates the sign-user from the designatum. The sign recalls the object because it incarnates the refusal of the object."[24] Thus a blank opens up, since the difference between the sign and its referent can never be bridged, and the originary event therefore manifests itself as center and periphery—a constellation that forever dissociates human beings from the center which they crave to occupy. The impossibility of ever overcoming the blank that differentiates the center from the periphery proves to be the driving force that both generates and energizes human culture.

Although Gans demonstrates this continually interchanging relationship between center and periphery in ritual, social, and economic terms, it nevertheless finds its most tangible expression in literature which, for him, becomes the signature of high culture. This is primarily because it brings the originary impulse of the sign to full fruition. Literature, for him, is declarative language. "The declarative describes the absence of an object the significance of which was established by the imperative, whose expression of this significance was supposed to make the object appear" (121). As this is the basic structure of literature, it becomes the epitome of high culture (171 ff.), since it is not a model of life in general, but rather a model of desire through which human culture first comes to life.

Such a model of desire is already paradigmatically expressed in Greek tragedy,[25] in which we may see ourselves in the place of the central protagonist and are given the opportunity to examine him from the safety of the periphery. The imaginary sacrifice of this central figure consoles us for our lack of centrality; at the same time, it teaches us, through example, the paradoxical nature of our own desire for centrality. If literature thus provides an imaginary model of human desire, it also highlights both difference and resentment as the constitutive components of human desire. Resentment, according to Gans—and in this respect he joins hands with Nietzsche[26]—powers the generation of culture insofar as the position of the center is denied to those who find themselves on the periphery (173, 198). Expressed resentment, however, turns into sublimation,[27] which allows human beings to entertain a relationship to their basically paradoxical desire: to be different from what they covet, and to undermine this difference as it is the source of resentment. Thus literature produces something that is irrevocably absent in the life that humans lead, and at the same time, by presenting what is absent, it makes the workings of human culture transparent (301).

In this respect, literature provides an almost indispensable compensation for the lack of any transcendental stance which, whenever postulated, exists outside human culture, and only predicates what the latter is supposed to be. Instead of being beyond culture, literature is inside it, functioning as a monitoring "device" and allowing us to observe the driving forces out of which culture arises. However, only a fiction is able to function in this way, not least as the endemic resentment—proceeding from the opposition between center and periphery—exhibits the paradoxical nature of human desire in all its shifting modes.[28] As sublimation, literature appears to provide at least momentary satisfaction through its forms of representation—representation which, as the avoidance of conflict, defers the real to the unreal. The disequilibrium inherent in desire is resolved for a fleeting, illusory moment, so that a psychological equilibrium may be enjoyed. For this enjoyment, however, the paradoxicality of desire is a necessary prerequisite, as it allows human beings to be simultaneously with themselves and outside themselves. Thus literature does two things at once: it both bridges the ineluctable difference between center and periphery, and it upholds that difference. Only a fiction is able to perform this paradoxical task, because it presents in simultaneity what are mutually exclusive.

If the interchange between interdiction and resentment appears to be the general matrix of culture, such a matrix can be qualified in cognitive terms as negativity. Negativity is dual by nature: the negation of something enables something else. Every negation entails a tacit motivation lying behind the negating act—a motivation, however, that cannot be logically or causally derived from what is negated. This makes negativity into a generative matrix, as the negating impulse does not necessarily condition the enabling feature, let alone shape it. The negating act only attends to or aims at what is interdicted or resented, and is not concerned with the outcome of a suspended interdiction or a cancelled resentment.

This dual aspect of negativity can be visualized or presented only through literature. The imagery of literature portrays the way in which interdictions and resentments are transcended, thus offering a sublimation that is impossible within the differential structure of human reality. Sublimation, however, is not only an escape hatch from the peripheral position; it also furnishes a stance inside culture from which to monitor culture's driving forces. For sublimation is double-edged: psychologically it is a form of escape, but in its original sense as the sublime it is also an emulation of desire, and hence a means of overcoming it.[29] Thus literature allows for something otherwise impossible: the reading of culture. What opens literature up to such a reading is the disclosure of its fictionality, which prevents it from turning into myth. It is a means of spelling out the way in which the life of culture proceeds; it thus offers a transparency and does not equate its narratives with the origin of culture, as myths are prone to do.

The prominent status accorded to literature and the "esthetic" in Gans's generative anthropology makes them appear double-sided. Do literature and the "esthetic" serve as explanatory fictions necessary for grasping human culture, or are they already conceived as a literary anthropology, exhibiting features of humans that are not brought out into the open anywhere else?

If we read sentences like the following, we get the impression that the "esthetic" is an indispensable prerequisite for human self-creation:

> The esthetic offers an internal solution to resentment; the esthetic oscillation between representation and imaginary presence defers resentment by preventing the stabilization of the resentful opposition between center and periphery. . . . Without the esthetic moment, the originary scene would collapse in conflict; the human would not have been preserved, for no knowledge of the center would have been acquired.[30]

The function exercised by the "esthetic" in the originary scene is, after the instituting of declarative language, taken over by literature, which plays out the interchange between center and periphery into the unforeseeable possibilities that with hindsight present themselves as the course of human history. In this respect a generative anthropology turns into a literary anthropology, as it creates a vivid perception of what human beings, in their ordinary activities, are so inextricably caught up in. What remains an open question, however, is why there is a need for the self-monitoring that literature appears to provide. Is the sublimation of resentment all that literature has to offer? If so, this would make literary anthropology shrink to a rather one-dimensional revelation of human life, and not furnish a great deal more than what psychoanalysis has come up with. At best, literary anthropology would help to uncover a psychology of human history, as Gans has done so splendidly.

But human history elucidated by the mirror of literature serves, in the final analysis, as a visualization of what is "nonconstructible": the originary event. If the history of culture is an exegesis of the nonconstructible originary event from which it has ensued, then the underlying pattern of a generative anthropology begins to emerge. Just as the originary event has generated the history of culture, the latter, in turn, lends plausibility to the positing of such an event. In other words, event and history are tied together by transactional loops. The "nonconstructibility" is made to loop into the history of culture, and the continual shifts of representation as avoidance of conflict are made to loop into the originary event, whose nonconstructibility perpetuates itself in the unforeseeable turns taken by the relationship between center and periphery. Literature becomes the beacon which allows us to monitor these unforeseeable turns, and hence reveals itself as the overall explanatory fiction. Since there is no stance outside both the originary event and human culture, the fictionality of literature becomes an innerworldly transcendence allowing us to comprehend what otherwise exceeds any and all cognitive frameworks. If there is an exploratory side to this otherwise explanatory use of fiction in Gans's enterprise, it comes to the fore in the construal of a cultural history. Such a construal aims at finding out what may have been the roots of culture, and how these roots have branched out into cultural patterns and institutions.

Is that all a literary anthropology may achieve, or are there other aspects of literature beyond the function of serving as an explanatory fiction enabling us to comprehend the life of culture? In the cases discussed so far, the use of fiction was explanatory, because the existence and the development of human culture are indisputable facts to whose enlightenment the fictions were applied. Fictions had to make the given comprehensible.

What distinguishes Gans from Geertz is that Geertz stays closer to the welter of given data, and fictions have to be made up in order to grasp these observations; Gans does not pay very much attention to ethnographical details, hence he makes literature into an overall construct: the explanatory fiction of culture itself. In concocting his fictions, Geertz takes from literature at best only an actor-oriented scenario for his enterprise, whereas Gans takes the fictionality of literature as the all-encompassing explanatory pattern for something which could otherwise not be fathomed. But Gans, like Geertz, acknowledges that there is something given: the constellation of center and periphery, which he considers a universal that is discernible from the revolutionary inception of mankind right through to postmodernism.

What distinguishes the literary fiction from fictions used in anthropological research is the fact that it is not meant to grasp anything given; instead of instrumentalizing the explanatory capabilities of fictions, fictionality in literature functions basically as a means of exploration. This distinction between different types of fiction is indicative not only of the manifold uses to which fictions can be put, but also of the specific demands that they have to meet.

Literary fictions are first and foremost "as if" constructions, and in this respect are almost the exact opposite to what Geertz had in mind when expressly stating that for his purpose they are not "merely 'as if' thought experiments." Whatever reference a literary text may make to any extratextual reality, the "as if" signals that such a reality is put in brackets, and is not meant as a given but is merely to be understood as if it were given.[31] Consequently, all the extratextual fields of reference that are reproduced in a fictional text are outstripped, as is indicated by their being bracketed. This runs counter to the actor-oriented scenario Geertz devised when trying to explain the covert implications of the interaction between a Berber chieftain, a Jewish merchant, and a French soldier in an incident observed in Morocco in 1912. Similarly, the opposition of center and periphery as the underlying blueprint of Gans's generative anthropology is certainly not to be taken for a mere "as if" construction; rather, it is a universal, not to be outstripped by literature, but to be illustrated in its kaleidoscopically shifting operations through literature, which thus becomes mimetic. Whenever fictions are used for explanatory purposes, they function as a means of integrating the data to be grasped. Whenever fictions deliberately disclose their fictionality—thus presenting themselves as mere "as if" constructions—they function as a means of disordering and disrupting their extratextual fields of reference. Explanatory fictions are integrative, whereas literary fictions, as instruments of exploration, are dissipative.

Dissipation occurs first and foremost through the inroads made by the fictional text into the referential fields to which it relates. Texts make these inroads by stepping beyond their own boundaries, lifting elements out of the extratextual systems in which they fulfill their specific functions. This applies both to the world of discourses and to the existing body of literature, from which fragments are incorporated into every new literary text in such a way as to decompose the structure and the semantics of the systems concerned. Such a disruption is almost the exact opposite of the integrative function exercised by explanatory fictions. When these truncated elements and dislocated fragments are assembled in the text, strange combinations are bound to occur, and since all these are made up by the fictional text itself, the question arises as to whether the literary text—being a fiction—actually consists of a plurality of fictions. All the scraps of material selected from outside and then imported into the text become related, interconnected, interlinked, telescoped, etc., and thus result in compositions of decomposed structures and disjointed meanings that have no equivalent outside the text itself. Consequently, whatever appears to have a resemblance to any extratextual reality should only be taken *as if* it were such a reality, since it is not meant to be one, and has therefore been put into brackets. This applies equally to all the universals still postulated in anthropological studies, especially when an explicit reference is made to them in a fictional text.

The very fact that literary fictionality consists of a plurality of fictions again sets it off from explanatory fictions, which are basically undifferentiated and cohesive; otherwise they would scatter what they have to integrate. The plurality described above is augmented in a literary narrative, for instance by a fictive narrator—who may be omniscient, first person, or continually self-effacing—or by the fiction of an implied author. Something similar happens with regard to the potential addressee, who may figure as a fictional, implied, intended, ideal, or contemporary reader. Equally, all the characters are fictions, maneuvered more often than not into a head-on collision by a fictional plotline. These fictions and their many variants form yet another category within the plurality encompassed by the literary text. This plurality is something which an integration-oriented explanatory fiction could not allow itself to indulge in.

What inferences might be drawn from the difference between the explanatory fiction as a unified construct and the literary fiction as a dispersive plurality? Explanatory fictions are meant to comprehend the welter of data that one is given to observe. Literary fictions decompose existing organizations outside the text, and recompose them in order to overstep given boundaries. Explanatory fictions have an implicit teleology, which the "as if" of the exploratory fiction deliberately suspends in order to plumb the unfathomable. The different activities of these two types of fiction entail different operational modes as well. Explanatory fictions—as we have seen—operate in recursive loops which explain the development of culture as an externalization of humans and the fashioning of humans as cultural artifacts. Humans transport themselves into what they are not and, in turn, are impacted by their "extragenetic, outside-the-skin control mechanisms," thus launching themselves into a process of self-fashioning. Transporting themselves into and simultaneously being affected by their own external-izations allows human beings to fathom how they negotiate the gap between themselves and their environment.

Recursive looping also characterizes generative anthropology, although there are two gaps to be negotiated: that between humans and their envi-ronment, and that which is designated as the originary scene. Consequently, the whole of human history is made to loop into the originary scene in or-der to establish its plausibility, and the scene itself is made to loop into this very history in order to account for its structural unfolding. The less an-thropological studies are based on field work, the more gaps open up for the explanatory fiction to negotiate.

The literary text as a plurality of fictions is virtually teeming with gaps that can no longer be negotiated by the procedures of explanatory fictions. Recursion, therefore, cannot be an operational mode for the interrelation-ships that develop within such a plurality. This is all the more obvious as lit-erary fictions are not concocted for the comprehension of something given. On the contrary, they dismantle what can be perceived as a given reality, or discourse, or social and cultural system. Recursion aims at control and thus at narrowing existing gaps; the multiplicity of fictions militates against con-straints and therefore generates gaps. What, then, is the relationship among these fictions within the text, bearing in mind that each of them has only other fictions as its environment? Instead of them looping into one another, they actually play with one another.

Recursion versus play marks the operational distinction between ex-planatory and exploratory fictions. Play is engendered by what one might call "structural coupling,"[32] which forms the pattern underlying the plural-ity of fictions in the literary text. This is most obvious in the operation of the fictional strategies, as the narrator is coupled with the characters, the plot-line, the addressee, and so forth. Such coupling is equally discernible with the truncated material imported into the text, derived from all kinds of ref-erential fields including existing literature. The fragments are interlinked, most strikingly in what has come to be called intertextuality. Structural cou-pling results in friction among the intertwined fictions, causing encroach-ment, perturbation, disturbance, infringement, etc. These consequences of structural coupling have to be acted out, and in that sense the plurality of fictions play with one another. The gaming which thus ensues is structured by a countervailing movement. It is free play insofar as it reaches beyond what is encountered, and it is instrumental play insofar as there is some-thing to be achieved. The actual play itself is permeated by all the features of gaming: it is agonistic, unpredictable, deceptive, and subversive, so that the multiple fictions find themselves in a state of "dual countering."[33] Such a state, however, reveals the difference in function which offsets this kind of fiction from that conceived as an explanatory construct. Dual countering acted out as gaming is—according to Heidegger—the hallmark of the art-work. Heidegger called it "jenes Gegenwendige" that arises out of and is powered by the "rift," which is the ineluctable condition for enabling by de-composing, for the rift is not in the nature of a straightforward conflict: "rather, it is the intimacy with which opponents belong to each other."[34]

If the dual countering effected by structural coupling characterizes the artwork as an interplay between plural fictions, what are the anthropological implications of such a structure? In contradistinction to the inherent tele-ology operative in recursive looping, the "movement of play," as Gadamer once remarked, "has no goal that brings it to an end," and this endlessness indicates that play has "no substrate."[35] Hence the gaming plurality of the literary text does not represent anything located outside the text, but rather produces something that arises out of all the fictions playing with and against one another. Continuous gaming creates disturbances and clashes between the fictions involved, and these generate the complexity of the text con-cerned. The complexity, as we have seen, is not representative of anything given, but it is an emerging phenomenon fueled by the perturbations that occur in the mutual impinging of fictions upon one another. This makes the literary text into an autonomous system, in the sense that such a system has "no project external" to itself.[36] Small wonder that the literary text has so frequently been likened to the human organism. However, this artificially created autonomy is not to be taken for the mirror image of the human body as a self-organizing system, since the complexity emerging from the interplay of fictions does not provide the necessary self-maintenance to which a great many operations within a truly autonomous system have to contribute. The interplay of literary fictions does not have such an opera-tive drive; it issues into a continual transgression of what each of the fictions implies. Instead of reducing the text play to an underlying pattern which is supposed to power it, the play itself turns out to be a generative matrix of emerging phenomena that can be qualified as ontological novelties. They are novelties insofar as they did not hitherto exist, and they are ontological insofar as they provide access to the hitherto unknown.

This leads us to what Ernst Mayr once called "the thorny problem of 'emergence,'" whose "principle" he stated "dogmatically" as follows:

"When two entities are combined at a higher level of integration, not all the properties of the new entity are necessarily a logical or predictable conse-quence of the properties of the components." This difficulty is by no means confined to biology, but it is certainly one of the major sources of indetermi-nacy in biology. Let us remember that indeterminacy does not mean lack of cause, but merely unpredictability.[37]

This unpredictability applies to the literary text insofar as the dual countering of fictions cannot be totally controlled. What emerges from it leads to an ontological novelty, which makes the literary fiction not only exploratory, but also a paradigm of "emergentism."

Emergence as an umbrella concept is a form of order, although it bears the inscription of unpredictability since it cannot be traced back to any underlying basis. Furthermore, it cannot be directly derived from the components that have been coupled with one another. Emergence as an unpredictable new order thrives on the transformation to which the components (here the gaming fictions) have been subjected. The plurality of interconnecting fictions in the text gives rise to a complex dynamic order of phenomena.

At this juncture we must switch from an operational to a symbolic description [38] if we are to spell out what emerges from the gaming fictions within the literary text as the overall fiction. An operational description is concerned with the inner workings of the exploratory fiction, while a symbolic one relates to the domain targeted by such an exploration, elucidating what emerges. The following remarks cannot possibly cover all that the exploratory fiction may reveal, but they may exemplify what emergence—generated by the dual countering of fictions—brings to light. [39]

Each text is a rewriting of other texts, which are incorporated and stored in the text concerned. Such a rewriting is a transgression of boundaries, and the fragments brought back from the inroads made into other texts are pitted against one another, thus erasing their contexts, cancelling their meanings, and telescoping even what may be mutually exclusive. The ensuing interconnection may be agonistic, deceptive, subversive, and indeed unprecedented, and this interplay will tease out a semantic polysemy that had never existed before.

Such storage of what has been pillaged from other texts is an effort to rescue what is past from its ultimate death. It is the catastrophe of forgetting that is counteracted by this assembly of dislocated fragments from a cultural heritage. Thus intertextuality forms the basic pattern of cultural memory—a memory that operates through multifarious interrelations. Each segment of the text is at least dually coded; it refers to another text, and it transforms this reference by making whatever elements have been stored in the text play against one another. Furthermore, intertextuality also encompasses the lacunae that exist between the reference text and the manifest text. These empty spaces, or temporal gaps, puncture the interplay of the transcoded fragments, thus spotlighting alienations, condensations, and overdeterminations. The dissipation of meaning, the dismantling of structures, and the disfiguring of contexts transmutes the reference text into a mass of segments out of which ever new combinations are made to arise. Therefore, intertextuality is not just a representation of human culture; it also enacts the largely hidden operations of memory, and thus allows for a vivid perception of how cultural memory functions.

There are two noteworthy aspects of this emergent order of cultural memory. On the one hand, it is marked by an ineluctable duality: references and allusions to other texts are both dissipated and used for a recomposition of unforeseeably changing relationships. On the other hand, only such a dissection of the cultural heritage allows diversified facets of the past to be brought together, thereby giving presence in simultaneity to what may be worlds apart. Cultural memory, which thus emerges out of the structure of intertextuality, presents itself as a tangible new order fueled by the multifarious forms of interplay between the dislocated fragments lifted out of previous literature.

Cultural memory as an emergent phenomenon may be read as an indication that whatever has "interested living men and women," and whatever "the creative minds of all generations . . . are . . . building together"—to use Pater's terms—should always be available.[40] The more comprehensive such a concern turns out to be, the more intense is the urge to have everything in one instant. Intertextuality—the memory of the text—is the road to this kind of satisfaction, not least as it permits recipients to be drawn into the workings of the interconnecting nodes that organize the shifting relations of this network, thus making them experience a presence which has never before been real or present to them. Could it be that such virtual presences, unattainable though longed for in everyday life, reveal a basic human urge?

What distinguishes these virtual presences is the fact that they defy deconstruction, which would otherwise unmask any presence as an interest-governed assumption to be exposed for what it is: an illusion. The craving, however, for such an unattainable presence in the midst of life, given a palpable shape by the exploratory fiction of the literary text, adumbrates a division in the human makeup itself. Since the cultural past can never become a real presence, only a literary fiction offers the potential recipient the opportunity to be in two different presences at the same time. To have the virtual presence of the past in one's own present may contribute to the stabilization of our humaneness. The past was, after all, manmade, and hence to be in a virtual presence which is outside one's real present provides a transgression of the limitations by which human beings are otherwise hedged in. Thus the literary fiction offers the chance to be with oneself and simultaneously outside oneself, which may well mean that in such a state the human being enjoys what is never achieved in life, namely to be and to have oneself. The argument could also be reversed by maintaining that it is the exploratory fiction that allows the elucidation of such a basic human disposition.

Cultural memory, which is collective memory that cannot be genetically transmitted, is by no means the only emergent phenomenon generated by the textual play. Dismantling the meanings, structures, and contexts of a cultural past is not meant to cancel them out, but rather is designed to encompass diversified ranges of the past, which can only be given presence by foreshortening what is invoked. Such a procedure is all the more necessary since the past is a domain of multiple organizations, whereas the future, in contradistinction, is entropy. If culture—as shown by ethnographical research—is an emergent phenomenon generated by the conversion of entropy into information, the exploratory character of literary fictions does not exactly function as a catalyst for such a transition, but it does throw light on the processes involved.

The interplay among the plurality of fictions generates a penumbra of possibilities, which are presences just as virtual as the cultural memory produced by intertextuality. These possibilities are distinctive insofar as they adumbrate an order that can only arise out of the interplay, although they cannot be logically or even causally derived from the fictions themselves. Since the possibilities are not extensions of what is depicted by the fictions of the text, the emergent order is not a utopian fantasy, and yet it is fantastic, because the possibilities generated are to a large extent unpredictable. Such unforeseeability springs from the transgressive effect produced by the reciprocal impinging of fictions upon one another. However, the transgression lacks a precise intentionality, not least because the multifarious moves of the textual play inhibit any definite intention. Furthermore, even a fairly consistent intention is unable to control the play's target.

Still, the emergent order—not to be equated with the components from whose interactions it has issued—is able to chart an open-ended and, in the final analysis, entropic future. It may even be a reassuring guarantee for such charting that it cannot be derived from the interacting components that have made it possible. At any rate, an entropic future has to be split into the duality of order and contingency, or one may just as well say that an open-ended future thus inscribes itself into the text. The future cannot be transgressed, but can only be fantastically charted by drawing on what has been transgressed. Therefore the possibilities are not counter-images to existing realities; instead, they delineate a limbo between what has been and the unfathomableness of what may come. This limbo functions as a buffer, allowing us to conceive how open-endedness might be dealt with.

There are two inferences—albeit symbolic ones—to be drawn from this intermediate state that literature is able to create. First, literature testifies to a transgressive urge that does not shrink from any kind of conflict, because, one might argue, lifting boundaries and overcoming what appears insurmountable are vital necessities of human self-preservation. The transgressive thrust only illustrates how humans have to master the contingencies of a challenging environment. Second, to observe the unpredictable transgressions that literature portrays is not only reassuring, but also protective, in the sense that humans may become aware of the unforeseeable plenitude they are able to spin out of themselves. It is this duality of an endangering transgression and a reassuring protection effected by the unforeseeable possibilities that makes this limbo a place of simultaneous torment and bliss.

The unpredictable possibilities of an emerging order as the signature of literature point to the basic operation of what Castoriadis once called "the radical imaginary."[41] As long as it is not activated, the imaginary lies dormant in the human mind. It has to be prodded into action by agents from outside itself, which trim and channel it according to the purpose it is meant to serve. The all-out stimulation of the "radical imaginary" is certainly exercised by entropy, as evinced by the reciprocal relationship between humans and the culture which they create and by which they are created. The emerging order of unpredictable possibilities arising out of the plurality of fictions at play with one another enacts such a process. Literature draws the whole of the human past into itself, and out of it arises a continuously shifting cultural memory which, in turn, is transgressed in an effort to chart open-endedness.

As a concomitant phenomenon of human development, literature appears to be the mirror that allows humans to see themselves reflected in their manifestations. Such a view of oneself may not result in any immediate practical consequences, especially since this self-perceiving is inauthentic, highlighted by the fictional "as if." This inauthenticity, however, does not seem to invalidate this self-examination, since humans never cease to perform it.

What might be the reason for such self-confrontation? Is it an unfulfilled longing for what has been irrevocably lost, or is it a prefiguration of what it might mean to be and simultaneously to have oneself? In the end, neither of these alternatives may apply. Instead, it may be the duality into which the human being is split, suspended between self-preservation and self-transgression, that makes us wander with undiminished fascination in the maze of our own unpredictable possibilities. With literature as Ariadne's thread, human beings try to keep track of their self-exploration, always on the verge of losing themselves between their alternatives.

NOTES

1. Clifford Geertz, *The Interpretation of Cultures* (New York: Basic Books, 1973), 5.
2. Ibid., 47, 49.
3. Arnold Gehlen, *Der Mensch. Seine Natur und seine Stellung in der Welt* (Bonn: Athenaeum, 1958), 21, 35, 89, 383; André Leroi-Gourhan, *Gesture and Speech,* trans. Anna Bostock Berger (Cambridge, Mass.: MIT Press, 1993), 76–83, 85, 88–89, 137; Eric Gans, *The End of Culture: Toward a Generative Anthropology* (Berkeley: University of California Press, 1985), 103 ff.
4. Geertz, *Interpretation of Cultures,* 51.

5. Leroi-Gourhan, *Gesture and Speech*, 308, 311.

6. Geertz, *Interpretation of Cultures*, 11.

7. For thick vs. thin description, see Geertz, *Interpretation of Cultures*, 3–30, especially 6–7, 9–11, 12, 14, 16, 25, 26, 27, 28.

8. Leroi-Gourhan, *Gesture and Speech*, 91.

9. Geertz, *Interpretation of Cultures*, 15–16.

10. Ibid., 44.

11. This is the way Geertz characterizes his enterprise (*Interpretation of Cultures*, viii).

12. Norbert Wiener, *The Human Use of Human Beings* (Garden City, N.Y.: Doubleday, 1954), 33.

13. Quoted by Geertz, *Interpretation of Cultures*, 70–71.

14. See Francisco J. Varela, *Principles of Biological Autonomy* (New York: North Holland, 1979), 86–91.

15. Geertz, *Interpretation of Cultures*, 50.

16. Jurij M. Lotman, *Aufsätze zur Theorie und Methodologie der Literatur und Kultur*, ed. and trans. Karl Eimermacher (Kronberg: Scriptor, 1974), 413, my translation.

17. Geertz, *Interpretation of Cultures*, 46.

18. Ibid., 24.

19. Francis Bacon, *The Advancement of Learning and New Atlantis*, ed. Thomas Case (London: Oxford University Press, 1974), 96.

20. Gans, *End of Culture*, 19–38.

21. See Eric Gans, *Originary Thinking: Elements of Generative Anthropology* (Stanford: Stanford University Press, 1993), 117–219.

22. See Gans, *End of Culture*, pp. 179–300. Further citations will be made parenthetically in the text.

23. Geertz, *Interpretation of Cultures*, 26.

24. Gans, *Originary Thinking*, 104.

25. See Gans, *End of Culture*, 227 ff., and *Originary Thinking*, 132 ff.

26. Gans differs from Nietzsche insofar as he does not share Nietzsche's moral nihilism.

27. See Gans, *End of Culture*, 223–24, 225–26, 229–30, 232–33, 244, 295, 302.

28. Gans, *Originary Thinking*, 177–219, has outlined such a process.

29. For the dual nature of sublimation see Paul Ricoeur, *Freud and Philosophy: An Essay in Interpretation*, trans. Denis Savage (New Haven: Yale University Press, 1970), 497–98, 514 ff.

30. Gans, *Originary Thinking*, 125.

31. For further details, see Wolfgang Iser, *The Fictive and the Imaginary: Charting Literary Anthropology* (Baltimore: Johns Hopkins University Press, 1993), 7–21.

32. For the meaning of this term, see Varela, *Principles of Biological Autonomy*, 33, 48, 211, 236, 246.

33. For further details, see Iser, *The Fictive and the Imaginary*, 222–38, 247–73.

34. Martin Heidegger, *Holzwege* (Frankfurt/Main: Klostermann, 1950), 43; *Poetry, Language, Thought*, trans. Albert Hofstadter (New York: Harper and Row, 1975), 63.

35. Hans-Georg Gadamer, *Truth and Method*, rev. trans. Joel Weinsheimer and Donald G. Marshall (New York: Crossroad, 1989), 103.

36. See William R. Paulson, *The Noise of Culture: Literary Texts in a World of Information* (Ithaca: Cornell University Press, 1988), 140.

37. Ernst Mayr, *Toward a New Philosophy of Biology* (Cambridge, Mass.: Harvard University Press, Belknap Press, 1988), 34–35.

38. For such a distinction see Varela, *Principles of Biological Autonomy,* 66, 70, 73, 79.

39. These remarks supplement what I have outlined in *The Fictive and the Imaginary,* 1–21 and 296–303, and in "Staging as an Anthropological Category," *New Literary History* 23 (1992): 877–88.

40. Walter Pater, *The Renaissance: Studies in Art and Poetry* (London: Macmillan, 1919), 49; *Appreciations with an Essay on Style* (London: Macmillan, 1920), 241.

41. See Cornelius Castoriadis, *The Imaginary Institution of Society,* trans. Kathleen Blamey (Cambridge: Polity Press, 1987), and my discussion of his concept of "the radical imaginary" in *The Fictive and the Imaginary,* 204–22.

CHAPTER TEN

"A Self-Unsealing Poetic Text":
Poetics and Politics of Witnessing

Jacques Derrida

Translated by Rachel Bowlby

> *The world becomes its language and its language becomes the world. But it is a world out of control, in flight from ideology, seeking verbal security and finding none beyond that promised by a poetic text, but always a self-unsealing poetic text.*
> MURRAY KRIEGER, *A Reopening of Closure: Organicism Against Itself*

> *[I]t is the role of art to play the unmasking role—the role of revealing the mask as mask. Within discourse it is literary art that is our lighthouse. . . . It would seem extravagant to suggest that the poem, in the very act of becoming successfully poetic— that is, in constituting itself poetry—implicitly constitutes its own poetic. But I would like here to entertain such an extravagant proposal.*
> MURRAY KRIEGER, *Ekphrasis: The Illusion of the Natural Sign*

Signing, sealing, divulging, unsealing. This will be about bearing witness.[1] And about poetics as bearing witness—but testamentary witness: attestation, testimony, will. A poem can "bear witness to" a poetics. It can promise it, it can be a response to it as to a promise in a will or testament. Indeed it must, it cannot not do so. But not with the idea of applying a previously existing art of writing, nor of referring to one as to a charter written somewhere else, nor of obeying its laws like a transcendental authority, but rather by itself promising, in the act of its happening, the foundation of a poetics. Thus it would involve the poem "constituting its own poetics," as Krieger puts it, a poetics which must also, as if *across* its generality, *become, invent, institute, offer* for reading, in an exemplary way, signing it, both sealing and unsealing it, the possibility of this poem. This would come about in the event itself, in the verbal body of its singularity: at such and such a date, at the both unique and repeatable moment of a signature which opens the verbal body onto something other than itself, in the reference which carries it beyond itself, towards the other or towards the world.

As testimony to warm gratitude, I would therefore like to take a certain risk in my turn, so as to share it with Murray Krieger—the risk of "entertain[ing] such an extravagant proposal." And to try it out, I would like to put to the test this experience of bearing witness. Wanting to recall places where, for over ten years, I have enjoyed living near Murray Krieger, I chose to go back over some texts by Paul Celan that I read with my students at the University of California, Irvine, for a course of seminars about witnessing. And especially about responsibility, when it involves a poetic signature, at a particular date. Hypothesis to be verified: all responsible witnessing involves a poetic experience of language.

I

Without giving up thinking about the secret in the perspective of responsibility, far from it, how is it that one has to come up against the question of witnessing (*testimonium*)? And why is the question of *testimonium* no different from that of the *testamentum*, of all the testaments, in other words of surviving in dying, of surviving, living on, before and beyond the opposition between living and dying?

> *Aschenglorie* [. . .]
>
> · · ·
>
> *Niemand*
> *zeugt für den*
> *Zeugen.*
>
> Ash-glory [. . .]
>
> · · ·
>
> No one
> bears witness for the
> witness.[2]

If we want to keep for them that poetic resonance to which, already, on the page, they mean to respond, we must remember that these words come to us in German. As always, the idiom remains irreducible. This invincible singularity of the verbal body already introduces us into the enigma of witnessing, beside that irreplaceability of the singular witness which indeed may well be what this poem is speaking to us about. It thus speaks *of itself,* signifying itself in speaking to the other about the other, signing and designing itself in a single gesture—"sealing and unsealing itself"—or again, to quote and displace a little the words of Murray Krieger: *sealing while (by, through) unsealing itself as a poetic text.*

This idiom is untranslatable, ultimately, even if we translate it. These three lines resist, and resist even the best translation. What's more, they come to us at the end of a poem which, however little certainty there may be about its sense, about all its senses and all its possible meanings, it is difficult not to think of as also related, through an essential *reference,* to dates and events, to the existence or the experience of Celan. The poet is *the only one who can bear witness* to these "things" which are not only "words," but he does not name them in the poem. At any rate the possibility of a secret always remains open, and this reserve is inexhaustible. It is more so than ever in the case of the poetry of Celan, who continually encrypted ("sealing, unsealing") these references. Some people have been able to bear witness—just so—to this, like Peter Szondi, friend and reader-interpreter of Celan, who shared at least some of his experiences, not that such testimony exhausts or, crucially, proves what he speaks of, far from it. This poem also remains untranslatable to the extent that it can be related to events of which the German language will have been a privileged witness, namely the Shoah, which some call by the proper name (and metonymic name—a huge problem which I leave hanging here) of "Auschwitz." The German language of this poem will have been present at everything that could destroy by fire and reduce to "ashes" (*Aschenglorie*, Ash-glory, is the first word of the poem, a word double and divided) existences of innumerable number—innumerably. Innumerably but also unnameably, thus incinerating, with the name and the memory, even the *assured* possibility of bearing witness. And since I have just said "the *assured* possibility of bearing witness," we will have to ask whether the concept of bearing witness is compatible with a value of certainty, of assurance, and even of knowing as such.

Ashes are that which annihilates or threatens to annihilate even the possibility of bearing witness to annihilation. Ashes are the figure of annihilation without remains, or without a readable or decodable archive. Perhaps that would lead us to think of this fearful thing: the *possibility* of annihilation, the *virtual* disappearance of the witness, but also of the capacity to bear witness, that is, of what would be the only condition of bearing witness, its only condition of possibility as condition of its impossibility—paradoxical and aporetic. When bearing witness seems assured and so becomes a demonstrable theoretical truth, when there is a piece of information or a report, a procedure of proving or even an exhibit in a trial, it risks losing its value, its sense or its testimonial status. That comes down to saying—always the same paradox, the same paradoxopoetic matrix—that as soon as it is assured, certain as a theoretical proof, a testimony cannot be assured *as* testimony. For it to be assured as testimony, it cannot, it must not be absolutely certain, absolutely sure and certain in the order of knowing as such. This paradox of "as," "as such" (*comme tel*) is the paradox we can experience—and there is nothing fortuitous about this—apropos of the secret and responsibility, of the secret of responsibility and the responsibility of the secret. How can a secret be shown *as* secret? To take up Murray Krieger's words again, how can a mask be revealed as mask? And in what way might a poetic work be called upon to put this strange operation to work?

So it is necessary first to hear these lines in their language, and to see them in their space. Necessary out of respect for their spacing but first of all because the spaced writing of this language does not admit of translation into a simple *speech*, French or English. We see indications already of the poignant question of untranslatable testimony. Because it must be linked to a singularity and to the experience of an idiomatic mark, for example that of a language, testimony resists the test of translation. It thus risks not even being able to cross the frontier of singularity, if only to deliver its meaning. But what would be the worth of an untranslatable testimony? Would it be a non-testimony? And what would a testimony that was absolutely transparent to translation be? Would it still be a testimony?

Ashes, we were saying, annihilate or threaten to annihilate even the possibility of testifying to annihilation itself.

It happens that Celan's poem has as its title its own *incipit*. Thus its first line speaks of ashes, and it appears reasonably open to translation. It is *Aschenglorie*, in a single word, which André du Bouchet translates, in *three* words, as "*Cendres-la gloire*," and Joachim Neugroschel in *two* words, as "Ash-glory." *Word-for-word* translation is already impossible. Infidelity has begun, and betrayal and perjury, from the very threshold of this arithmetic, with this accountability of the incalculable. The poetic force of a word remains incalculable, all the more certainly so when the unity of a word ("*Aschenglorie*") is that of an *invented* composition, the inauguration of a new body. All the more certainly so when the birth of this verbal body gives the poem its first word, when this first word becomes the verb which comes at the beginning. *En arkhe en o logos* [In the beginning was the word]. And if this logos was a light, for John, here it was a light of ashes. In the beginning was (the word) "*Aschenglorie*."

This glory of the ashes, this glory of ash, this glory which is that of the ashes but which is also of ash, in ash—and glory is minimally the light or the shining brightness of fire—here it is lighting a poem that I shall not even attempt to interpret with you. Light is also knowing, truth, meaning. Now *this* light is no more than ashes *here*, it becomes ashes, it falls into ashes, as a fire goes out. *But* (it is the mobile and unstable articulation of this "but" which will be important for us) ashes are also glory, they can still be re-nouned, sung, blessed, loved, if the glory of the re-noun is not reducible either to fire or to the light of knowing. The brightness of glory is only the light of knowing [*connaissance*] and necessarily the clarity of knowledge [*savoir*].

Why not even attempt to *interpret* this poem? I am quite willing to try to explain this limit. What matters is not what this poem means, or that it means, or that it bears witness to this or that, nor even *that* it names and *what* it names—*elliptically* as always. Ellipsis and caesura and the cut-off breathing presumably mean here, as always in Celan, that which seems most *decisive* in the body and in the rhythm of the poem. A *decision*, as its name indicates, always appears *as* [*comme*] interruption, it decides as [*en tant que*] a tearing cut.

What counts, then, is not the fact that the poem *names* some themes which we know in advance must be at the heart of a reflection on responsibility, witnessing, or poetics. What matters most of all is the strange limit between what can and cannot be determined or decreed in *this poem's witnessing to witnessing*. For this poem says something about bearing witness. It bears witness to it. Now in this witnessing to witnessing, in this apparent meta-witnessing, a certain limit makes meta-witnessing—that is, absolute witnessing—both possible and impossible.

Let us try to put ourselves in the region of this limit, at the passage of this line. We will be guided by a hypothesis: this line is perhaps also that line of necessary "extravagance" which Murray Krieger speaks of.

We have just alluded to some motifs which are in some way signalled by this poem, and which we know in advance intersect at the heart of the questions of responsibility, of the secret, of witnessing.

What then are these motifs? Well, one example would be the *three,* the figure of everything that takes itself beyond two, the duo, the dual, the couple. Now *three* is named twice, in the first stanza and close to the final stanza which is the one that names the *Aschen* (*Aschenglorie,* to repeat, in *a single word* in the first line, but *Aschen-glorie,* cut by a hyphen across two lines, near the end). Both times, there is a tripleness affecting both the road (*Weg*) and the hands (*Händen*), the *knotted* hands (we should also keep hold of the knot, the knotting of the link and the hands).

> *ASCHENGLORIE hinter*
> *deinen erschüttert-verknoteten*
> *Händen am Dreiweg.*

Let us quote both French and English translations; they are not wholly satisfying, but no one can teach a lesson to anyone else here, by definition:

> *CENDRES-LA GLOIRE revers*
> *de tes mains heurtées-nouées pour jamais*
> *sur la triple fourche des routes.*

> Ash-glory behind
> your shaken-knotted
> hands on the three-forked road.

It would also be possible to translate into French as follows:

> *Gloire pour les cendres, derrière*
> *tes mains défaites effondrées—toutes nouées*
> *à la fourche des trois voies.*

> [Glory for ashes, behind
> your demolished collapsed hands—all knotted
> at the fork of the three ways.]

I am not happy with this "*pour les cendres*" ("for ashes"), for it is just as much about the glory *of* ashes as the glory promised *to* ashes; and if, as I considered doing, we translated as "*gloire* aux *cendres*" ("glory *to* ashes"), it would be necessary to understand not only the glorification of ashes, but, as one might say of a still life, the figure of glory surrounded by ashes, on a background or an ornament of ashes. Which amounts to so many ways of noting the poetic stroke of genius in this untranslatable "*Aschenglorie.*" Untranslatable the word remains, word for word, one word for the other, where the composed vocable does not decompose. For in the original version it is not divided, as it will be lower down, near the end, disarticulating and unifying itself to itself, this time, at the end of the line, by a strange hyphen. A hyphen of this kind is also an act of poetical memory. It points out the beginning *in* return; it gives a reminder of the initial undividedness of *Aschenglorie:*

> *Aschen-*
> *glorie hinter*
> *euch Dreiweg*
> *Händen.*
>
> *Cendres-*
> *la gloire, revers*
> *de vous—fourche triple,*
> *mains.*
>
> Ash-
> glory behind
> your three-forked
> hands.

One could also translate another way:

> *Gloire*
> *de cendres derrière vous les mains*
> *du triple chemin.*
>
> [Glory
> of ashes behind
> you hands
> of the triple road.]

Thus "*euch*" (*vous,* you) has just replaced the "*deinen*" of the second line ("*deinen erschüttert-verknoteten / Händen am Dreiweg,*" yours, your hands, the hands which are yours). The addressee of the apostrophe has gone into the plural. At any rate, it is no longer simply the same, it is no longer reducible to the being in the singular, masculine or feminine, to whom the first stanza is addressed. The two stanzas turn, they *turn round,* as a stanza [*strophe*] and an apostrophe always do. The two stanzas apostrophize more than one addressee. They turn round from one to the other, they turn themselves away from the one to others.

Why point out, if not more than that, this allusion to the *three*, whether in connection with road (*Dreiweg*) or hands (*Dreiweg / Händen*)? Because in fact we will soon be coming up against this motif of the third in the scene of possible/impossible testimony, of bearing witness that is possible *as* impossible. In its Latin etymology, the witness (*testis*) is someone who is present as a third person (*terstis*). We would have to look very closely at this to understand what it might imply. *Testis* has a homonym in Latin. It usually occurs in the plural, to mean "testicles." It even happens that Plautus plays on the word in *Curculio,* and exploits its being a homonym. *Testitrahus* means both complete and male, masculine. Some feminists, men or women, couldn't deprive themselves, enjoying or unjoying [*s'en jouant ou sans jouer*], of deriving from this an argument about the relations between a certain way of conceiving of the third person and bearing witness, on the one hand, and the chief, the head and phallocentric capital on the other. It is true that, in English, *testis, testes* has kept the sense of testicle—which could be an incitement to militancy.

In his *Vocabulaire des institutions européennes* [*Dictionary of European Institutions*], in the chapter on "Religion and Superstition," Benveniste analyzes a word, "*superstes,*" which can mean "witness" in the sense of survivor: someone who, having been present then having survived, plays the role of witness. Benveniste makes an association between *superstes* and *testis* but also distinguishes them:

> We can see the difference between *superstes* and *testis.* Etymologically, *testis* is someone who is present as a "third" (*terstis*) at a transaction where two persons are concerned; and this conception goes back to the Indo-European period of civilization.[3]

As always, Benveniste analyzes the etymology by following the line of a genealogical recollection which goes back to institutions, customs, *practices, arrangements.* In this valuable but profoundly problematic work which, as we see, wants to be a "dictionary of Indo-European *institutions,*" the words are selected and then placed in a network according to the *institutional* figures of which they are also assumed to be, precisely, the witnesses. The words *bear witness* to the institutions; the vocabulary *attests* to an institutional sense. But even if we suppose that the sense exists before and outside these words (an improbable or virtually meaningless hypothesis), it is at any rate certain that the sense does not exist without these words, which is to say without that which bears witness to it, in a sense of bearing witness which still remains highly enigmatic, but inescapable here. If the words *bear witness* to a usage and an institutional practice,[4] the paradox here is concentrated in the analysis of the word *testis, terstis,* which attests, with regard to knowledge, thus making way for assumed knowledge, to an institution or a practice, a social organization, a "conception"—that is Benveniste's word—which, he says, "goes back to the Indo-European period of civilization." In order to illustrate, in reality to *establish* this filiation, to prove this fact, Benveniste adds:

> A Sanskrit text says: "Every time two persons are present, Mitra is there as a third"; thus the god Mitra is by nature the "witness." But *superstes* describes the "witness" either as the one who "subsists beyond," witness at the same time as survivor, or as "the one who holds himself to the thing," who is present there. We see now what can and must be meant theoretically by *superstitio,* the function of the *superstes.* This will be the "property of being present" as a "witness."

Benveniste's statements here open onto the larger context that we could reconstitute, in particular around *superstes,* the survivor determined *as* witness, and around *testis, terstis,* determined as a third. The witness is the one who will have been present. He or she will have *attended,* in the present, the thing of which he is witness. Every time, the motif of presence, of being-present or of being-in-presence, turns out to be at the center of these determinations. In *Le Différend,* a book in which the question of the witness plays a large role, Jean-François Lyotard approaches this question of the witness as third person a number of times, without reference to Benveniste or to Celan. But by privileging the example of Auschwitz and the debate around "revisionism" (which is naturally a debate about the status of testimony or bearing witness and of survival), he problematizes the idea of God as absolute witness.[5]

Quite obviously, we must take into account an undeniable fact: like the institutions to which it is thought to refer, which it ought to reflect, represent, or incarnate, Latin semantics (*testis, terstis, superstes*) only denotes one etymologico-institutional configuration among others—and even one among others for "us," assuming that we can say "we" Westerners. It is not, for example, to be found in German as well. The family *Zeugen, bezeugen, Bezeugung, Zeugnis,* translated as "witness," "to bear witness," "testimony," "attestation," belongs to a completely different semantic network. One would be hard put, in particular, to find in it an explicit reference to the situation of the third, or even to presence. In the family of what we will not risk simply calling homonymy are all the words we have just read in the Celan poem (*Zeug, Zeugen, Zeugung*). Elsewhere, they also mean tool, procreation, engendering, and indeed generation—both biological and familial. After what the word "*témoin*" [witness] (*terstis, testis*) bears witness to [*témoigne*] by its supposed genealogy, we have what is also *witnessed* to by the word *Zeugen* in its supposed genealogy or generation, etc. If we take account of the witness as *terstis superstes,* as surviving third, and even as inheritor, guardian, guarantee, and legatee of the will and testament, ultimately of what has been and has disappeared, then the crossover between *on the one hand* a genealogical or generational semantics of *Zeugen,* and *on the other hand* the semantics of *terstis superstes,* becomes fairly vertiginous.

Crossover of a *vertiginous* filiation, yes, perhaps. But it is vertigo which turns our head, vertigo in which we are going to turn and let ourselves be turned round, and not only between the tropes and stanzas of Celan.

In English, the Latin root does of course remain, with *testimony* and *to testify, attestation, protest, testament.* So it articulates together for us the two themes of survival and of witnessing, etc. But the family of *witness* and *bearing witness* is quite different, presumably opening out onto the aspect of seeing, and thus towards another semantic and poetic space in the final words of Celan's poem in translation: "No one / bears witness for the / witness." Finally—but this is where we should have begun—Greek makes no explicit reference to the third person, to surviving, to presence, or to generation: *martus, marturos,* the witness, who will become the martyr, the witness to faith, does not literally imply any of these values (third, surviving, presence, generation). *Marturion* means, to follow the institutional usage, "testimony," but also evidence or "proof."

Here we touch on a sensitive and heavily problematic distinction between testifying, bearing witness [*témoignage*], the act or experience of witnessing as "we"[6] understand it, and, on the other hand, proof; between testifying and, on the other hand, theoretical-constative certainty. This is both an essential distinction and one that is in principle insurmountable. But in practice the confusion always remains possible, so fragile and easily crossed can the limit sometimes appear, and whatever language and word is used. For this is not reserved for the Greek *marturion* alone: the Latin *testimonium*—bearing witness [*témoignage*], giving evidence, attestation—can come to be understood as proof. So language cannot of itself alone, as a lexicon or dictionary would do, be guardian and guarantee of a usage. A pragmatic slippage from one sense to the other, sometimes in the passage from one sentence to the other, can always occur. We should ask for what necessary—not accidental—reasons the sense of "proof" regularly comes to contaminate or divert the sense of "bearing witness." For the axiom we ought to respect, it seems to me, even though it may be problematized later, is that *bearing witness* is not *proving.* Bearing witness is heterogeneous to the administration of a legal proof or the display of an object produced in evidence. Witnessing appeals to the act of faith with regard to a speech given under oath, and is therefore itself produced in the space of sworn faith ("I swear to speak the truth"), or of a promise involving a responsibility before the law, a promise always open to betrayal, always hanging on this possibility of perjury, infidelity, or abjuration.

What does "I bear witness" mean? What do I mean when I say "I bear witness" (for one only bears witness in the first person)? I mean not "I prove," but "I swear that I have seen, I have heard, I have touched, I have felt, I have been *present.*" That is the irreducibly *perceptible* dimension of presence and past presence, of what can be meant by "being present" and especially "having been present," and of what that means in bearing witness. "I *bear witness*"—that means: "I affirm (rightly or wrongly, but in all good faith, sincerely) that that was or is present to me, in space and time (thus, perceptible), and although you do not have access to it, not the same access, you, my addressees, *you have to believe me,* because I am committed to telling you the truth, I am already committed to it, I tell you that I am telling you the truth. Believe me. You have to believe me."

The addressee of the witnessing, the witness of the witness, does not see for himself what the first witness says he has seen; the addressee has not seen it and never will see it. This direct or immediate non-access of the addressee to the object of the witnessing is what marks the absence of this "witness of the witness" to the thing itself. This absence is therefore crucial. It thus hangs on the speech or the mark of testimony inasmuch as it is dissociable from what it bears witness to: the witness is not present either, of course, present in the present to what he recalls, he is not present in the mode of perception, inasmuch as he bears witness, at the moment when he bears witness; he is no longer present, now, to what he says he was present to, to what he says he perceived; even if he says he is present, present in the present, here, now, by what is called memory, memory articulated in a language, to his having-been-present.

II

This "you have to believe me" must be understood. "You have to believe me" does not have the sense of the theoretico-epistemic necessity of knowledge. It is not presented as a convincing demonstration, the result of which is that you cannot not subscribe to the conclusion of a syllogism, to the connections of an argument, or even to the manifestation of something present. Here, "you have to believe me" means "believe me because I tell you to, because I ask it of you," or, equally well, "I promise you to speak the truth and to be faithful to my promise, and I commit myself to being faithful." In this "it is necessary to believe me," the "it is necessary," which is not theoretical but performative-pragmatic, is as determining as the "believe." Ultimately, it is perhaps the only rigorous introduction to the thought of what "to believe" might mean. When I subscribe to the conclusion of a syllogism or to the delivery of a proof, it is no longer an act of belief, even if the one who conducts the demonstration asks me to "believe" in the truth of the demonstration. A mathematician or a physicist, a historian, as such, does not seriously ask me to *believe* him or her. He does not appeal in the last analysis to my belief, at the moment when he presents his conclusions. "What is believing?"—what are we doing when we *believe* (which is to say all the time, and as soon as we enter into relationship with the other): that is one of the questions that cannot be avoided when one tries to think about bearing witness.

In spite of the examples invoked to begin to make things a little clearer, bearing witness is not altogether and necessarily discursive. It is sometimes silent. It has to involve something of the body which does not have the right of speech. We should thus not say, or believe, that bearing witness is entirely discursive, thoroughly a matter of language. But we will not call something bearing witness that is not open to the order of the *"comme tel,"* of the present or having-been-present *"comme tel,"* *"en tant que tel,"* of the *"as such"* or of this which indeed Murray Krieger stresses—as truth itself, the truth of the lie or the simulacrum, the truth of the mask—in the sentence quoted in the epigraph ("the role of revealing the mask *as* mask").

This "as such" is presupposed by language, unless on its side it presupposes at least the possibility of a mark, or a prelinguistic experience of the mark or the trace "as such." This is where the whole formidable problem of the apophantic opens up—of the *as such,* of presence and language. We will not enter into it directly here in its own right.[7]

Whoever bears witness does not bring a proof; he is someone whose experience, in principle singular and irreplaceable (even if it can be cross-checked with others to become proof, to become conclusive in a process of verification) comes to attest, precisely, that some "thing" has been present to him. This "thing" is no longer present to him, of course, in the mode of perception at the moment when the attestation happens; but it is present to him, if he alleges this presence, as *re-presented* in the present in memory. At any rate, even if—something unusual and improbable—it was still contemporary to the moment of the attestation, it would be inaccessible, as *perceived* presence, to the addressees who receive the testimony. The witness marks or declares that something is or has been present to him, which is not so to the addressees to whom the witness is joined by a contract, an oath, a promise, by a pledge of sworn faith whose performativity is constitutive of the witnessing and makes it a pledge [*gage*], an engagement. Even perjury presupposes this sworn faith which it betrays. A perjurer does indeed threaten all witnessing, but this threat is irreducible in the scene of sworn faith and attestation. This structural threat is both distinct and inseparable from the finitude which any witnessing also presupposes; for any witness can make a mistake in good faith, he can have a limited, false perception, one that in any number of ways is misleading about what he is speaking about; this kind of finitude, which is just as irreducible and without which, also, there would be no place for bearing witness, is nonetheless other, in its effects, than the kind which makes it obligatory to believe and makes lying or perjury always possible. There are thus two heterogeneous effects here of the same finitude, or two essentially different approaches to finitude: the one which goes by way of error or hallucination in good faith, and the one which goes by way of cheating, perjury, bad faith. Both must always be *possible*, at the moment of bearing witness.

But the very possibility of lying and perjury (lying being a kind of perjury) attests that for us, bearing witness, if there is such a thing, gains a sense only before the law, before the promise, the commitment. It has a sense only in regard to a cause: justice, truth as justice. Here we will merely situate this difficulty at the moment where in fact we encounter in the same word, *marturion*, and in a way that is not accidental, two heterogeneous meanings: 1. *on the one hand*, bearing witness, testimony, attestation (which belongs to the space of believing, of the act of faith, of engagement and signature; and we will constantly have to ask and re-ask ourselves, what does *"believe"* mean?); and 2. *on the other hand*, proof, certain determination, the order of knowledge. It is always the alternation between *Glauben und Wissen*, the title of a work of Hegel's, but also of an interminable debate between Kant and Hegel.

Whether it is phenomenological or semantic, we will not go so far as to say that *in fact* this distinction between *testimony* or *bearing witness* and *proof* "exists," in the strong and strict sense of the word. We will not go so far as to say that it *holds in reality, now or at present*. We are dealing here with a frontier that is both rigorous and inconsistent, unstable, hermetic, and permeable, uncrossable *de jure* but *de facto* crossed. The whole problem consists in the fact that the crossing of such a conceptual limit is both forbidden and constantly practiced. But if there is testimony and if it answers properly, *incontestably*, to the name and the sense intended by this name in our "culture," in the world which we think we can, precisely, inherit and bear witness to, then this testimony must not essentially consist in proving, confirming a knowledge, in assuring a theoretical certainty, a determining judgment. It can only appeal to an act of faith.

To complete this inspection of the Greek vocabulary, next to *marturion*, *marturia thesthai* refers to the action of giving a deposition: it is the attestation, the evidence set down by a witness. *Martureisthai* is to call to witness, to invoke witnesses, call upon as witness. A lovely example of this "call upon as witness," a sentence from the *Civil Wars* of the historian Appian of Alexandria, says this: *"marturomenos emauton tes philotimias,"* "calling on myself as witness to my zeal, to my ambition, to my taste for honors." Another common translation: "calling on my conscience as witness to my ambition." Someone bears witness before the others, since he is speaking, since he is addressing himself to the others; but he calls on the others as witness to him by calling on *himself* first of all as witness to his being sufficiently conscious, present to himself, to bear witness before the others of *what* he bears witness to, to the *fact that* he is bearing witness and to *that which* he is bearing witness to—first of all before himself.

Why this translation? Why this example? Because in it we encounter one of the irreducible folds of witnessing and presence, of attendance, of attendance in existence as presence: it is the fold of presence *insofar as it is* presence *to oneself*. A witness can only invoke having been present at this or that, having attended this or that, having tried out or experienced this or that, on condition of being and having been sufficiently present *to himself, as such*, on condition of claiming, at any rate, to have been sufficiently conscious of himself, sufficiently present to himself, to know what he is talking about. There is no longer any mask here. If there still were one, the masks would be exhibited *as* masks, in their mask-truth. I can only claim to offer reliable testimony if I claim to be able to testify to it before myself, sincerely, without mask and without veil, if I claim to know that what I have seen, heard, or touched, is the same as yesterday, to know what I know and mean to say what I mean to say. And thus to reveal or unveil—beyond the mask or the veil. In witnessing, presence to oneself, classic condition of responsibility, must be coextensive with presence to something else, with having-been-present to something else, and with presence to the other, for instance to the addressee of the testimony. It is on this condition that the witness can be answerable, responsible, for his testimony, as for the oath by which he commits himself to it and guarantees it. In the very concepts of perjury or lying *as such* it is presupposed that the liar or the perjurer is sufficiently present to himself; he has to keep the sense or the true sense of what he is dissimulating, falsifying, or betraying, present to himself, in its truth—and he has to be able, accordingly, to keep its secret. Keep it *as such*—and the keeping of this safe-keeping is the movement of *truth* (*veritas, verum, wahr, wahren,* which means to keep; *Wahrheit:* the truth).

What we have here is one of the joints linking the problematics of the secret, of responsibility, and of testimony. No lie or perjury without responsibility, no responsibility without presence to oneself. This presence to oneself is of course often interpreted as self-consciousness. Under this head, bearing witness before the other would involve bearing witness before one's own consciousness; this can lead to a transcendental phenomenology of consciousness. But this presence to oneself is not necessarily the ultimate form of consciousness or of self-consciousness. It can take other forms of existence, that of a certain *Dasein* for instance. Think of the role (phenomenological in another sense) which the value of testimony or attestation can play in Heidegger's *Sein und Zeit,* especially around the passages concerning, precisely, *Dasein*'s attestation (*Bezeugung*) to its originary possibility and its authenticity (*Eigentlichkeit*).[8] *Dasein* must be able to testify about itself: here we have, in *Sein und Zeit,* the axiom or the testimony of the existential analytic of *Dasein*. From the beginning, Heidegger announces the bringing to light, the manifestation, the phenomenological presentation (*Aufweis*) of such a testimony (*der phänomenologische Aufweis einer solcher Bezeugung*), namely the phenomenology of an experience which is itself phenomenological, in other words which consists in a *presentation*. It is the presentation of presentation, the testimony: here there is witness for the witness, testimony for the testimony.

To return now to the Celan poem, let us again stress this double reference to the attestation (*Bezeugung*), in "*Niemand / zeugt für den / Zeugen,*" as a reference to the enigmatic and recurrent figure of the three. While taking note of this crossover between the semantics of the witness and that of the "three" or the third, let us beware of being overhasty. Let us not pre-interpret this co-occurrence of the two motifs in the Celan poem. Although this crossover is irreducible a priori wherever there may be a question of both the witness and the three, nothing allows us to go beyond this a priori in the reading of this poem.

The same is true for the reference to the *oath*. The poem names the oath and the *petrified* oath, that which roars deeply at the bottom of the petrified oath, of the oath of stone, of the oath become stone:

> *Pontisches Einstmals: hier*
> *ein Tropfen,*
> *auf*
> *dem ertrunkenen Ruderblatt*
> *tief*
> *im versteinerten Schwur*
> *rauscht es auf.*

Published translations:

> *Pontique une fois: ici*
> *telle une goutte,*
> *sur*
> *le plat de la rame submergée,*
> *au profond*
> *du serment mué en pierre,*
> *sa rumeur.*

> Pontic once-upon: here
> a drop
> on
> the drowned oar-blade,
> deep
> in the petrified vow,
> it roars up.

Another possible translation:

> *Autrefois Pontique: ici*
> *une goutte*
> *sur*
> *la palme d'une rame noyée*
> *au fond*

du serment pétrifié
bruit.

[Once Pontic: here
a drop
on
the palm of a drowned oar
at the bottom
of the petrified vow
sounds.]

Suppose that we refrain, as I would like to do here, from "commentary" on this poem. But even before doing this, in any case, and whatever the poem or its signatory *means to say,* whatever he means to be testifying to, one cannot not a priori link this figure of the oath to that of testimony which comes up at the end. There is no testimony without some involvement of oath (*Schwur*) and without sworn faith. What distinguishes an act of testifying from the straightforward transmission of knowledge, from straightforward information, from the straightforward statement or the mere demonstration of a proven theoretical truth, is that in it someone *commits himself* in regard to someone, by an oath that is at least implicit. The witness *promises* to say or to manifest something to another, his addressee: a truth, a sense which has been or is in some way present to him as a unique and irreplaceable witness. This irreplaceable singularity links the question of testifying to that of the secret but also, indissociably, to that of a death which no one can anticipate or see coming, nor give or receive in the place of the other. With this attestation, there is no other choice but to believe it or not to believe it. Verification or transformation into proof, contesting in the name of "knowledge," belong to a foreign space. They are heterogeneous to the moment peculiar to testifying. The experience of testifying as such thus presupposes the oath. It happens in the space of this *sacramentum.* The same oath links the witness and his addressees, for example—but this is only an example— in the scene of justice: "I swear to speak the truth, the whole truth, and nothing but the truth." This oath (*sacramentum*) is sacred: it marks acceptance of the sacred, acquiescence to entering into a holy or sacred space of the relationship to the other. Perjury itself involves this sacralization in sacrilege. The perjurer only commits perjury *as such* insofar as he keeps in mind the sacredness of the oath. Perjury, the lie, the mask, only appear as such (*"the role of revealing the mask as mask"*) where they confirm their belonging to this zone of holy experience. To this extent at least, the perjurer remains faithful to what he betrays; he pays homage of sacrilege and perjury to sworn faith; in betrayal, he sacrifices to the very thing he is betraying; he does it on the altar of the very thing he is thereby profaning. Whence both the wiliness and the desperate innocence of him who would say: "in betraying, in betraying you, I renew the oath, I bring it back to life and I am more faithful to it than ever, I am even more faithful than if I were behaving in an objectively faithful and irreproachable way while forgetting the inaugural *sacramentum.*" For the secret that cannot be shared of the oath or perjury, for this secret that cannot even be shared with the partner in the oath, with the ally of the alliance, there is consequently only testimony and belief. Act of faith without possible proof. The hypothesis of proof does not even make sense any more. But on the other hand, because it remains on its own and without proof, this testimony cannot be authorized through a third person or through another testimony. For this witness there is no *other* witness: there is no witness for the witness. There is never a witness for the witness. This is also what the Celan poem might mean. It is also this that can always be alleged, inversely, by all the "revisionisms" in the world when they refuse all testimonies on the pretext that testimonies will never, by definition, be proofs. What should be the response to an allegation that might be translated like this: I can testify to this before my conscience, I am betraying you, I am lying to you, but in doing this I remain faithful to you, I am even more faithful than ever to our *sacramentum?* No objection can be made, nothing can be proved either for or against such a testimony. To this act of language, to this "performative" of testimony and declaration, the only possible response, in the night of faith, is another "performative" consisting of the saying or testing out, sometimes without even saying it, of an "I believe you."

How can this belief be thought? Where should we situate this faith, which does not necessarily have to take on the grand appearances of so-called religious faith? This act of faith is involved everywhere there is participation in what are called scenes of witnessing. And in truth the moment you open your mouth. The moment you open your mouth, the moment you exchange a look, even silently, a "believe me" is already involved, which echoes in the other. No lie and no perjury can overcome this appeal to belief; they can only confirm it; in profaning it, they can only confirm its invincibility.

Can this "believe" be thought? Is it accessible to the order of thought? The reason we referred to *Sein und Zeit* and to what it demands of *Bezeugung,* of the phenomenology of attestation, and precisely on the subject of the authentic *being-able-to-be-oneself* of *Dasein,* is that elsewhere Heidegger constantly excluded or at least dissociated the order of faith or belief from that of thinking or philosophy. He did this very often, but in particular in an abrupt, later statement, from *"Der Spruch des Anaximander."*[9] This statement radically excludes the order of belief from that of thought in general. Heidegger then touches on a problem of translation. (I point it out because we too are caught up, right here, in the scene of translation and testimony, and of the translation of the poem by Celan on testimony, of a poem that is virtually untranslatable and which testifies on the subject of testifying.) It is for Heidegger precisely a question of the translation of a *Spruch. Spruch:* word of honor, sentence, judgment, decision, poem, at any rate a speech which is not a theoretical and scientific utterance and which is linked to some language in a way that is both singular and "performative." Now what does Heidegger say in a passage which is also concerned, precisely, with presence (*Anwesen, Praesenz*), that presence which is the foundation of the classical value of testimony, and this time presence as representation, in the "representation of representing" ("*in der Repraesentation des Vorstellens*")? After proposing a translation for Anaximander's aphorism, Heidegger declares: "Belief has no place in the act of thinking (*Der glaube hat im Denken keinen Platz*)." This sentence is taken from an argument which must be reconstructed, at least in part:

> We cannot prove (*beweisen*) translation scientifically, nor should we, in virtue of some authority, have faith in it [give it credit, believe it, *glauben*]. The reach of proof [understood: "scientific" proof] is too short (*Beweis trägt zu kurz*). Belief has no place in the act of thinking. Translation can be rethought [reflected, *nachdenken*] only in the thinking [*im Denken*] of the judgment [word of honor, *Spruch:* it is necessary to think the *Spruch*, that speech of commitment as poem, judgment, decision, commitment, to think, rethink, starting from there, the possibility of translation, and not the other way around]. But thought (*das Denken*) is the *Dichten* [the poem, poetizing, the poetical act or operation, the poetic which Krieger is perhaps speaking of in the passage quoted as epigraph—but the words "act" and "operation" are not suitable: there is something other than the activity of a subject, perhaps we should say "the event," the "coming" of the poetic—] of the truth of being (*der Wahrheit des Seins*) in the historical conversation [dialogue, dual language] of thinkers [*geschichtlichen Zwiesprache des Denkenden*].

Heidegger thus dismisses scientific proof and belief back to back, which could let it be thought that to that degree he is giving credit to a non-scientific witnessing. In this context, the believing of belief is the credulity which accredits authority, the credulity which shuts its eyes to acquiesce dogmatically in authority ("*Autorität*" is Heidegger's word). Heidegger extends with no less force and authority the assertion according to which believing has no place in thinking. Is this believing foreign to that which in thought itself (in particular, the thought which thinks in the *Zwiesprache* and holds itself in relation to the *Spruch* of a thinker, in the experience of thinking translation) concerns the *Bezeugung*, the attestation which *Sein und Zeit* speaks of? Is there not a belief in the recourse to attestation (*Bezeugung*), in the discourse which brings it into play? And in the experience of thought in general, thought as Heidegger refers to it, is there not an experience of *believing* which is not reducible to that credulity or that passivity before authority which Heidegger here excludes so easily from thinking? And doesn't the authority of some "believing," "making [someone] believe," "asking to believe" always necessarily insinuate itself in the invocation of a thought of the truth of being? What, in that which is not proof, holds the place of this *Glauben* in the thought which Heidegger means to think at the very moment when he is excluding belief or faith?

III

"Raise your right hand and say 'I swear it.'" To these words a witness must respond, when he appears before a French court. Whatever the meaning of the raised hand, it does in any case engage the visible body in the act of the oath. The same is true for the wedding ring worn on the finger. Now *"Schwurfinger"* means the three fingers that are raised in taking an oath. That is perhaps not unrelated to the *"Händen am Dreiweg"* or the *"Dreiweg-Händen"* which return on two occasions in the Celan poem. They are first of all tied to the *tie,* the knot (*knoten, verknoteten*). One can imagine that these "knots" are not unrelated to the ties of the oath, for instance the oath of stone the poem mentions: *"im versteinerten Schwur."* Secondly, they are linked to the knots of the hands (*erschüttert-verknoteten Händen*) and of pain (*Schmerzknoten*).

Stricto sensu, determined by a culture, the *inherited* concept of testimony implies, we were saying, some kind of oath, some swearing to a law or faith. This is the reference to the *sacramentum,* namely to what is at issue between the parties involved in a trial, or in a contest. This issue is entrusted, during the hearing, during the procedure known as *per sacramentum,* to the Pontiff. "Pontiff" is not far from *Pontisches,* *"Pontisches Einstmals"* ("Pontic once-upon") which we will have occasion to speak about again.

But that does not necessarily mean that for every testimony we have to raise our hands and swear to speak the truth, the whole truth, and nothing but the truth. That does not necessarily mean that every time we do what is called *témoigner* or *déposer sous la foi du serment* [give evidence on oath] (*unter Eid bezeugen, unter Eid aussagen,* or *to testify* or *to bear witness*—which almost always has of itself the weight of "attesting on oath," before the law), we do it ritually. No, but even when the scene is not formalized in this way by an institutional code of the positive law which would oblige you to observe this or that rite, there is in every testimony an implication of oath and of law.

This extension of the implied oath just mentioned may appear extraordinary and abusive, even extravagant, but I think it legitimate, meaning incontestable. Logically, it makes it obligatory to take any address to another for a testimony. Each time I speak or manifest something to another, I am testifying to the extent that even if I neither say nor show the truth, even if, behind the "mask," I am lying, hiding, or betraying, every utterance implies "I am telling you the truth, I am telling you what I think, I testify before you to that to which I testify before me, and which is present to myself (singularly, irreplaceably). And I can always be lying to you. So I am before you as before a judge, before the law or the representative of the law. As soon as I testify I am before you as before the law, but, as a result, you who are my witness, you who bear witness to my bearing witness, you are also judge and arbiter, judge and party as much as judge and arbiter." We will come back to this essential possibility of the judge's becoming-witness or the witness's becoming-judge and becoming-arbiter.

I have already admitted: I will not attempt to interpret this poem. Not even its last lines:

Niemand
zeugt für den
Zeugen.

No one
bears witness for the
witness.

What then are we doing with this poem? And why are we quoting it? Why are we invoking its poetic force? Why are we borrowing its force when in fact, and no doubt because of this, beyond all we might decode of this poem we don't finally know *to what* it is bearing witness? What we are calling here the force of the poem, and first of all in its language, is what makes us have to quote it, again and again, by an irresistible compulsion. For it is quoted and requoted, it tends to be learned by heart when you know you do not know what, in the last resort, it means, when you do not even know *of what* or *for whom* and *for what* it is testifying. Because we do not know, even if we can know a lot and learn a lot about it, and learn a lot from it. We can "read" this poem, can desire to read, quote, and requote it, while giving up on interpreting it, or at least on going over the limit beyond which interpretation encounters both its possibility and its impossibility. What we have here is a compulsion to quote and requote, to repeat what we understand without completely understanding it, feeling at work in the economy of the ellipsis a force stronger than that of meaning and perhaps even than that of truth, of the mask which would manifest itself as mask. The reciting compulsion, the "by heart" desire, is because of this limit to intelligibility or transparency of meaning.

Is not this limit that of a crypt, and thus of a certain secret? In bearing witness for witnessing and for the witness, the poem says that there is no witness for the witness. It is presumably an indication, a descriptive statement, but also, implicitly perhaps, a prohibiting prescription: no one does in fact bear witness for the witness, no one can, it is true, but first of all because no one should. No one can, because it must not be done.

The poem bears witness. We don't know about what and for what, about whom and for whom, in bearing witness for bearing witness, it bears witness. But it bears witness. As a result, what it says of the witness it also says of itself as witness or as witnessing. As poetic witnessing. Can we not, then, here transfer to witnessing, to this poetic witnessing, as to that which in all witnessing must always appear as "poetic" (a singular act, concerning a singular event and engaging a unique, and thus inventive, relationship to language), that "extravagant proposal" of Murray Krieger's: "the poem, in the very act of becoming successfully poetic—that is, in constituting itself poetry—implicitly constitutes its own poetic"?

Moreover, *taken on its own,* the last stanza

Niemand
zeugt für den
Zeugen.

No one
bears witness for the
witness.

may vacillate or pivot, it seems to turn-re-turn around the axis of its own syntax. To the point of vertigo. The "for" (*für*)—what does it mean?

We can offer at least three hypotheses on this subject.

1. Is it about bearing witness in *favor* of someone (I bear witness for you, I bear witness in your favor, I am a witness for the defense, etc.)? *Zeugen für jenen* does in fact generally mean to testify *in favor of* someone, as opposed to *zeugen gegen jenen,* to testify against someone.

2. Is it rather about "bearing witness for" the other in the sense of "in the place of" the other? And here invalidating this possibility, this power, this right, by recalling that no one can bear witness *in the place of* another, any more than anyone can die *in the place of* another? In this impossibility of substitution, we are testing out an alliance between death and the secret. The secret always remains *the* experience of bearing witness, the privilege of a witness for whom no one can be substituted, because he is, in essence, the only one to know what he has seen, lived, felt; he must thus be *believed,* taken at his word, at the very moment when he is making public a secret which anyway remains secret. A secret *as* secret. Now even if we cannot say anything definite about it, "*Aschenglorie*" clearly remains a poem of death and the secret. The poem survives by bearing witness, through this alliance, to the surviving of the *testis* as *superstes.*

If no one can replace anyone as witness, if no one can bear witness *for* the other as witness, if one cannot testify for a testimony without taking from it its worth as testimony (which must always be done in the first person), is it not difficult to identify the witness with a third person? We readily represent the third person as anyone, as a replaceable first person: the third is a singular "I" in general. In fact nothing is more substitutable but nothing is less so than an "I." The question introducing itself on the horizon is indeed that of what one calls a first person, a discourse in the first person (singular or plural, *I* or *we*). Who is the "I" of the poem? This question displaces itself; it gets divided or multiplied, like the question of the signature, between the "I" of which the poem speaks, or to which the poem refers, reflexively (and which can also sometimes be a *mentioned* or even a *quoted* "I," if we want), the "I" who writes it or "signs" it in all the possible ways, and the "I" who reads it. How then is it determined, this self-referentiality, the autodeictic quality always posited or alleged by whoever says "I," thereby demonstrating, even if he is masked, that the speaker is showing himself and referring to himself? The form of this self-referential self-presentation is not only grammatical; it can be simply *implied* by discourses which are not conjugated in the first person of the present.

3. But there is still a third possibility: to testify "for" someone not in the sense of "in favor" or "in the place of" but "for" someone in the sense of "before" someone. One would then testify for someone who becomes the addressee of the testimony, someone to whose ears or eyes one is testifying. Then the sentence "no one bears witness for a witness" would mean that no one, no witness, bears witness before someone who is also a(nother) witness. A witness, as such, is never in a position to receive the testimony of another, nor entitled to do so. The judge or the tribunal, the representatives of the law, assumed to be neutral and objective, can certainly receive a testimony, but another witness cannot, since he is as singular and as involved as the first witness. The judge or the tribunal, the arbiters, those who judge and decide, those who conclude, are not mere witnesses; they must not, should not be only witnesses, in other words subjects who find themselves strangely in the situation of being present at or participating in that which is attested to. They would be suspected, as any witness is suspect, of being interested parties, partial subjectivities, interested, situated in the space described by the testimony. The judge, the arbiter, or the addressee of the testimony is thus not a witness: he cannot and must not be. And yet at the end of the day the judge, the arbiter, or the addressee do have to be *also* witnesses; they do have to be able to testify, in their turn, before their consciences or before others, to what they have attended, to what they have been present at, to what they have happened to be in the presence of: the testimony of the witness in the witness box. It is only on the basis of this testimony that they will be able to *justify* their judgment. The judge, the arbiter, the historian also remains a witness, a witness of a witness, when he receives, evaluates, criticizes, interprets the testimony of a survivor, for instance a survivor of Auschwitz. Whether he accepts or contests this testimony, he remains a witness of a witness. He remains a witness even if he contests the first testimony by alleging that, since he has survived, the survivor cannot be a certain and reliable witness to what happened, in particular of the existence for this purpose, a purpose of putting to death, of gas chambers or ovens for cremation—and that therefore he cannot bear witness *for* the only and true witnesses, those who have died, and who by definition can no longer

bear witness, confirm or disprove the testimony of another. In this context, *"Aschenglorie"* can also offer for hearing, between the words, mounting from the light of the ashes, something like a desperate sigh: no witness for the witness in this perverse situation which will permit all the judges, arbiters, historians to hold the revisionist thesis to be fundamentally indestructible or incontestable.

Although he cannot be a witness "in the box," the judge-arbiter-historian must also and further testify, if only to what he has heard attested. He must bear witness to the experience in the course of which, having been present, put in the presence of the testifying, he has been able to hear it, understand it, and can still reproduce the essence of it, etc. There would be a third person and testimony to testimony, witness for the witness.[10]

Niemand / zeugt für den / Zeugen: "Für" is thus both the most decisive and the most undecidable word in the poem. Nothing prohibits any of these three readings. They are different, but not necessarily incompatible. On the contrary, they can accumulate their potential energy deep in the crypt of the poem, thereby giving it its force of appeal and inducing our compulsion to cite-recite it without knowing, beyond knowledge. In these *three* readings of *"für,"* which intensify the three that we have not finished with, even the verb of the stanza vacillates as well. Its tense vacillates, it makes its mood and the negation to which it is subject (*Niemand zeugt*) vacillate with it. The present indicative can signify a fact to be stated: no one bears witness. . . . But as is often the case (in French too, especially when there is question of law), "no one bears witness" implies: "no one can bear witness," "no one can, has been able, and will ever be able to bear witness for the witness" (with the three possible senses of "for" that we have just invoked). And as a result, this being able, this "not being able" is displaced and translates easily into an "ought not to" or a "to have not to": no one can, which is to say no one must, no one should bear witness for the witness, replace the witness, defend the witness, bear witness before the witness, etc. One cannot and (in addition or moreover or above all) one should not bear witness for the witness, in all the senses of "for." One cannot and should not (claim to) replace the witness of his own death, for instance someone who perished in the hell of Auschwitz (but that does not mean that this poem is a poem on Auschwitz — and for the very reason that I am in the process of pointing out again, namely that no one bears witness for the witness). One neither can nor should replace (thus bear witness *for*) the witness of his or her own death, or the witness of others' deaths, the one who was present and survived, for instance at the hell of Auschwitz.

And yet, in its own way, the poem does bear witness to this impossibility. It attests to this prohibition which is imposed on bearing witness, in the very place where one has to go on appealing to it. This impossibility, this prohibition appears as such. Non-appearance appears (*perhaps*) *as* non-manifestation. Is this possible? How? How should we understand this "perhaps"? Its possibility or its necessity?

It is a matter of death, if death is what one cannot bear witness to for the other, and first of all because one cannot bear witness to it *for oneself.* The survival of surviving, as place of witness and as testament, would here find both its possibility and its impossibility, its chance and its threat. It would find them in this structure and in this event.

That this is a poem on *the subject of death,* a poem *of* death, a poem which speaks death *as such,* can be maintained at no great risk. It can be maintained where one cannot separate questions of the secret, the crypt, and witnessing from questions of survival and death. It can also be affirmed by taking as testimony the naming of ashes, of course. There are ashes there but they are of glory. Or again, there is glory, light, fire, but already in ashes. Double possibility of the "but"—the ash, certainly, and death, but glorious; glory, certainly, but of ash and death without memory. The double possibility of this implied "but" is, indeed, implied, in the hyphen, which *is now stressed* at the end of the line to articulate and disarticulate the relationship between ashes and glory,

> Aschen-
> glorie

(double word: we don't know which is the subject and which the predicate), and *is now effaced,* in a single, simple word, as in the opening (*"Aschenglorie"*). There too, one does not know whether the glory is of ashes or the ashes are glorious, ashes of glory. This explains du Bouchet's French translation, which prefers *"Cendres-la gloire"* ["Ashes-glory"] to *"Gloire de cendres"* ["Glory of ashes"]. "Ashes" is always in the plural, of course: ashes never gather together their dissemination and that is just what they consist in. They consist in not consisting, in losing all consistence. They have no more existence, they are deprived of any substance that is gathered together and identical to itself, of any relationship to themselves.

That is confirmed (perhaps) via the association of the *Dreiweg* with the *Pontisches,* with the petrification of the oath in its crypt, especially with the Tartar moon (*Tatarenmond*). There are at least two proper names in that (*Pontisches* and *Tatarenmond*) whose referent seems unavoidable. Namely, perhaps, the goddess Hecate. Here is the stanza we have not yet read:

> (*Auf dem senkrechten*
> *Atemseil, damals*
> *höher als oben,*
> *zwischen zwei Schmerzknoten, während*
> *der blanke*
> *Tatarenmond zu uns heraufklomm,*
> *grub ich mich in dich und in dich.*)

The published translations say:

> (On the perpendicular
> breath-rope, at that time,
> higher than above
> between two pain-knots,
> while the shiny
> Tartar moon climbed up to us,
> I burrowed into you and into you.)

> (*Perpendiculaire, alors,*
> *sur cette corde le souffle,*
> *plus haut que le faîte,*
> *entre deux noeuds de douleur, cependant*
> *que la blanche*
> *lune tatare jusqu'à nous se hisse,*
> *je m'enfouis en toi et toi.*)

It could also be translated:

> (*Sur la corde verticale*
> *du souffle* [*corde vocale?*] *autrefois* [*damals*, which echoes *Einstmals* above; once
>   upon a time],
> *plus haut qu'en haut,*
> *entre deux noeuds de douleur, pendant que*
> *La nue (luisante, lisse) lune tatare se haussait (s'élevait) vers nous*
> *je m'enfousissais (je m'enterrais, je m'encryptais) en toi et en toi.*)

> [(On the vertical cord
> of the breath [vocal chord?], long ago,
> higher than on high,
> between two knots of pain, while
> the bare (shiny, smooth) Tartar moon was raising itself (rising) towards us
> I buried myself (I interred myself, I encrypted myself) into you and into
>   you.)]

The name of the goddess Hecate is not pronounced. It remains, it will perhaps remain ineffaceable, beneath the surface of this poem, because of the association of the moon, the Pontic, and the three of the *Dreiweg*. However little one knows about the goddess Hecate, the first thing one remembers is that her most important trait is the three—and the tripleness of the way or road. She is *trimorphic,* she has three forms and three faces (*triprosopos*). She is also the goddess of the crossroads, in other words, as the name both indicates and does not indicate (*quadrifurcum*), of a road branching off in four rather than three directions. Of course, but apart from all the Oedipal associations which multiply with every crossroads, we know that a crossroads can be made of the crossing of two, three, or four roads, hence in three ways. Now Hecate, goddess of crossroads, is called *trioditis* (a word which comes from *triodos,* three ways: it is the adjective from *triodos,* honored in the crossroads). She protects roads and she is polyonymous, she has lots of names. We are only selecting the features which matter to us here. An account of Hecate could be prolonged *ad infinitum.* For this goddess of the *Dreiweg* also has a privileged relationship with fire, with brightness, with burning—and so with consumption or ashes as much as with glory. Her mouth exhales fire, she is *pyripnoa* (breath of fire) (*Atem,* that word dear to the author of *Atemwende,* the title of the collection that includes "*Aschenglorie,*" *Atem* that we also come across here again in "*Atemseil*"). Her hands brandish torches. The Chaldaean Oracles associate her with implacable thunderbolts and call her "flower of fire." Transporting fire from on high (think of the verticality and "*höher als oben*" in Celan), she is life-giving and fertile. But another chain of associations inverts these meanings and turns Hecate towards the aspect of the moon and death. Her signs and her triadic nature then couple her with Mene or Selene, the moon, the goddess of the moon—which we see appearing in Celan's poem. Some prayers to the moon invoke Hecate and Selene as one and the same goddess (three heads, crossroads, etc. . . .): "This is why you are called Hecate of many names, *Mene,* you who split the air like Artemis the arrow-darter. . . . [I]t is from you that all proceeds and in you, who are eternal, that all comes to an end."[11] Elsewhere, she becomes Aphrodite, universal procreator and mother of Eros both low and high "in the Underworld, the abyss and the aion (the forever, being in all times, the eternal)." Goddess of light but also of night, she keeps her festival in the crypts and the tombs. So this is also a goddess of death and the subterranean underworld, a goddess of Hades. This is the guise in which Hecate appears in *Macbeth,* at any rate. Apart from the general knowledge that one might have of this, we know that Celan also translated Shakespeare. What can be stressed in a completely distinctive way in the apparition of Hecate (Act 3, Scene 5) is that the three surfaces again there in the form of the three witches who meet her and speak with her ("Why, how now, Hecate! you look angerly!"). Hecate's reply is about nothing else than death ("How did you dare / To trade and traffic with Macbeth/In riddles and, affairs of death"); glory ("or show the glory of our art"); the "pit of Acheron"; the moon ("Upon the corner of the moon"); etc.

With Acheron, or the Styx, we could return to Celan's poem, to "*Pontisches Einstmals,*" the only time that we cross the waves of the Black Sea. Because it is only once that we cross them. The "Pontic once-upon" perhaps designating the passage of death. That is also where Odysseus is only authorized to pass through a *single time* to go and see the dead, when he goes to consult Tiresias. At the moment of death—and to reassure themselves about their fate after death, even if they were cremated—the Greeks needed a witness.

They had to go by way of a *trivium* which would decide on the route and the place of their destination.

There would be much to say here, in particular on the subject of Odysseus, of Elpenor, his drunkenness and his oar, to which there is *perhaps* a reference, we will never know, in the words *"ertrunkenen Ruderblatt,"* the blade of a drowned or drunken oar. There would be much to say as well on the subject of the vertical cord, the breath-rope (*Atemseil*), which perhaps, *perhaps,* alludes to the death of Tsvetaeva. We know what she represented for Celan. Tsvetaeva hanged herself in 1941 *unwitnessed*. She lived in the Tartar republic. So that the Tartar moon (*Tatarenmond*) may condense at least two encrypted allusions, thereby—as is most often the case—foiling the unity of reference, and thus of reading, and thus of witnessing, without however effacing the singularity of each event, of each date thereby re-lated, re-marked.

Whatever their probability or improbability, the "perhaps" of these singular references which all make appeal to dated evidence (for example, we have to know who Tsvetaeva was and who she was for Celan, and how, where, and when she killed herself, she too, like him, etc.), we can say a priori that this poem speaks of death (for which there is no witnessing), perhaps of suicide, and that the *"grub ich mich in dich und in dich"* may mean not only "I dig myself in, I burrow," but also "I bury myself, I encrypt myself within you inside you": *graben, grub;* and *Grab* is the tomb: you are my tomb, my own tomb, you to whom I address myself, whom I take as witness, if only to say (to you) "no one bears witness for the witness."

Beyond or before everything that could be thought, read, or said of this poem, according to the "perhaps," the probability and the act of faith which is a poetic experience, beyond or before all the possible translations, a mark remains and is here re-marked: it is a certain limit to interpretation. Ultimately, it is in all certainty impossible to put a stop to the meaning or the reference of this poem, the meaning or the reference to which it testifies or responds. Whatever one might say about it, and that can be deployed *ad infinitum, there is a line.* It is not marked only by the poem. It is the poem, poetics, and the poetics of the poem—which dissimulates itself by exhibiting its dissimulation *as such.* But it is this "as such" which turns out to be doomed to the "perhaps." Probable and improbable (possible but removed from proof), this "as such" takes place as poem, as this poem, in it, and *there* one cannot reply in its place, *there* where it is silent, *there* where it keeps its secret, while telling us that there is a secret, revealing the secret it is keeping as a secret, not revealing it, while it continues to bear witness that one cannot bear witness for the witness, who ultimately remains alone and without witness. In *Le pas au-delà*, Blanchot speaks of a "word still to be spoken beyond the living and the dead, bearing witness for the absence of attestation."[12]

It is of this essential solitude of the witness that I would have liked to speak. It is not a solitude like just any solitude—nor a secret like just any secret. It is solitude and secrecy themselves. They speak. As Celan says elsewhere, the poem, it speaks, secretly, of the secret, through the secret, and thus, in a certain way, in it beyond it: *"Aber das Gedicht spricht ja! Es bleibt seiner Daten eingedenk, aber—es spricht"* ("But the poem it speaks! It keeps its dates in mind, but in the end—it speaks").[13] It speaks to the other by keeping quiet, keeping something quiet from him. In keeping quiet, in keeping silence, it is still addressing itself. This internal limit to any witnessing is also what the poem says. It bears witness to it even in saying "no one bears witness for the witness." Revealing its mask *as* a mask, but without showing itself, without presenting itself, perhaps presenting its non-presentation as such, representing it, it thus speaks about witnessing in general, but first of all about the poem that it is, about itself in its singularity, and about the witnessing to which any poem bears witness.

Left here to itself, in its essential solitude, in its performance or in its happening, the poetic act of the work perhaps no longer derives from the presentation of self *as such*.

NOTES

1. Translator's note: In the course of this essay on the subject of *témoignage*, Derrida discusses the implications of differences between French and English (and other languages) in their respective vocabularies in this semantic field. For a translation from French to English, particular problems of non-symmetry presented themselves. The English noun "witness" roughly corresponds to the French *témoin*, but the verb "to witness" is not equivalent to *témoigner:* to witness is primarily to see or hear for oneself, whereas *témoigner* means to bear witness in the way that a witness does in a court of law, for instance to testify, to give evidence. Similarly, the noun *témoignage* means testimony, giving evidence, bearing witness; in some contexts, it can be simply evidence: that which of itself bears witness, is an indication.

However, the English verb "witness" also has a transitional sense, or rather one that encompasses both meanings. When someone formally "witnesses" a signature, or some other official event, the witnessing is not only seeing the deed done (witnessing in the first sense), but also, by giving a witness's signature, *attesting* (the second sense) to *having witnessed* in the first sense. For this reason, I have sometimes translated *témoignage* as "witnessing," rather than "bearing witness" or "testimony," where the context makes it clear that that is the sense implied.

2. Paul Celan, "Aschenglorie," in *Atemwende* (Frankfurt am Main: Suhrkamp, 1967), 68; English trans. by Joachim Neugroschel in Celan, *Speech-grille and Selected Poems* (New York: Dutton, 1971), 240; French trans. by André du Bouchet in Celan, *Strette* (Paris: Mercure de France, 1971), 50.

3. Emile Benveniste, *Vocabulaire des institutions européennes* (Paris: Minuit, 1969), 2:277. The continuation of this passage, quoted below, is from the same page. This book was translated by Jean Lallot and Elizabeth Palmer as *Indo-European Language and Society* (London: Faber and Faber, 1973); see 526 for the passage under discussion.

4. There are occasions when Benveniste himself uses the word "witness" [*témoin*] to characterize a word or a text inasmuch as it attests to a custom or an institution. See for instance 1 : 92, in a chapter on hospitality: "Witness this text . . . ," says Benveniste.

5. Jean-François Lyotard, *Le différend* (Paris: Minuit, 1983), 103, 158.

6. "We," meaning a traditional community—I would not in fact say an institutional one in Benveniste's sense. This community must have been constituted out of a heritage in which language, linguistic feeling, is neither dominant nor just one element among others, and in which the history of Greek, Roman, Germanic, and Saxon systems of meaning is inseparable from either philosophy, Roman law, or the two Testaments (and in fact from all the testaments of which this tradition of witnessing is made).

7. I have tried to do so elsewhere, in particular around questions of the animal, of the life of the living creature, of survival and death—especially in *Of Spirit*, trans. Geoffrey Bennington and Rachel Bowlby (Chicago: University of Chicago Press, 1989), and *Aporias*, trans. Thomas Dutoit (Stanford: Stanford University Press, 1993).

8. Martin Heidegger, *Sein und Zeit* (Frankfurt am Main: Klostermann, 1977), vol. 2, paragraph 54, and the whole of chapter 2.

9. Martin Heidegger, *Holzwege* (Frankfurt am Main: Vittorio Klostermann, 1950), 343.

10. On this being-witness or rather on this becoming-witness of the judge or the arbiter and, conversely, on this being- or becoming-arbiter of the witness, which will lead to so many problems, obscurities, and tragic confusions, appeal should again be made to Benveniste (*Vocabulaire des institutions indoeuropéennes*, vol. 2, ch. 3, "*Ius* et le serment à Rome" ["*Ius* and the Oath at Rome"]).

11. "Hécate—dans l'esotérisme grec," in *Dictionnaire du mythologie,* ed. Yves Bonnefoy (Paris: Flammarion, 1981), 485–86.

12. Maurice Blanchot, *Le pas au-delà* (Paris: Gallimard, 1973), 107.

13. See "Der Meridian," in Paul Celan, *Gesammelte werke III* (Frankfurt am Main: Suhrkamp Verlag, 1983), 3 : 196; I interpret this passage in *Shibboleth* (Paris: Galilée, 1985), 20 ff.

CHAPTER ELEVEN

My Travels with the Aesthetic

Murray Krieger

For many years, during the heyday of modernism and for a while beyond, I traveled with the aesthetic as its fortunes were rising in the criticism around me, so that it long seemed to me that my career and the fortunes of the aesthetic went hand in hand. Because of my devotion to literature, the companionship of the aesthetic brought with it the need to defend the literary as a mode of discourse whose workings persuade us to distinguish it from other (presumably non-poetic) modes.[1] In recent years, however, the role of the aesthetic, and consequently the distinct existence of the literary, have been widely put in question, if not altogether denied. But even in these last years I have not joined with those who have turned against the aesthetic: I have not acquiesced in the diminishing—indeed in many places the utter collapse—of its fortunes. I have tried to resist the reigning orthodoxies and their ideological implications, as earlier I had worried about being too much in step with fashion.

But of course such resistance has come at a cost: because it has refused to desert the aesthetic, my recent work no longer mirrors what has become dominant in the criticism around me. Indeed, it may seem to be moving in a reverse direction from the one in which criticism has been going. For, far from indulging in the widespread rejection of the aesthetic, it was my intention to extend its function beyond the hedonistic—indeed leisure-class and escapist—character too often ascribed to it as if we were still in the fin de siècle of a hundred years ago. I wanted not merely to help save the aesthetic, but to make it worth saving by broadening our sense of what at its best it has been, of how it always has served its culture. Nevertheless, during these last years, for the aesthetic and for me in our journeying together, it has become a bumpy ride.

To the extent that my travels through the realm of theory have been a mirror—at one time faithful and more recently inverse—of general trends in academic literary criticism, I believe it would be worth tracing the development of these trends as they are reflected—or rejected—in my work throughout its span of more than four decades. So I will proceed, even as I recognize that much of the historical recital that follows may show the effects, and probably distortions, of hindsight as I look back at—and perhaps unconsciously reshape—my earlier thinking from where I am now sitting.

Just after World War II, as a very young army returnee, I suffered a brief attachment to the left's idolatry on behalf of the phrase "art as a weapon" in the political arena. (I say "suffered" because it was, I later came to realize, an ascetic attachment that celebrated anger as well as pain, quite probably an outgrowth of my need to respond to the horrors I had witnessed in India from 1943–1945.) [2] I have elsewhere treated the ascetic and the aesthetic as opposed alternatives that, throughout the history of literary commentary, have preconditioned each writer's critical disposition. These alternatives have so functioned for me, although I have—increasingly in recent years—been working to close the gap between them.[3] But I have no doubt, as I look back, that my immediately postwar commitments were ascetic in their exclusive concern with the moral and political uses to which literature was to be put, at whatever cost to—indeed to the purposeful neglect of—its aesthetic attractions. My attitude back in the mid-forties seems now to have been an earlier version of—and in its theoretical grounding not very different from—the sort of politicized criticism so much with us today.

It did not take long, however, for my graduate courses at the University of Chicago to force me to recognize the affective energies within the manipulation of language, narrative, and figuration that could, and did, rivet my attention to the innate powers of the literary text, and that persuaded me of more things in its heaven and earth than could be contained by any of the political programs I was trying to make them serve. I suppose that today this change could be dismissed as simply a move to formalism, and to some extent it was.

Certainly what the dogmas of the University of Chicago neo-Aristotelian critics taught in those days was an extreme version of formalism. Through an expansion of Aristotle's *Poetics* that could be applied to all literary genres, the governing method required us to search out in every text the structure that shaped the sequence of incidents, or of internal movements, or of any other developing element (which they termed the "plot-form") that enabled the work to have the unique effect that a proper reading would sponsor. This was my introduction to the prospects of an aesthetic reading of texts, and an introduction also to linking the aesthetic with the notion of a closed form and, beyond that, with some version of organicism.

It was an organicism derived from Aristotle's theory of plot or action, in which any accidental chronological sequence is to be transformed into a teleological structure: every before and after ("*post hoc*") is to be transformed into an antecedent and its consequence ("*propter hoc*"). In effect, the time line of any random series of events is turned back upon itself into the circle of intertwinings between the presumed beginning and the apparent end, until these very oppositions are dissolved into one another. Thus in any properly aesthetic text the analysis by the reader was to be derived exclusively from the mutual interrelations between part and whole within a self-created formal closure.[4]

The reader, then, was to trace the manipulations of all the elements that created the poem's self-enclosed form, as these elements were geared, through their formal interaction, to effect the special pleasure peculiar to its genre. Consequently, for the Chicago version of Aristotelianism, all questions of meaning or of theme, of any commentary or judgment the poem might be suggesting concerning the world of human experience, were outside the scope of—indeed irrelevant to—the properly "literary" (really "poetic," in Aristotle's sense) function, and hence literary value, of the drama or poem or novel under consideration. And such questions were accordingly outside the scope of what was considered a proper reading.[5]

This heavily imposed method was at the farthest extreme from the political program with which I had come armed to Chicago. Subjecting myself to it did teach me how crudely I had been ready to make an absolute division between form and content, and ready to insist on taking the content of a text (what I thought of as its "message") as an independent statement to be judged—and put into political use—on its own. My newly learned awareness of the inadequacy of the form-content dichotomy did open the way for me to reconceive how poems worked. But while the brilliance of the Chicago method in the hands of Ronald Crane, or Elder Olson, or Norman Maclean, was enough to make me discredit my politicized view of the poetic "weapon," I found that method thoroughly inadequate in its disdain for *any* thematic interest in literature, an interest I still retained.[6] My previous inclination would hardly let me go so far in the other direction.

I came to see the neo-Aristotelian alternative, in the form in which it was presented by the Chicagoans, as a literary analogue to the theory in the visual arts offered by pure and thin formalists like Clive Bell and Roger Fry, and I found it utterly inadequate to a verbal medium as immersed in human living and dying as I found the several literary genres to be. For me, literature would have to reflect the problems of existence, but it would have to do so in its own way because of the special lens created by its form. So, lest I was to allow literature to be trivialized by what seemed to me a narrow aestheticism, any formalism I could propagate would have to be strongly tempered by continuing thematic concerns in a search for a broader notion of the aesthetic that could blend the content into the form. And, thanks to

Arnold Bergstraesser and then to Eliseo Vivas, both of them also my teachers at Chicago, I made progress in that search.

With Bergstraesser I was introduced to an intensive study of late-eighteenth- and early-nineteenth-century German idealism and romanticism, both in themselves and in the ways they were related to British thinking. I became immersed in several versions of the romantic opposition between science and poetry, I learned about the complex functions of romantic irony, and, above all, I wandered through the several confusing layers in a varied body of Coleridgean texts, which, as a strange mixture of dualistic and monistic thinking, were derived from an array of German writers from Baumgarten and Mendelssohn to Kant to the two Schlegels, Schelling, Fichte, and Hegel.

Through these pre-Kantian, Kantian, and post-Kantian studies I came to understand what I meant by the aesthetic and how it would function in my theorizing. The aesthetic was to be placed between pure sensory experience and the conceptual. More organized than raw experience but not subject to the rigors of systematic discourse as in the conceptual, the aesthetic was to provide a perceptual form—a form that is pre-conceptual—through which we might grasp the flow of experience, grasp the particular *as* particular. Thus I saw the mission of the aesthetic to be that of resisting control by external concepts while still working to impose its own form upon experience.

In accordance with this notion of the aesthetic, I struggled with the attempt to show how form and meaning could be *seen* as *immanent* in properly literary works, works that resist any *transcendent* meaning—directed from outside the verbal structure and directing it—which characterizes other texts. Thus I came to see the interrelationship in the Western tradition between an interest in the aesthetic and the commitment to organicism. I explored the extent to which organicism, as a potentially misleading metaphor, had to be packed and unpacked if it was to serve as the basis for an aesthetic.[7] Most of all, perhaps, I learned to forgo easy, totalizing definitions of organicism for one that fully retained its complex call for a give-and-take dynamic between material and form, between part and whole. This organicism always pressed both sides of the call for *unity* in *variety*. It remained alert to the need for variety, with all its implications of openness, while persisting—despite all contradiction—in the conventional call for closure that was implied by the demand for unity.

Working under Vivas, I learned that the way to get to the aesthetic in literature was to begin by acknowledging the mixed nature of our response to texts, compounded as it was of elements we might single out as moral, cognitive, and aesthetic. If we wished to analyze that compound for theoretical reasons, we could seek definitions of each of those elements, so long as we understood that none usually appears in a pure state, so that these would be heuristic and not "real" definitions of our aesthetic, moral, or cognitive experiences. Nor is there any suggestion that it would be more valuable to have a pure experience devoid of other elements, were it possible, than the mixed experiences we normally have. With those caveats, we can go on to speak of the aesthetic element or the cognitive element or the moral element within our experience of a text, as well as what the aesthetic experience itself (or one of the others) would have to be, if we could have one.[8]

Moving out from these assumptions, Vivas defined our aesthetic experience of any symbolic construct as a "state of rapt, intransitive attention" to the text in all its potential complexities, in contrast to the cognitive and the moral modes of experience, both of which, in their different ways, require a transitive attention that pierces through the symbols at hand to a constellation of meanings and consequences beyond. This is not at all to claim that the aesthetic is superior to other modes, only that it can be defined as different from them and that we can say what its characteristics are.

Now any text might be subjected to any of these experiences, depending on the reader and how the reader chooses to read. That is, since the definitions are not real ones, we should not speak ontologically about an "aesthetic object." We might, however, want to move from these definitions of the several elements within the mixed experience to claim that there is an agency in the text that sponsors one or another of them. We could then be reading a textual construct *as if* it were aesthetic by claiming to find in it properties worthy of being read intransitively, properties that appear to seek self-enclosure. As would-be aesthetic critics, we would have to maintain that those properties encouraged us, even induced us, to respond aesthetically to them.

We would go on to claim that those characteristics were there to be perceived by others as well, that ours was not an idiosyncratic response, not a reading-in that we could not expect to be repeated by other readers coming to the text. In that way, our hypothetical, heuristic procedure would lead us to bestow aesthetic features upon the text, what Vivas termed "factors of control," which, by keeping us searching within the text, solicit the aesthetic element of our experience from a knowing and compliant reader whom the text traps within its constructed attributes. So the circle of the hypothetical definition can be closed: *if* we want to define what the aesthetic response would be, and *if* we then want to define the characteristics in a text that appear designed to invite an aesthetic response rather than any other, then we can seek in the text those features, largely formal, that would lead us in that direction. And we can make aesthetic judgments of those texts that we choose to read within these criteria. In this scheme, the advantages maintained for literary texts are clearly established, although the reader may choose to read other texts according to the aesthetic model that literary texts may seem especially designed to satisfy.

Besides teasing out for me this notion of what the aesthetic would be, both in our experience and in texts, Vivas introduced me in a disciplined way to the history of aesthetics in all of its theoretical variations, as well as to a literary analysis that shrewdly discriminated the intricate ways in which philosophy does and does not make its way into literary form. I came to appreciate his notion that the properly literary text rivets itself onto what he termed "the *primary* data of experience" and works to prove itself resistant to the conceptual (as secondary), which, coming *after,* sifts that primary data in accord with the dictates of logical, propositional, and perhaps generally didactic or specifically political schemata.[9] The literary search was for an order, a form, that could precede the logically guided constraints of the conceptual and yet, on the other side, did not surrender to the welter of raw experience itself.

Indebted to Bergstraesser and Vivas, then, I was groping my way toward a related version of the aesthetic. Although it was not until I had written several books that I found ways to formulate it,[10] I was moving in this direction from my earliest work at Chicago, by tracing the aesthetic's twentieth-century development through an intensive reading of Kant and the work of aestheticians like Benedetto Croce, A. C. Bradley, I. A. Richards, D. W. Prall, Samuel Alexander, and John Dewey, guided by Vivas's reading of them.[11] Following them in my search to define the peculiar and peculiarly resistant character of literary form, as distinguished from conceptual form, I was led to a profound and lasting awareness of the constructive role of the aesthetic medium in the artist's creative process. It was an awareness that showed me how to turn the nineteenth-century definitions of organicism into a critical method.

In the case of any of the arts, I came to understand the extent to which the artistic medium—language in the specific case of literary art—together with the conventions that became attached to it over the centuries, generates a resistance to the intentions that the artist thought he or she had going into the process. This resistance forces the transformation of those intentions, in a give and take between the artist and that historically conditioned medium out of which the growing poetic entity is to emerge. These transformations are thus to be seen as helping to constitute a finished product that is fully interpretable only when we take account of either what that medium, in its resistance, permitted, or what, being forced to slacken that resistance, it yielded up to the artist's original intentions. In the latter case the product would be judged as less successfully organic, to the extent that its final version reflected an external control rather than a development that was generated internally, through the mutual interaction of its parts, which, indeed, could hardly be taken separately as independent elements. As Vivas had put it, whatever meanings the poem finally presents are meanings that have come, not merely through language (as in non-poetic discourse), but "*in and through* language," so that they can be found only there, in the poem, and cannot be conceptually extrapolated from it without loss.

Consequently, any interpretation was to proceed by granting that the transformative role of the medium should have forced the artist to create a freestanding product, which could not be reduced to what he or she brought to it at the outset of the creative process. Words, with their multiple possibilities of both sound and sense, singly and in interaction; metaphor, which can transmute an intended literal meaning; internal relations among narrative elements, which can alter the apparent meaning of an incident, a character, or a statement; literary conventions, which can both constrain and enable every current version of them—all these were to be seen as opening the form to pressures that both limit it and allow it to recreate itself as it moves along. In accordance with such argument, and also by analogy to the more material plastic arts to which the literary art was now made companion, it is not surprising that the word "object" was attached to the texts that were to be approached as organically complete "works of art." Consequently, interpretation was practiced as the attempt to discover the complex intertwinings that "object" exhibited to the "close reader."

Here I found the grounds for an aesthetic that could distinguish poetic discourse and its potential for meaning from those kinds of discourse in which such struggles with the medium need not take place in these complex ways, "non-poetic discourse" in which the intended argumentative meanings might be unimpeded in their absolute control. An aesthetic that allowed for this special role for poetry as a distinctive mode of discourse was indeed a far cry from the anti-aesthetic I had been looking for in literature when I came to Chicago from the army: that had called for an unresisted expression of political ideology, in effect collapsing the literary into the political functions of discourse generally. But, from the other side, as I viewed this organic aesthetic, it still left room for literature to exude a thematic substance such as the Chicago Aristotelians would have precluded from their purely formal analysis.

So I came away from my studies with Bergstraesser and Vivas searching for a theory of reading poems in whose organicism the give and take between form and experience struggled to reconcile the attempt to complete the form, to close it off, with the challenge to accommodate experience by remaining open to what was alien to—apparently unaccommodatable by—that form. I suppose I was intellectually ready for the call in 1948 to teach at Kenyon College, which was then the center of the thinking we associate with the New Criticism. Under the spiritual leadership of John Crowe Ransom, the college—but far more importantly for me, the national summer program in criticism he founded there as The Kenyon School of English—gave an institutional base to that movement.

I used my year there, and the following summer at the Kenyon School of English studying under Allen Tate and René Wellek, to create a theoretical ground for those aspects of the New Criticism that reflected an organicist aesthetic. But it was, I guess, Cleanth Brooks who offered the most explicit attachment to organicism in his readings and his essays justifying those readings, while Ransom offered a dualistic opposition (Kantian, he called it) and Tate wandered back and forth between the two poles they represented. With Wellek I also entered the world of Russian and Prague School Formalists, with their emphasis on the poet's "making strange" of language, his or her use of "defamiliarization" in order to force poetry to be taken as a distinctive mode of discourse, in contrast to their notion of "normal discourse." Hence their assigning to the critic the task of uncovering in each poetic text the key to its "literariness" or "poeticity" by focusing on its deviations from the norms of discourse. Much of this thinking entered my early attempts to work toward an organic theory that would differentiate the literary from the non-literary. It was later that I discovered how artificial and unempirical a concept "normal" discourse was, and how blurred was the separation between the literary and the non-literary. Consequently, as will be seen in what follows, I had to shift the distinction from one about objects to one about reader responses.

After that year and summer, I was ready to return to work under Eliseo Vivas, first on co-editing *The Problems of Aesthetics* (1952) with him, and then on my dissertation, which later grew into *The New Apologists for Poetry* (1956). That book was to serve as a probing (or was it my construction?) of a theory, or conflicting theories, that might lie behind the New Criticism, whose members for the most part attended to individual texts and preferred not to grapple with theoretical issues. In this way *The New Apologists* was to uncover the theoretical weaknesses of that movement even while it praised its role in the history of criticism. At the root of those weaknesses—and my own as I exposed them—was their ambivalence, and mine, in dealing with the consequences of organicism. How was one to reconcile the desire to treat the self-defined and self-fulfilled object as a self-sealing system with the need to remain fully conscious of its relations to the verbal and literary traditions that precede it, as well as the need to break it open for his or her understanding and postliterary commentary? Indeed, I remember even then being disturbed by, and dissatisfied with, the New Critics' overcommitment to an unmodified doctrine of aesthetic closure.

In these days of dispute about the reactionary and hence repressive role of canons, I still must confess that the New Criticism, as well as my early attachment to it, was motivated in large part by the New Critics' desire to recreate the canon and to institutionalize their version of it. It was to be a canon made up of works that were seen as responding to their organicist readings, or at least that could be made by the ingenious critic to be seen that way. Be-

cause of their peculiar character, the poems of John Donne, or rather a se-
lect few among those poems, had a paradigmatic role bestowed upon them.
If I may venture an extreme statement, one might think of the method of
the New Criticism as the canonization of Donne's "The Canonization." That
poem served as the master-text (or perhaps as the metatext) for at least two
generations of New Critics. Indeed, Cleanth Brooks borrowed his title from
a crucial passage in "The Canonization" when he wrote *The Well Wrought Urn*
(1947), the book that, as much as any other, shaped the direction to be
taken by the New Criticism.

For the New Critics, this poem celebrated both the verbal distinction and
the poetic collapse of the distinction between the sacred and the profane,
between the intelligible and the sensible, between paradox and logic, between poetic discourse and rational discourse. For they would make the profane verbally sacred and give linguistic perception access to the intelligible,
thereby finding at once a self-enforcing logic that encompasses the paradoxical and a poetic discourse that creates its own strange reasonability. They
argued for these distinctions, at once asserted and collapsed in the poems
they treated, as a defining element in the use of language in the literature
of both the Renaissance and high modernism, the two periods whose union
had been first manufactured by T. S. Eliot and systematically justified in criticism and theory by Cleanth Brooks. In *The Well Wrought Urn,* besides drawing from "The Canonization" to furnish his title, Brooks used his analysis of
that poem as his opening chapter, on which his other analyses of all the
other poems from many later periods treated in that book were modeled.
This canonization ("Canonization"?), in effect, creates his canon for him.

More than they may have known, this poem and the use to which it was put
by New Critics represented the culmination of the difference between literary criticism as it had been practiced and a new, revolutionary criticism that
would sanctify—and hence canonize—a whole new order of poetry. It was
no accident that Cleanth Brooks wrote *The Well Wrought Urn* as a follow-up
to his *Modern Poetry and the Tradition* (1939), which in its final chapter called
for a revision of the history of English poetry based on a reading method
that *The Well Wrought Urn* was shortly to demonstrate—with "The Canonization" leading the way. And when I wrote *The New Apologists for Poetry* as my
summary book, my elegy to the New Criticism that I was helping to bury, it
was also my model treatment of "The Canonization," pushed into a metapo-
etic extension even more explicitly than in Brooks, that furnished the substance of my own introductory chapter. This book, too, celebrated a new
order (or at least a newly considered order) of poetizing and of criticizing
that which had been poeticized. And, perhaps all too much like Brooks's
work, which it in part criticized, it sought to create the framework for instituting a poetic canon for our culture—a canon whose members were to be

canonized in accord with the theoretical conclusions found in (or read into) Donne's poem.

But even at that early stage of my writing, though without a sure sense of the theoretical reasons that warned me off, I was aware of the dangers of an organicism that overemphasized the closed system, and I tried to fall back from the excesses of the claims of metaphorical identity by retaining some residue of the concern with difference that I also found in the poem. So, although I probably overemphasized the aesthetic requirement of poetic closure, I did make some allowance for our double vision—of enclosure and of the disruption from outside—as we read the extravagances of Donne's figures. We were to indulge them, enter their trap, and yet resist a total and uncritical entrapment, with some help from the poem, which also undercuts itself:

> although the reader has been fooled by the absurdities which have been concealed under the seeming rationality of the poem and has taken the vehicles of the metaphors seriously instead of remaining within the confines of the tenors, nevertheless the poem has forced him also to take rationality along with him as a beguiling, covert guide. After all, sexual intercourse is not quite the conversion to sainthood . . . nor are love verses meant to be regarded only as hymns to saints. And the lovers do not in any obvious way affect the business of the world, which can never forsake its "rage." The ambiguities prove that the reader was not meant only or merely to be fooled all the way. On the other hand, neither is he to look upon the poem merely as faulty argument or as a joke. For in one sense—through the operation of its language—it *has* proved its case. (17–18)

Whether as true double vision or only as uncertainty, I was expressing what I saw as the critic's need to feel both the monistic and dualistic poles—the metaphoric and metonymic poles—of the figure-making daring of the poet: both the closure and the openness to the challenge to the would-be organic whole by all that would break through it. I perceived that the New Critics failed to theorize that doubleness and so were again and again trapped by it, and it was then my theoretical ambition to sustain it and ride with it, even while I retained an attachment to the doctrine of aesthetic closure.

As a result of my distrust of what I viewed as the all-controlling pressures applied by the conceptual realm of discourse, or, to put it another way, as a result of my distrust of universals and my love of poetry's particulars, it was not surprising that I should have felt the attractions of the existentialism that was captivating midcentury Europe. Existentialism was not a common influence among my American New-Critical colleagues, but to me it seemed inevitable as the means of binding a formal aesthetic to the world of our subjective experience, thereby giving meaning to that world.[12] That influence fills my commentaries, and the theory behind them, in *The Tragic Vision* (1960);[13] and, I suspect, despite many changes in my thinking, I have never altogether lost that attachment. In the concluding chapter of that book I struggled to make firm the tie between existentialism and my organicist aesthetic, and I theorized it explicitly in the essay "The Existential Basis of Contextual Criticism."[14]

What my version of existentialism and my aesthetic of literature had in common were the rejection of constricting and oppressive universals for the particularity of experience, and the insistence that the philosophical pursuit of the thinness of essence, at the expense of the density of existence, had a totalitarian inhumanity about it. Consequently, it also seemed to me that the pursuit of an existentialist "philosophy" was a self-contradictory enterprise: if it was philosophy, and hence a conceptual system, it could not be existentialist; and if it was living, breathing existentialism, it could not be a philosophy. Literature, then, would constitute the only thoroughly existential discourse, and it was the commentator's task to preserve its resistance to universals by resisting the temptation to extrapolate propositional messages from all the complexities that the text provided.

I had inherited from the New Critics the celebration of the two-sidedness, if not the multiplicity, of possible meanings—usually meanings in conflict—in poetry. At times they termed it "irony," at times "ambiguity," at times "tension," at times "paradox." These were devices that freed the text from the repressive dominance of the Platonic universals—in practice the ideological controls—that would confine all its wayward elements. In giving full play to these devices, I found my first sense of literature's subversive potential, which could be revealed only through a formalistic reading that reveled in the text's two-sidedness.

In dealing with the novels I treated in *The Tragic Vision,* I tried to show how the particular text resisted being reduced to a single set of universal propositions, not only by furnishing the grounds for a contrary, if not contradictory, interpretation, but also by leading the reader to sustain the two at once. I referred to this double vision of existence as a vision of "the Manichean face of reality," and called this opposition "thematic dualism," even while claiming that the literary text that contained it was serving an "aesthetic monism." Here was a working-out of the dynamics of organicism that combined the move toward the domestications of closure with the receptive exposure to the alien other. For what the aesthetically perceived text was seeking to enclose was at the same time opened outward by an ineluctable thematic opposition. This combination—an aesthetic monism that somehow was to reflect an unyielding thematic dualism—then seemed to me the way to have an organicism that could avoid the suffocating Hegelian pressure to be all-embracing, such as we feel in the realm of political dogma. Yet I must concede that I still could be seen as giving special indulgence to the notion of the aesthetic as a holding-together—a making of a whole—of the thematic oppositions that should splinter its unity.

When I turned to the theoretical consequences of my examination of Shakespeare's sonnets in *A Window to Criticism: Shakespeare's Sonnets and Modern Poetics* (1964), I discovered in Renaissance typology and, consequently, in the Renaissance use of metaphor, another source of the special power I was seeking to attribute to the literary. One obvious place where the figurative meaning is immanent in the literal, I saw, was in the miracle of the Christian sacrament arising out of the divine-human paradox figured in the person of Jesus: his body *in* the bread, his blood *in* the wine. Here indeed was a literalization of metaphor. I began to understand the extent to which the extravagance of Renaissance metaphorical claims to the verbal miracle— with one meaning sliding into and *becoming* another in the poetic act of figuration—was related to the typological habit behind the Christian semiotic that flowed through the language usage of Renaissance poets. And the critic would need a Christian hermeneutic, flowing from the divine-human paradox as it invades our habit of responding to metaphor, if he or she was to grapple successfully with the poems in our tradition.

But secular love poems in the Renaissance imposed this semiotic practice, the move toward a verbal miracle, while undercutting any claim to an accompanying sacred substance. That is, in the Christian sacrament the metaphor, as a miraculous transubstantiation, can be confirmed only by faith; in the poem's metaphor the identity forged in the poem between differentiated words is offered as an illusion—a trick permitted by verbal manipulation within the poetic context—that produces an impossible miracle, sustained only *pour l'occasion* through the aesthetic moment of the fiction. If the identity was not impossible, I urged, it would hardly seem a miracle; and yet, within the workings of the poem, the miracle appears to have been worked. Here, in the limited commitment called for by the aesthetic moment, I found a reinforcement for my sense of the double vision of poetry, of its self-contradictory character.

As I then argued, the reader may use the fictional illusion momentarily to inhabit a world in which such transformations, such identities forged from ineluctable differences, have meaning, though without depending on any attendant substantive belief, as in the Christian literalizing of metaphor. In this way, metaphor in these secular poems, both a borrowing from and a parody of the Christian model metaphor, serves aesthetic purposes, earned in the interstices of the poem since it has been stripped of any external claim to validation provided by an accompanying faith. Later I came to see this linguistic paradigm as controlling the function of metaphor beyond the Renaissance, throughout our poetic and our recent critical traditions. Thus, more generally, it served for me as another indication of how poems attempt to enclose us within their almost magical aesthetic powers, even while they remind us of their limitations by covertly gesturing toward the world of language—and indeed the experiential world itself—beyond. Clearly, I was not altogether deserting the existentialist motif in my work.

There was yet more aesthetic magic to be accounted for. My *Window to Criticism* also reflected the influence of Erich Auerbach's work on the *figura*,[15] based on the typological intertwinings between the mortal narratives of the Old Testament and their figural transformation in the eternally present Christian story of the New Testament. Such intertwinings defied contradiction: an Old Testament "figure" did not cease being a limited mortal prefigure even as he participated in his figured fulfillment within the New Testament's metaphysical story beyond history. It seemed clear to me that this was no mere allegorical relationship, since differentiated entities were simultaneously to be seen both as distinct and as fused, as we later found in the Coleridgean-Crocean organicist definition of the symbol. Like the poetic metaphor that it presaged, the *figura* could be explicated as a linguistic device only by a hermeneutic laden with the Christian mystery, with its three-in-one miracle of separate and yet fused entities, rather than by the dualistic separation projected by the Platonic or Hebraic hermeneutics.

Like other Renaissance scholars, when I applied this device to the widespread uses of typology in the Renaissance I began to see typology everywhere, but nowhere more strongly than in poems that developed the intertwinings of the language of sense and the language of spirit by means of metaphor as a microcosmic reflection of the figural habit of language. Metaphor, like the *figura*, represented the literary capacity to bring together, as identities, elements whose absolute differentiation was being subliminally acknowledged. By their secularization of the sacred, humanization of the divine, sensualization of the spirit, and the mutual reflection they urged between microcosm and macrocosm, these poems, as I read them, reflected the Renaissance humanist drive toward heaven on earth, though only while transforming the sublime terms of the divine into a sublunary language, the language of these poems, a language whose intense internal activity created an illusion that substituted for the external authorization of faith.

I found that the extravagance of the daring of these poems was again and again joined, though often obscurely, to the constraints of their retreat.[16] Thus, in the *figura* as in the specific instances of Renaissance metaphor, I witnessed the capacity of poems to enlarge the range of their meanings—indeed to create self-conflicting meanings beyond the limits of normal language usage—through a self-licensed growing power forced upon the words by both the poet and his or her tradition. And I seized upon these marvels as yet another corroboration of the powers recognized by an organicist aesthetic.

It was several years later that I found in the work of my friend and ally, Rosalie Colie, a theoretical ground for the double movement I had for some time been trying to describe, an explication of the poem's self-undercutting action at its highest moment of self-assertion. Colie termed it the poem's "unmetaphoring" act, subtly performed in resistance to its own metaphorical extravagance at the peak of its self-fulfilling exuberance. We are to look out for the poem's underside that reminds us of the illusion we are willingly undergoing. It thus becomes a self-demystifying illusion even while it works to maintain its illusionary character.

To explain this unmetaphoring countermovement within the poem, Colie, under the influence of E. H. Gombrich, argued that our interpretation should take account of poetry's habit of self-reference: the poem commits itself and us to its total metaphorical indulgence only while it is also conceding its own "merely" metaphorical condition by referring to its own status as make-believe, as a fiction. The metaphor is engaging in what I have called a systematic duplicity: the two elements that the metaphor uses its language to proclaim as one, it also acknowledges—outside this moment— as two. And the aesthetic liberality of our perception allows us to grasp as one this double vision for our contemplation—like an "impossible picture" of M. C. Escher—as if there were no discord between its two aspects.

By the time of *The Classic Vision* (1971), my critical method, in its fealty to the aesthetic, had forsaken the exclusive concentration on closure usually associated with the New Critics. In order to account for our experience of the self-revealing mysteries of literary texts, that method yielded to the need to invoke the paradox of a closure always in the process of being reopened. I called upon an anti-Hegelian model to provide an anti-synthetic alternative to the unifying reconciliation of textual elements that New-Critical readings had regularly worked to find. Instead of forging a synthetic identity out of differentiated, and even opposing, elements, the texts, as I read them, were responding to the twin pressures of polarity and identity, allowing the reader the paradoxical perception of polarity *as* identity.[17] Every *both/and* was accompanied by a *neither/nor,* and at the same perceptual moment both sets of oppositions held. My readings in *The Classic Vision* had reflected this model, and in the epilogue to that book I sought explicitly to summarize the couplings of metaphoring and unmetaphoring moves that I had been tracing in each of the texts studied. It was the special gift of the literary way of reading, under the license of the aesthetic, to make possible these impossible simultaneities of discursive response.

I pressed another version of these impossible simultaneities in my extensive work on ekphrasis that I began in 1967 and did not complete until the publication of my book with that title in 1992.[18] With the oxymoronic motto of "the still movement of poetry," I used poetry's representation of spatial and pictorial objects of art as an opening to my claim about the poem's simultaneous exploitation of the utter sweep of movement and the fixity of stillness. What we had in these poems, I argued, was a stillness that was still moving, always in motion, as well as a motion that was always in the process of being stilled. Form was to be viewed only as movement, though as movement that the aesthetic would permit us to grasp even as it was slipping away. And I freely ranged outward from ekphrastic moments in poetry, and from ekphrastic poems, to theorize about this self-contradictory element in poetry generally, finding in the ekphrastic principle an echo of my earlier claims about poetry's systematic duplicity.

In *Theory of Criticism* (1976), the book that followed *The Classic Vision,* I tried to systematize what I had been doing as well as to show its relation to the theoretical tradition within which—and, I thought, beyond which—I had been working. Nevertheless, with whatever qualifications, my primary fealty to the aesthetic remained dominant in this book.

In it, however, I had to confront the overwhelming challenge from the rising tide of structuralist and poststructuralist thinking. However revolutionary this change in theoretical perspective was proving to be, by this time in my development I did not regard it as antagonistic to my own direction. The shifting sands beneath my own theorizing led me to believe that much of this new emphasis had already been reflected in my work, though in quite different terms and with a different emphasis. For example, I could think of many ways in which what, after Colie, I termed the "unmetaphoring" of metaphor would be consistent with some of the moves being made by those now called deconstructionists. Similarly, I had been emphasizing the need to display, at least by implication, the uncontrollable "variety" that challenges, even explodes, every attempt at an all-controlling "unity" in the very act of its being asserted; to match every centripetal move, which threatens to be repressively all-encompassing, with a centrifugal drive that claims freedom from it.

It seemed to me that while a deconstructionist like Paul de Man and I both argued for an emptiness within metaphorical fullness and an absence within poetic presence, I was stressing the fullness and presence while he stressed the emptiness and absence. Still, both of us made concessions to both sides. But just as I could not altogether forgo the metaphor's drive toward identity in the teeth of difference, I would not forgo the "presence" of the literary text, although I had departed from the New Critics by recognizing that my notion of textual presence, illusionary as it was, carried with it the concession to emptiness and absence that texts also prompt a reader to sense, often all the more strongly because of the extent to which they make their presence felt. I continued to argue for this sort of presence in texts that we read as poems.[19] In them the context of verbal elements, as they were being worked by the poet (and, in turn, by the reader), had a heft and a density that sought to lock us in on their "corporeality,"[20] although that very density of interpretive possibilities blocked us from relating them to their references or even from feeling that literal references existed within them.

For full as they may be to our perception of them *as* complex verbal elements, they are, from another perspective that they also allow us, empty: mere signifiers whose illusionary realm openly betrays itself as such.

The practice I was calling for in reading all texts we intended to treat as literary seemed to me not very different from deconstructionist readings of just about all texts of any sort. But then by using these reading methods, derived from habits of interpreting literature, upon all texts, deconstructionists were, in effect, bestowing upon them what I would think of as a literary character. So to me the deconstructionists' similar treatment of all sorts of texts seemed, despite their rejection of the "aesthetic," as an aestheticizing of the reading method, as the establishing of a reading intentionality that obliterated the distinction between the literary and non-literary, but only by ceding hegemony over all texts to the literary. Nor did I find this imperialistic enlarging of the domain of the literary bothersome, since I myself had for some time been moving from the notion of the poem as a firmly fixed aesthetic object with objectively discoverable characteristics (as in the New Criticism) to the phenomenological notion of the text as an intentional object, responding to the way in which the reader intends it, as his or her text, to be read. This notion of course enlarges the category of the texts we may choose to include within the literary domain since it is we, in effect, who put them there once we choose to read them in ways learned and adapted through the reading of what the canon has handed down to us as more narrowly literary texts. Despite areas of increasing agreement, however, it has become clear that my own fidelity to the illusion of presence and metaphorical identity in the single text that one claims as literary, and my attentiveness to its singularity, kept me and keep me at some distance from those who, as followers of Paul de Man, work as textual deconstructionists.

Still, increasingly in my essays over the years that followed, I have had to confront the war on the aesthetic from other, more antagonistic quarters. Perhaps in reaction against the antihistoricist theorizing of the New Critics followed by the structuralists—and their successive domination over the critical arena—several varieties of sociohistorical theorists came forcefully to reject any association with the aesthetic. They have become the most dominant force in the field, and month by month, year by year, threaten to increase that dominance. These theorists, often with political motives, forcefully reestablished the historicist perspective, granting it the exclusive role in interpreting all writings, literary and otherwise, which were to be seen only within the determinants of that perspective. To me it was as if I was being revisited by the political ghosts of my pre-Chicago critical attitudes, though here and there newly sophisticated by the language of poststructuralist theories of textuality. Nor is there any sign that their power is waning. Indeed, reinforced by many coming from all sides—cultural and feminist and minority theorists—who have felt excluded or repressed by two millennia of literary and critical history, they have only been strengthening their hold on the critical realm, replacing theory with historicism and the aesthetic with the sociopolitically ascetic.[21]

But I have held onto the aesthetic as a liberating force, despite the fact that for some years historicists of several varieties have almost routinely charged the aesthetic with being a respectable and ostensibly innocent front for a reactionary politics. One source that theorists have repeatedly used to link the aesthetic with the political right is Walter Benjamin's claim about fascism's "aestheticizing of politics."[22] Working from Benjamin, current political theorists condemn this use of the aesthetic as a surreptitious way of imposing Hegel's all-unifying dream, fully realized in the wholly dominating, totalitarian nation state. As Benjamin had foreseen, the Marxist reaction is rather to politicize the aesthetic in a way that leads to its condemnation. The relation of the aesthetic to nineteenth-century organicism, and of both to the totalizing tradition we associate with German idealism in general and Hegel in particular, has nourished this association and the political rejection of the aesthetic that follows from it.

While undoubtedly there are such prospects in organicism, and these can surely lead, and often have led, to a reactionary politics, I had long struggled to show organicism's other side and with it the other side of the aesthetic.[23] My view of organicism emphasized the uniqueness of the text's internal development of a language system that would resist the intrusion of any universal language from outside. Meaning had to be immanent and not imposed by a transcendental authority. This was hardly a prescription for totalitarianism. It must be conceded that authoritarian—especially some fascist—thinkers have used another version of organicism in a way that deserves Benjamin's charges.[24] Emphasizing the all-incorporating power of the whole at the expense of the particularity of the part, they insisted that the latter fall in line and surrender any autonomy to the universal, with nothing held out.

But my work stresses a big difference between organicism in a text, whose verbal system (as I define it) resists externally imposed universal meanings and works to be ideology-free, and the political claim to an organicism that would absorb everyone and everything into the workings of the nation state. One resists assimilation and the other would forcibly assert it. The latter organicism is hardly a give-and-take negotiation between part and whole within the constraints and enablings of a verbal medium, so that it is hardly open to the creative transformations that indulge the alien elements that would resist assimilation. The dangers of some political uses of organicism are too acute for us to blur it with the liberating consequences of the aesthetic uses of organicism.

As I read him, Bertolt Brecht seems to have followed Benjamin's prescription about the aesthetic in his attack on the traditional drama, which he terms the theater of illusion. And I find his attack on illusion, as an effect of the aesthetic, similarly misdirected and for similar reasons: Brecht also fails to comprehend the duplicity of illusion's hold on us. Because the "reality" projected onstage wraps us in illusion, leading us to mistake the actors and their actions for "natural signs," Brecht claims that this theater is serving the dominant political power structure as a model and a metonym of *its* illusions, in which it would enclose its audience. Consequently, for him such theater creates in the audience a habit of perception that will accept as reality the socio-political-economic illusions that power would foist upon them. A repressive society, according to Brecht, tries to use its art rhetorically to persuade the audience to take as real the illusionary naturalizing of the authorization of its power. So one must fight the aesthetic impact of theater as one must fight the political impact of destructive ideological illusions—by the reaction of "alienation."

But I had come to see that Brecht was wrong, and too naively accepting of illusionist drama: at its best the theater, like trompe l'oeil painting, is not trying actually to take us in. Instead, its devices slyly point to itself: it undercuts its apparent illusionary claims with its textual or subtextual references to its artifice, to the art of theater. In his espousing the anti-illusionary call for alienation, it was Brecht—and not necessarily the rest of us—who was being taken in by traditional theater. Here he is representative of the politicized theorists who would take *us* in by locking us within the ideological limitations of their claims. It is, I believed, the aesthetic that helps rescue us from such traps, because it alerts us to the illusionary, the merely arbitrary, claims to reality that authoritarian discourse would impose upon us; because, unlike authoritarian discourse, the aesthetic takes back the "reality" it offers us in the very act of offering it to us. It thus provides the cues for us to view other discourse critically, to reduce the ideological claims to the *merely* illusionary, since there is in other discourse no self-awareness of their textual limitations, of their duplicity—their closures, their exclusions, their repressions. I would agree with Brecht that illusion may frustrate, may baffle, may mislead us—but only until the aesthetic teaches us how to put it to use.

As I have reported earlier in this recital of my development, I had for some time been urging the anti-Hegelian uses of a duplicitous organicism that would be invulnerable to Benjamin's charge of using aesthetic totalization as a model for political closure.[25] Because of its fictional character, the literary would be free of any totalizing tendency toward the single-sided. For to me the danger of totalization, and its repressive force, emanates rather from the unrelenting controls that the conceptual—often in the guise of the political—would impose upon discourse. Thus for me it was the aesthetic that held the promise of freeing us from that repressive dominance: the drive to exclusion dictated by the monolithic claims of conceptual discourse can be happily evaded by the drive to inclusion provided by the duplicitous notion of the aesthetic as I had been developing it. The sociopolitical function of literature in its aesthetic dimension, then, is to *de*stabilize the dominant culture's attempt to impose *its* institutions by claiming a "natural" authority for them, and by using (as Brecht in this case properly sees) a false art (a conceptual rhetoric disguised as art) to create the ground for this illusionary naturalization of its claim to power. The aesthetic reveals the fraudulence, and thus the deception, of this attempt.

Within us there is indeed a semiotic desire for the natural sign, and it is to this desire that authoritarian discourse (including the pseudo-art that serves it) appeals in its claim to natural authority. It is to this desire that the aesthetic also appeals, but innocuously, since it reminds us of the illusionary character of the arbitrary sign's attempt to claim the sanction of nature, so that it implicitly warns us against any discourse that would impose this claim without self-awareness of its own duplicity. I saw that it is in the play of fictional illusion that we can indulge the freedom of the aesthetic. While it makes no commitment to the reality claims of its references and subliminally calls attention to its own illusionary status, the discourse we read as literary is bound by a form that allows it, in the very act of self-denial, to create an ever opening discourse. On the other hand, discourse that we are not to read as aesthetic, discourse that seeks to control our beliefs and our actions, must retain a claim for the cognitive adequacy of its signs. In effect, it affirms the power of its references, like the "natural-sign" claims I attributed above to Brecht. The discourse that represents political and thus cultural power uses its arbitrary signs to claim a natural-sign sanction. It would in effect claim the authority of natural signs in order to exercise their dominion over us. But only the aesthetic, as I continued to see it, permits us to indulge the semiotic desire for the natural sign without falling prey to it. Indeed, it provides an exposure of the monolithic dangers of such manipulative discourse. Thus, I saw the literary, functioning within the aesthetic dispensation, as providing a healthily subversive antidote to the political abuse of discursive power.

Despite the general attacks on the aesthetic we have been witnessing during the past two decades, I found at least one strain of poststructuralist thinking that suggested strong, if unexpected, support for my fidelity to the aesthetic. It may not be intended as in any way supportive of the aesthetic, indeed may very well seem anti-aesthetic, but I see it as a continuation of the theoretical tradition I have throughout my career been working to extend, sometimes in spite of the direction normally ascribed to it. But whether in the name of the aesthetic or not, this version of postmodernism shares my notion that a text should, as a subsidiary function, serve indirectly as a political agent for freedom from totalization—in other words, for the counterideological.

I felt especially responsive toward one of the major definers of the postmodern, Jean-François Lyotard, although he clearly had no interest in looking sympathetically upon what he could conceive as the "aesthetic." Indeed, he rather saw himself as a defender of the "sublime" (in Burke's and Kant's sense of the term) as an irrational disruption of any formal order. In his writings he called for autonomous "small stories" (*"les petites histoires"*), and resistance against any metanarrative that sought to contain them or control them. I saw this rejection of the metanarrative, together with his disdain, on a micro level, for the controlling discourse of the "sentence" that would impose itself on the errant mini-autonomy of the "phrase," as a counterideological argument for discursive freedom that echoes my own.

These claims found reinforcement in the earlier, but recently revived, work of Mikhail Bakhtin on behalf of the carnivalesque, dialogical function of the novel.[26] For Bakhtin the novel is the dialogical instrument because it is a conglomeration of incompatible genres; indeed, far from being itself a genre, it functions as an anti-genre. Within the novel all genres are allowed to range freely, regardless of any potential discursive conflict among them. This is the carnivalesque character of the novel: as a textual force it suspends hierarchy and exclusionary distinctions within its bounds, much as the moment of carnival, in an authoritarian society, throws up in the air a variety of otherwise incompatible possibilities, for the moment free of hierarchy and, in general, of authoritarian regulation and its ideologically controlled structure.

Carnival time is a momentary, unrestrained indulgence during which a culture is allowed to have access to what its ruling ideology, as a repressive agent, would normally forbid: that which is forbidden to be represented is, for the moment, permitted freely to display itself. The dominant culture still is maintaining itself free from harm, because the encapsulated moment of carnival controls the subversive forces by authorizing their emergence only *pour l'occasion* and thus domesticating them, bringing them within its calendar. Still, some subversive danger to the exclusively authorized vision of a culture lurks in the representation of the forbidden, because the loosing of subversive elements, even thus limited in time, allows them exposure as a vision other than its own, so that they may persist to haunt that culture long after the moment of carnival is past. Here, in Bakhtinian carnival, I found another way of stating my hope for the literary text to function as a counterideological force. As I had been insisting, the role of any text, when we allow it to function in an aesthetic mode for us, is not to counter one ideology with another, but rather, as with the moment of carnival, to reveal the inadequacies of ideology itself, as conceptual discourse, to deal with errant particularity.

Political theorists may with good reason charge that literature, so conceived and defended as a discourse that undermines ideological commitment, would be the enemy to action, and indeed would paralyze its reader, its self-conscious duplicity rendering the reader incapable of reacting single-mindedly to social wrongs. Thus recent politicizing critics, anxious to use the literary text, as they would any other text, as rhetorical reinforcement for their clearly specified objectives, are committed to argue against what may be termed the "aesthetics of dissent"—that is, against a valuing of the power of the text to stand free of all conceptual structures, all metanarratives, and thus, by implication, to function as a dissenting voice against them.[27]

Granted that this aesthetic might prove useful to malevolent forces who could use it to paralyze their opposition; still, enemies of the aesthetic could similarly use their antagonism to it to persuade us, in rejecting it, to follow *their* agenda for action, similarly exclusive and authoritarian. It is, I confess, the aesthetic that might well destabilize the opposition to an authoritarian ideology by showing it, as an alternative ideology, to be a mirror version of what it opposes. Paralysis alone ensues.

Of course the aesthetic need not be the only, or even the most socially useful, mode of response to a text.[28] Moral, political, or other sorts of responses surely have their value as well as their dangers. But I feel, as before, though now reinforced by theorists like Lyotard and Bakhtin, that the fictions we entertain within the aesthetic mode of response, thanks to the resistance to universals they engender in us, allow us an awareness of existence that enriches, as it softens, our humanity. In the everyday world of action, of decision-making, literature, unlike other discourse, does not help us decide so much as it warns us to distrust the decisions we must make. When we are required to choose one path rather than another, it reminds us to tread with a light foot and a heavy heart.

So, though a much warier companion than I used to be, I travel with the aesthetic still. For my engagement with poststructuralism has only strengthened my sense of the need to protect the reader's response to the extraordinary things that the poetic manipulations of language and the discourse of fictions can perform for us. Yet I am mindful of the charge from political quarters that this view of the aesthetic is hardly a theoretical claim independent of historical—and thus political—sources. In such quarters this view of the aesthetic is judged to be no more than an echo of the weak voice of a long failed traditional liberalism that now, too late in human history, still looks to find all sides in balance because it is reluctant to make a strong choice lest it have to act upon that choice. And it is thus charged with seeking to ignore or evade—or with vainly seeking to transcend—the inevitable pressures of ideology upon poet and critic alike, even while its posture continues to serve the existing power structure.

Despite my acknowledgment of such pressures, I have already recorded my resistance to any attempt to reduce all discourse, and all responses to discourse, to direct or indirect reflections of the political. Nor can I accept the attempt to inflict on us as writers or readers the historicist's sociopolitical determinism, which would deprive us of any measure of freedom from

environmental coercion in what we write or how we read. Indeed, no theoretical position more clearly reveals its own captivity by history's ideological
pressures than recent politicized historicisms, whether called new historicism, cultural materialism, or other names. They are themselves the victims
of the forces they would impose on others. So I continue to reject their ideologically imposed insistence that the literary text, under the aegis of the
aesthetic, is also absolutely, without reservation, subject to sociohistorical—
and thus political—control.

If I feel there is a greater freedom from historical determinism in poems,
it is because of my confidence in the creative power that asserts itself in the
complex struggle to make a literary text. Though so much of the text is
made by historical forces, I claim that it is this creative power, unlocked by
the interaction between the poet and the verbal medium, that allows the text
not merely to be history's receptacle, but also to free itself to be the source
of further history. It was for this reason that, since my earliest writings, I have
devoted so much energy to all that can happen as we immerse ourselves in
the rich interactions among the verbal meanings and sounds as they com-
mingle within a poem. I have not wavered in my admiration of the role played
by the language medium, in its collusion with—but also in its resistance
to—the author, as it complicates and thus transforms what the author may
have thought he or she meant the poem to express; or, in a drama, of the role
played by the interactions among characters and speeches, as well as the
give-and-take between our sense of reality and the make-believe of theatri-
cal representation. The text that emerges may well surprise history's—and
thus the reader's—expectations, and create its own as it goes along, if we allow ourselves to go with it.

In such texts I value the role of illusion making and illusion sustaining,
but always in the midst of illusion confessing. Whether it be the illusion of
a metaphor working toward an identity between its two elements while ambiguously conceding their distinctness from one another, or characters and
actions in a play imposing upon us to feel them as actual persons and hap-
penings while ambiguously forcing between them and us the aesthetic distance between stage and audience, or the play between chronicle and story
or between confession and narrative projection in prose fictions, in all these
cases we indulge both sides. The illusion *and* the retreat in our sense of make-
believe, full presentation *and* empty representation, the free-standing, bodily here *and* the "imitation" pointing there, the press toward metaphorical
identity *and* the concession to metonymic difference—all these, for the
wary and fully attentive reader, alternate, collide, and yet cohabit. For theirs
is the aesthetic realm, in which such incompatibilities are rendered compatible by the poet, but only if we allow and—more than allow—pursue it.

It is this now-you-see-it-now-you-don't character of aesthetic illusion that
has led me elsewhere[29] to put forward the notion of the "shadow text," a

mock-text that is invisibly implied by, and subliminally stands like a shadow behind, the poetic text. These shadow texts are the generic texts that our reading habits and our interpretive discourse infer as we try to probe the mysteries of the text at hand. As readers, our limited language resorts to these shadows, and projects them upon the text in our effort to grasp it, to subdue it to our own terms. It is to these shadows—the shadow genre, the shadow "reality," the shadow ideology, all of these shadowing the text—that we refer as we seek to interpret it. But, to the extent that it provokes our aesthetic response, the text parodies, distorts, transforms, even—or especially—subverts these shadows and forces us to reject them as it moves beyond them toward becoming the dispersive self we watch being created.

So, as I look back at where I have been and think of where I am, I am still claiming that the aesthetic—together with the literary read within its terms—performs a number of indispensable functions for us and our culture. Like Wolfgang Iser, I claim for the literary a primary anthropological function in helping us see and feel beneath our systematic and generalized languages, and thus in protecting us from being misled by them. I have not, it seems clear, given up my commitment to the primary value of the immediacies of the existential as an alternative to the hazards of the conceptual. It is by virtue of its relation to the existential that I value the aesthetic in literary readings, for its capacity to free itself—and thus us—from ideology. I would hardly deny that all texts, including the poetic, can be shown to have their roots in ideology; but I argue that the poem is to bring into discursive prominence the subliminal ideological pushes and pulls within a cultural moment, and to undo the very mind-set (as well as language-set) that is victimized by ideology.

But the aesthetic serves other functions too. As I have tried to show, it permits us access to the illusionary with the luxury and thus the freedom of not being captured by it except as a momentary way of seeing. Thus the literary also serves an important psychological function, and in its way a cognitive function: by satisfying deeply human desires it provides a necessary alternative to the cognitive skepticism that accompanies our usual discourse, to our sense that discourse cannot deliver our internally felt experience to us. I am convinced that elementary desires are entailed in our need to move beyond the metonymies of language to the momentary metaphorical grasp that converges into a full apprehension of the identity that we dream.[30] This vision may indeed be momentary only (that is, caught only within the moment of aesthetic response), yielding that metaphorical identity as a reading of an elusive experiential "reality" which we know contains mysteries that evade the trimmed logic of our ways of speaking and writing. And only in what we read as literary can we glimpse it, if only momentarily.

The metaphorical grasp occurs while a broader awareness of the metonymic duality that surrounds the moment is obscurely being conceded. Still, that momentary vision satisfies our desire, our psychological longing, to have such moments, so that it generates pleasure to have this illusion, the illusion of a natural sign which insulates itself against any oppressive consequence by claiming only the imaginary rights of being a fiction. As with our visionary or dream experiences, the pleasure is only ephemeral. Here, in the aesthetic, it is ephemeral because it is tied to our simultaneous awareness, encouraged by our reading, of the merely metonymic and arbitrary way of the verbal sign that has for now captivated us by invoking a special magic. But because this genre of pleasure can be repeated again and again with each literary reading to come, such experiences can, thanks to the aesthetic, become an enduring source of psychic as well as cognitive satisfaction.

Looking back upon the paths I have taken, I see it is by reason of these functions that I have argued for placing literature within the family of the fine arts rather than within the family of discourse. From the mid-eighteenth through much of the nineteenth century, theorists were troubled about the place of literature within the aesthetic domain, as well as about its relation to the other arts, because their use of "aesthetic" was restricted to the source meaning of that term as deriving from the immediacies of sense perception. And the plastic arts and music, with their appeal to the eye and the ear, satisfied this restriction, whereas there were obvious complications in dealing with the verbal art because of the mediating role of language, with its primary appeal to the mind in its compounding of sound and meaning. Unlike the case with literature, the media of the other arts were not available outside those arts for the mundane functions of normal communication. Thus aestheticians struggled to find in the literary those elements that would distinguish it from other discourse, so that it would be allowed to join its fellow or sister arts and to interact with them as aesthetic artifacts subject to similar aesthetic analysis.[31] There followed a long and productive series of discussions of the literary as a fine art as a result of these interactions.

After more than a century, during which theorists carefully made the case for literature as a special mode of discourse, differentiated from other uses of language by its primary relation to the aesthetic, this move has been generally rejected in recent decades along with the aesthetic itself. Instead, the literary has been recaptured by the large and heterogeneous family of discourse, subject to the operational rules that apply to language generally. It could not be forced thus to join the family of discourse without having to renounce its sibling status within the family of the arts, without—in effect—renouncing the aesthetic. In this new domestication of its arrangements, it need no longer travel with the aesthetic, be exposed to the glories and the dangers along that road, resist or succumb to the misfortunes suffered by the arts in an inhospitable time.

But I am arguing—as I suppose I always have as I have traveled this road—for another judgment about where the literary belongs, about its specialness as a mode of our response and, thus, for its being taken by us as if there were a specialness in it as a mode of discourse. In view of my emended version of the ways in which the aesthetic can function for us, it is not, I hope, only a belated gesture for me to summon others to travel this road with me.

NOTES

1. Of course the range of the literary could be broadened, since room was always to be left open for texts (ostensibly non-poetic) which we choose to read *as* literary, and so apply literary ways of reading to them. Subsequent criticism over recent decades has shown that this is a broad range indeed.

I must add the obvious note that I am using "literature" or "the literary" and "poetry" or "the poetic" interchangeably, in accordance with the Aristotelian definition of "poetry" as relating to all fictions, whether in verse or prose.

2. Among the many outrages I observed, I cannot overemphasize the traumatic effects on me and others of witnessing the Bengal famine of 1943–1944, in which, it was estimated, some four and a half million people died, many of them left lying about the streets of Calcutta until picked up by the death carts. What young person could not be utterly transformed after witnessing such horrors firsthand?

3. This distinction between the ascetic and the aesthetic is central to my essay "The 'Imaginary' and Its Enemies," to be published in *New Literary History*. The subtitle of the second part of that essay is "The Ascetic vs. the Aesthetic."

4. A passage in chapter 8 of Aristotle's *Poetics* is the most likely support for this critical attitude:

> As therefore, in the other imitative arts, the imitation is one when the object imitated is one, so that plot, being an imitation of an action, must imitate one action and that a whole, the structural union of the parts being such that, if any one of them is displaced or removed, the whole will be disjointed and disturbed. For a thing whose presence or absence makes no visible difference, is not an organic part of the whole.

Aristotle follows this in chapter 10 with his call for firm logical interrelations among the parts of a tragedy instead of a reliance upon a mere chronological relationship among them: "what follows should be the necessary or probable result of the preceding action. It makes all the difference whether any given event is a case of *propter hoc* or *post hoc*." I grant that the Butcher translation (1895) I am using here, reflecting as it does late-nineteenth-century intellectual traditions, is anxious to press organicist language upon the first passage. But this flavor in the Butcher translation did help shape the Aristotle that was inherited by our century. And earlier, in the Renaissance, Ben Jonson had commented in the spirit of just this Aristotelian organicism that in a drama "it behooves the action . . . to be let grow till the necessity ask a conclusion" (from "What the Utmost Bound of a Fable," in *Timber: or Discoveries Made Upon Men and Matter* [1641]).

5. According to Aristotle's careful distinctions among the disciplines, such issues were matters reserved for the category of "thought," and hence would be more

properly considered under the *Rhetoric,* or perhaps the *Nicomachean Ethics,* than the *Poetics.*

6. There are several formalistic attacks on thematic analysis in the neo-Aristotelian essays opposing the New Critics (in *Critics and Criticism, Ancient and Modern,* ed. R. S. Crane [Chicago: University of Chicago Press, 1952]). I will quote one representative example from Elder Olson's "A Symbolic Reading of the *Ancient Mariner,*" an unfavorable review of Robert Penn Warren's essay on *The Rime of the Ancient Mariner:* "We may indeed worry about whether, on the contrary, it is not an absurdity to conceive of a poem—i.e., any imitative poem—as *having* a theme or meaning. The words have a meaning; they mean the poem; but why should the poem itself have any further meaning? What sense is there in asking about the meaning of something which is itself a meaning?" (139).

7. The following are some of the more obvious quotations that shaped my notion of the organic: (1) From Coleridge, the following unacknowledged appropriation from August Wilhelm von Schlegel in his "Shakespeare, a Poet Generally":

> No work of true genius dares want its appropriate form, neither indeed is there any danger of this. As it must not, so genius cannot, be lawless; for it is even this that constitutes its genius—the power of acting creatively under laws of its own origination. . . . The true ground of the mistake [of claiming Shakespeare had no "judgment" to impose laws to control his "genius"] lies in the confounding mechanical regularity with organic form. The form is mechanic, when on any given material we impress a pre-determined form, not necessarily arising out of the properties of the material;—as when to a mass of wet clay we give whatever shape we wish it to retain when hardened. The organic form, on the other hand, is innate; it shapes, as it develops, itself from within, and the fullness of its development is one and the same with the perfection of its outward form. Such as the life is, such is the form.

(2) From Benedetto Croce's formidable restatement of Coleridge, in establishing his distinction between symbol and allegory (*Aesthetic,* chapter 4, in the Douglas Ainslie translation):

> the *symbol* has sometimes been given as the essence of art. Now, if the symbol be conceived as inseparable from the artistic intuition, it is a synonym for the intuition itself, which always has an ideal character. There is no double bottom to art, but one only; in art all is symbolical, because all is ideal. But if the symbol be conceived as separable—if the symbol can be on one side, and on the other the thing symbolized, we fall back again into the intellectualist error: the so-called symbol is the exposition of an abstract concept, an *allegory;* it is science, or art aping science.

(3) And from T. E. Hulme's adaptation of Henri Bergson ("Bergson's Theory of Art," in *Speculations*): "Now vital or organic is merely a convenient metaphor for a complexity of a different kind, that in which the parts cannot be said to be elements as each one is modified by the other's presence, and each one to a certain extent is the whole. The leg of a chair by itself is still a leg. My leg by itself wouldn't be."

8. The two key essays in which Vivas works out his position on the aesthetic experience are "A Definition of the Aesthetic Experience," *Journal of Philosophy* 34 (1937): 628–34, and "A Natural History of the Aesthetic Transaction," in *Naturalism and the Human Spirit,* ed. Yervant H. Krikorian (New York: Columbia University Press, 1944), 96–120. The phrase quoted in the following sentence is from "A Definition of the Aesthetic Experience," 628.

9. Vivas's notion of "the primary data of experience" seems theoretically related

to John Crowe Ransom's desire for poetry to reveal in its fullness "the world's body" (the title of his book published in 1938), in contrast to science's concern only for one or another ordering of the world's skeleton.

10. It was later that I traced in detail this in-between status of the literary text (as a formed version of experience that avoided the forms of propositional statements on the one side and unformed raw experience on the other), as well as the special difficulties that status created for the language of the literary interpreter: see the first (and title) chapter of *The Play and Place of Criticism* (Baltimore: Johns Hopkins University Press, 1967), 3–16.

11. I recall being influenced especially by the following texts: Croce's *Aesthetic* (1901), A. C. Bradley's "Poetry for Poetry's Sake" (1909), I. A. Richards's *Principles of Literary Criticism* (1925), D. W. Prall's *Aesthetic Judgment* (1929), Samuel Alexander's *Beauty and Other Forms of Value* (1933), and John Dewey's *Art as Experience* (1934).

12. To the influence of Continental existentialism I should add my attempt also to accommodate the related writings of Georges Poulet and the so-called "critics of consciousness." I passed through this group, but only after finding in them reinforcement for my need to accord importance to the role of the subjectivities of consciousness. However, I always qualified any concession to the immediacies of subjectivity by insisting on the mediating role of the fixed object that was to contain them. See my "Mediation, Language and Vision in the Reading of Literature," in *Interpretation, Theory and Practice,* ed. Charles Singleton (Baltimore: Johns Hopkins University Press, 1969), 211–42.

13. See especially chapter 1. My drift toward existentialism owed far more to Kierkegaard and Berdyaev than to either Sartre or Heidegger. It was Kierkegaard's focus on the inadequacy of the "ethical" (the realm of Hegelian universals, and of language), and on the need to go beyond the ethical—and in spite of it—to where normal language could not lead, that led me to him, though I would find in poetry an access to language that he would deny. I assigned to poetry a representational form of what for Kierkegaard is the religious person's "leap of faith," which, because it is a leap, cannot be bridged by verbal representation. So for me the "aesthetic" was to be a post-ethical distortion, beyond normal language, rather than, as in Kierkegaard, a pre-ethical hedonism. In literature the leap was to be bridged by the miraculous claim to metaphor, though, like the leap of faith, it acknowledges its own impossibility, as well as its unavailability to the realm of a shared language, except when language is distorted into the literary. As I used it, existentialism was made to furnish another way of working toward the notion of literature as the attempt to represent the unrepresentable.

14. Originally published in *Criticism* 8 (1966): 305–17, it was reprinted in *The Play and Place of Criticism* (Baltimore: Johns Hopkins University Press, 1967), 239–51. This essay, like my other uses of existentialism, was intended also to make it clear that the theoretical grounds of the New Critics need not support the reactionary politics of many of those associated with them: Eliot, Wimsatt, Brooks, and most of the others among the southern Fugitive group. I sought to show that the existential may well be a more compatible consequence of their kind of organicism than was their own ideological call for the reinforcement of cultural traditions. Unfortunately, this call helped give the New Criticism, and organicism, a bad name, even if for the wrong reasons.

15. Many discussions can be found in Erich Auerbach's *Mimesis: The Representation of Reality in Western Literature,* trans. Willard R. Trask (Princeton: Princeton University Press, 1953). See the pages on Dante (194–202) and also 48, 73–76, 156–62, 247–48, and 555; see also his essay on *figura* in *Scenes from the Drama of European Literature* (1959).

16. I later developed a refinement of this coupling of daring and retreat, enclosure and reopening, in my treatment of Ben Jonson's "Why I Write Not of Love": "Presentation and Representation in the Renaissance Lyric: The Net of Words and the Escape of the Gods," in *Mimesis: From Mirror to Method, Augustine to Descartes,* ed. John D. Lyons and Stephen G. Nichols, Jr. (Hanover and London: University of New England Press, 1982), 110–31.

17. Twin diagrams of Hegelian and anti-Hegelian models, together with more detailed explanations of their differences and my reasons for urging the anti-Hegelian, appear in "Poetic Presence and Illusion II: Formalist Theory and the Duplicity of Metaphor," in *Poetic Presence and Illusion: Essays in Critical History and Theory* (Johns Hopkins University Press, 1979), 160–64.

18. My key essay, "Ekphrasis and the Still Movement of Poetry; or *Laokoön* Revisited," first appeared in *The Poet as Critic,* ed. Frederick P. W. McDowell (Evanston, Ill.: Northwestern University, 1967), 3–26, although these ideas were not fully developed until the completion of my book *Ekphrasis: The Illusion of the Natural Sign* (Baltimore: Johns Hopkins University Press, 1992).

19. De Man's comments on my treatment of Keats's "Ode to a Nightingale" may be a good indication of both the difference between our arguments and their overlapping. See my essay "'A Waking Dream': The Symbolic Alternative to Allegory," in *Allegory, Myth and Symbol,* ed. Morton W. Bloomfield, Harvard English Studies 9 (Cambridge, Mass.: Harvard University Press, 1981), 1–22, and de Man's responsive remarks, "Murray Krieger: A Commentary," in *Romanticism and Contemporary Criticism: The Gauss Seminar and Other Papers,* ed. E. S. Burt, Kevin Newmark, and Andrzej Warminski (Baltimore: Johns Hopkins University Press, 1993), 181–87.

20. The source of this term is found in the work of Sigurd Burckhardt, to which I am greatly indebted. See especially "The Poet as Fool and Priest: A Discourse on Method" and "Notes on the Theory of Intrinsic Interpretation," in *Shakespearean Meanings* (Princeton: Princeton University Press, 1968), 22–46 and 285–313.

21. I refer again to the second part of my forthcoming essay, "The Ascetic vs. the Aesthetic" (see note 3 above).

22. See Walter Benjamin's "The Work of Art in the Age of Mechanical Reproduction," in *Illuminations,* trans. Harry Zohn (New York: Schocken Books, 1969), especially 241–42.

23. I make my most explicit argument for this alternative view of organicism in my Wellek Library Lectures volume, *A Reopening of Closure: Organicism Against Itself* (New York: Columbia University Press, 1989).

24. See David Carroll, *French Literary Fascism: Nationalism, Anti-Semitism, and the Ideology of Culture* (Princeton: Princeton University Press, 1995). He makes a careful and persuasive case for the relationship between some versions of organicism (mainly those he calls "neoclassical") and fascism. But he does allow for a different reading of organicism that might be exempt from his charges (see 271, note 8).

25. See note 17 above, and the diagrams to which it refers.

26. Bakhtin's work from the earlier days of Russian formalism and its Marxist modifications has become, since its rediscovery, a major influence as a buttress to some forms of poststructuralist theory. Some of his writings claim as their authors the alternative names sometimes used by Bakhtin—V. N. Voloxinov and P. N. Medvedev (although the degree to which these writings can be attributed to Bakhtin remains unclear).

27. A most ambitious book-length attack on what he terms "the aesthetic of dissent" is John Rowe's recently published sweeping study of American literature, *At Emerson's Tomb: The Politics of Classic American Literature* (New York: Columbia University Press, 1996).

28. I suppose that my willingness to separate the aesthetic as a distinct, valuable, and irreducible way of reading, a possible alternative to other ways of reading, is my response to those who these days unabashedly put forth the claim that "everything is political."

29. See "The Anthropological Persistence of the Aesthetic: Real Shadows and Textual Shadows, Real Texts and Shadow Texts," *New Literary History* 25 (Winter 1994): 21–33.

30. Here, this late in my career, I am surprised to hear in myself this echo of Northrop Frye's language and ideas, even though I approach these from so different a perspective and for other theoretical purposes than his. I am thinking of his "anagogic phase," which involves "the total dream of man," the final phase in his "Theory of Symbols" in *Anatomy of Criticism* (Princeton: Princeton University Press, 1957):

> In the anagogic aspect of meaning, the radical form of metaphor, "A is B," comes into its own. Here we are dealing with poetry in its totality, in which the formula "A is B" may be hypothetically applied to anything, for there is no metaphor, not even "black is white," which a reader has any right to quarrel with in advance. The literary universe, therefore, is a universe in which everything is potentially identical with everything else. (124)

Of course, in my own view metaphor is far less consummate. As grasped within the aesthetic moment, it always involves an awareness of its metonymic underside that denies it. It is a metaphor that has known metonymy, so that no momentary grasp of identity leaves the illusionary transcendental dream undisturbed by the fall into difference.

31. My book *Ekphrasis* seeks to trace the theoretical consequences of such interactions between literature and the visual arts, considered within the domain of the aesthetic. See especially chapter 6, "Language as Aesthetic Material" (145–95).

NOTES ON CONTRIBUTORS

Hazard Adams is Professor Emeritus of Comparative Literature at the University of Washington. His latest books are *The Farm at Richwood and Other Poems* (1997) and *Many Pretty Toys: A Novel* (1999), the second part of his academic trilogy.

Ernst Behler died on September 16, 1997, having chaired the Department of Comparative Literature at the University of Washington for twenty years. He was editor of the *Friedrich Schlegel Critical Edition* (Schöningh, 35 volumes) and had begun editing the *August Wilhelm von Schlegel Critical Edition* as well as *The Complete Works of Friedrich Nietzsche* (Stanford, 20 volumes), and he was coeditor of *Nietzsche-Studien*. He was the recipient of two Guggenheims, the Alexander von Humboldt Research Prize in the Humanities, and other international awards; his later books include *Irony and the Discourse of Modernity* (1990), *Confrontations: Derrida/Heidegger/Nietzsche* (1991), *Frühromantik* (1992), *German Romantic Literary Theory* (1993), and, with Aldo Venturelli, *Friedrich Nietzsche* (1994).

Rachel Bowlby holds a chair in modern literature at the University of York. Her books include *Just Looking* (1985), *Still Crazy After All These Years: Women, Writing and Psychoanalysis* (1992), *Shopping with Freud* (1993), *Feminist Destinations and Further Essays on Virginia Woolf* (1988 and 1997), and *Carried Away: The Invention of Modern Shopping* (2000). She has translated books by Derrida and Lyotard, including Derrida's *Of Hospitality* (forthcoming from Stanford).

David Carroll is Professor of French and Chair of the Department of French and Italian at the University of California, Irvine. His works include *French*

Literary Fascism: Nationalism, Anti-Semitism and the Ideology of Culture (1995) and *Paraesthetics: Foucault, Lyotard, Derrida* (1987), as well as essays on nineteenth- and twentieth-century French literature, critical theory, and history and politics.

Michael P. Clark is Professor of English and Comparative Literature at the University of California, Irvine. He is the author of books on Michel Foucault and Jacques Lacan, and articles on the history of literary theory, Early American literature, and the impact of the Vietnam war on popular culture in the U.S.

Jacques Derrida is Directeur d'études à l'Ecole des Hautes Etudes en Sciences Sociales à Paris. Since 1987 he has also held a joint appointment as Professor in the Department of English and Comparative Literature and the Department of French and Italian at the University of California, Irvine. Among the most recent translations of his work are *The Gift of Death, Specters of Marx, Politics of Friendship, Resistances—of Psychoanalysis,* and *The Monolingualism of the Other.*

Denis Donoghue is University Professor and Henry James Professor of English and American Letters at New York University. His recent books include *Walter Pater: Lover of Strange Souls* (1995) and *The Practice of Reading* (1998).

Stanley Fish has recently become Dean of the College of Liberal Arts and Sciences at the University of Illinois at Chicago. The Thirtieth Anniversary edition of *Surprised by Sin: The Reader in Paradise Lost* (1967) won the 1998 Hanford Book Award from the Milton Society of America. *The Stanley Fish Reader,* edited by H. Aram Veeser, has just been published by Blackwell's. Forthcoming publications include *How Milton Works* and *The Trouble with Principle,* both from Harvard University Press.

Wolfgang Iser is Professor Emeritus at the University of Constance, Germany, and Professor of English at the University of California, Irvine. His recent books are *Staging Politics: The Lasting Impact of Shakespeare's Histories* (1993) and *The Fictive and the Imaginary: Charting Literary Anthropology* (1993). His forthcoming book is titled *The Range of Interpretation.*

Murray Krieger is University Research Professor at the University of California, Irvine, where he has taught since 1966. A founding Co-Director of the School of Criticism and Theory and founding Director of the University of California Humanities Research Institute, he is the author of thirteen books and editor of four others. His current work-in-progress is a personal history of developments in literary theory spanning the more than half century of his participation in them.

J. Hillis Miller is UCI Distinguished Professor of English and Comparative Literature at the University of California, Irvine. He has published many books and essays on nineteenth- and twentieth-century English and American literature and on literary theory. His most recent books are *Reading Narrative* (1998) and, with Manuel Asensi, *Black Holes* (1999). He is currently at work on a book on speech acts in Henry James, as well as a book on *Speech Acts in Literature*.

Wesley Morris is Professor of English and Chair of the Department of English at Rice University. He has published on contemporary literary theory and William Faulkner. At present he is writing a book on literature and performance theory.

Stephen G. Nichols is the James M. Beall Professor of French and Humanities at Johns Hopkins University, where he also chairs the Romance Languages Department. He has been Director of the School of Criticism and Theory (founded by Murray Krieger) since 1995. His most recent books are *Medievalism and the Modernist Temper* (with R. Howard Bloch, 1996) and *The Whole Book* (with Siegfried Wenzel, 1996).

INDEX

Text: 10/12 Baskerville
Display: Baskerville
Composition: G&S Typesetters
Printing and binding: Maple-Vail Book Manufacturing